The Conscious Closet

ALSO BY ELIZABETH L. CLINE

Overdressed:
The Shockingly High Cost of Cheap Fashion

The Conscious Closet

The Revolutionary Guide to Looking Good While Doing Good

ELIZABETH L. CLINE

PLUME

PLUME
An imprint of Penguin Random House LLC
penguinrandomhouse.com

Copyright © 2019 by Elizabeth L. Cline
Penguin supports copyright. Copyright fuels creativity, encourages diverse voices, promotes
free speech, and creates a vibrant culture. Thank you for buying an authorized edition of this
book and for complying with copyright laws by not reproducing, scanning, or distributing any
part of it in any form without permission. You are supporting writers and allowing Penguin to
continue to publish books for every reader.

Plume is a registered trademark and its colophon is a trademark of
Penguin Random House LLC.

Illustrations by Alexis Seabrook.

Rana Plaza photo by Sk Hasan Ali / Shutterstock.com. Onion-Skin Tie-Dyed T-shirt photo
courtesy of Cara Marie Piazza. All other photos courtesy of the author.

All Q&As and tutorials used with permission.

Fashion Manifesto courtesy of Fashion Revolution.

Library of Congress Cataloging-in-Publication Data
has been applied for.

9781524744304 (PB)
9781524744311 (ebook)

Printed in the United States of America
1   3   5   7   9   10   8   6   4   2

Book design by Kristin del Rosario

To my grandmothers,
Margarett and Routh

CONTENTS

The Conscious Closet

I'm just trying to change the world, one sequin at a time.

—LADY GAGA

Introduction

If **you want** to change the world, there's no better place to start than with the clothes on your back and the shoes on your feet. I'm not being dramatic. I believe it to my core. A look at the facts: Apparel is a 2.5-trillion-dollar business that holds up 3 percent of the global economy and employs *hundreds of millions* of people around the world, mostly young women.[1]

Clothes are our most personal and universal possession. I bet you're wearing the stuff right now.

And yet the clothing industry is a far cry from the empowering, innovative, and uplifting force it should be. It is instead among the world's largest carbon emitters, water polluters, and users of toxic chemicals. As much as 8 percent of carbon emissions are caused by fashion.[2] A third of the microplastic pollution junking up our oceans is coming from what we wear.[3] A garbage truck's worth of unwanted fashion is landfilled in the United States every two minutes.[4] And in an industry that makes some people so fantastically rich and famous, there are somehow only a handful of garment workers earning a living wage *anywhere*.

More people than ever are aware of clothing's negative social and environmental impacts and want no part of them. No one *wants* to feel guilty when they get dressed in the morning. We want and expect to feel good in our clothes.

As I've learned, building a more conscious closet takes effort. Anything worth doing does. But it isn't hard or unstylish or expensive. It can be easy and beautiful and accessible to anyone, including you. Beyond that, it will help you get off the fast-fashion treadmill, regain your shopping sanity, and uncover your personal style. All while saving you money. It *can* change the world. And it *will* change your life.

I know because all of this happened to me.

Eight years ago, I set out to write my first book, *Overdressed: The Shockingly High Cost of Cheap Fashion.* As I boarded a plane to investigate the sweatshops in Bangladesh and China, my closet was overflowing with clothes that I didn't like or care about. I recycled, shopped for organic food, used reusable shopping bags, and yet I was ignoring the enormous environmental crisis lurking in my closet. I rarely felt confident or happy in what I wore, despite owning 354 items of clothes. I was trapped in a sad clothing cycle, and I was eager to find a way out of it.

Overdressed was one of the first investigations to draw a straight line between our increasing consumption of fashion and the critical problems of climate change, pollution, and poor working conditions. Driving it all was the meteoric rise of "fast fashion," a hyperaccelerated cycle of making, consuming, and trashing clothes that is wrecking our environment and keeping workers locked in poverty. After the book came out, countless people turned to me wanting to know how to dress with their values. They asked, "How should I shop? What's okay to wear?" The truth is, I was often asking myself the same questions.

I struggled at first to build a conscious closet. I bought rainbow-colored eco-shoes and sewed a homemade lavender mesh top so amateurish it would have gotten me kicked out of home economics class. I stood up at a gathering of other conscious-fashion experts one winter's night after my first book's release and pleaded, "Please, someone just tell me what to wear!"

In recent years, struggle has become progress. Before my eyes, sustainable and ethical fashion has transformed from a niche cause to a worldwide movement (you'll hear plenty from and about those movement leaders in this book). New reports and fresh research, which I've drawn from, have outlined exactly where the environmental and social impacts of fashion happen, giving us a precise road map to how we can make changes on a personal, societal, and industry-wide level. There are new brands, retailers, and business models, which you'll learn about, making conscious fashion more accessible. We are on the cusp of an entirely new way of producing, selling, and consuming clothing that is already changing the world—and not a moment too soon.

But my philosophy of conscious dressing, the one you'll find in this book, crystalized after three life-changing experiences. The first happened as I hit the road to promote *Overdressed,* sharing my research at schools and in communities far and wide, from Milan, Italy, to Walla Walla, Washington. I've had hundreds of conversations and been asked hundreds of questions by all kinds of people about their clothes. Here are some of the queries I've heard time and time again:

"How do I know if my clothes were made in a sweatshop?"

"How can I tell if my clothes are good quality?"

"Is polyester or cotton worse for the planet?"

"How do I afford ethical fashion?"

"Can I shop ethically at X/Y/Z brand?"

These chats always mix an interest in sustainable and ethical consumption with a thirst for more practical knowledge about clothes. Many people are seeking information about how to consume clothes responsibly, but they also want to know how to consume them *well*!

Fast fashion swept away a certain kind of commonsense know-how and respect surrounding our clothing, from how to recognize a good buy and shop for quality to how to sew on a button and mend a hole in a favorite pair of jeans. I aim to do my part to resurrect these time-tested life skills. Not coincidentally, choosing well for our wardrobes and doing our part to extend the life of clothing is not only sustainable but these are some of the most emotionally rewarding habits we can cultivate in our everyday lives.

The Conscious Closet is also inspired by my experience digging through old clothes. For the past three years, I have collaborated with Wearable Collections, a New York City–based company that collects more than 2 million pounds of worn clothing and shoes each year for reuse and recycling. Founder Adam Baruchowitz is an open-minded guy with a passion for reuse, and thus I found myself sorting through a portion of his collections (which adds up to about a thousand pounds *per week*) with the goals of studying what's in New York's clothing waste stream and exploring solutions to our disposable clothing culture. I eventually spun part of this project into a small resale enterprise and even found myself traveling to Nairobi, Kenya, in 2016 to document where our used clothes end up.

You might imagine that New Yorkers have lavish garbage. That's what I thought, too. But alongside the small sliver of designer handbags and gowns, I saw enough fashion waste to scare me straight: dog-hair-covered jackets, gobs of T-shirts, "ugly Christmas sweaters," trendy dresses and tops, clearance items with the tags still on, and, yes, soiled socks and underwear. I came face-to-face with our unbelievable, catastrophic, and ecologically disastrous consumption of clothes. After having a front-row seat to how people buy, treat, and toss clothing, I learned just where we're going wrong and what we can do about it. My time working with Wearable Collections and in the secondhand industry not only gave me the conviction to keep fighting fast fashion, it earned me a veritable master's degree in both clothing quality and craftsmanship, and mending and repair, which informs *The Conscious Closet.*

Last but not least, *The Conscious Closet* is motivated by my own transformation from a life as an impulse shopper and fast-fashion addict to that of a conscious consumer of clothing. When I first considered the prospect of giving up my mindless deal-hunting habits, I could only think about what I would miss out on—the thrill of a shopping bag of new clothes, a half-off sale, or clicking Buy Now whenever I wanted. But, if I was honest with myself, the way I shopped wasn't bringing me any closer to a wardrobe I could feel good in. Once I tuned into my fashion choices and learned the full story behind what we wear, I was able to put together a wardrobe that I cherish and feel amazing in *for the first time in my life.* It feels better and can even look better to be a more mindful consumer of clothes. I discovered that conscious fashion is the secret—not just to avoiding harm toward other people and the planet but to loving, *truly* loving, and feeling good in your clothes—and I simply had to share what I've learned with others.

So what is a conscious closet? A conscious closet is a wardrobe built with greater intention and awareness of our clothes, where they come from, what they're made out of, and why they matter. *The Conscious Closet,* which you're reading, will help you transform your wardrobe and layer more ethical and sustainable clothing choices into your life with ease. Whether you're looking to find out about eco-friendly fibers, conscious brands, shopping for quality, green laundry habits, or how to pass on what you're not wearing in the best possible condition, this is the A-to-Z handbook that will help you look good, feel good, and do good through what you wear.

And by the final pages, you'll join the fashion revolution for change. In truth, conscious fashion isn't a product or a thing you have to buy. Conscious fashion is a mind-set, a movement, and a way of life. It is a manifesto and a call to action. Let's use the awesome power of fashion to change fashion itself and in turn we just might save the world!

The author in her happy place, sorting clothes for Wearable Collections.

How to Use This Book

The Conscious Closet is organized around strategies that fit a multitude of lifestyles and personalities. The reason for this is simple: Clothes are personal. We all have *very* different attitudes and needs when it comes to what we wear. Age, career, income, personal style, regional style, and our unique perspectives on life combine to shape how we feel about our clothes. Some of us love fashion and trends, and plenty of others just want to get dressed and get on with our day. No matter where you are on the fashion spectrum, this book is for you.

YOUR FASHION PERSONALITY TYPE

Your approach to building a conscious closet can be tailored around what I call the three Fashion Personality Types: the Minimalists, the Style Seekers, and the Traditionalists. Choosing a personality type will help you get the most out of your read and shift your consumption habits in a way that fits your lifestyle. The Fashion Personality Types are a loose framework that will help you dial in to your conscious-closet strategy, so don't overthink them.

- **The Minimalists.** At one end of the spectrum are the Minimalists. These personalities crave a finish line in fashion, buy for keeps, and tend to prefer a more timeless look. They want to cut the clutter out of their lives and build a tightly edited and attractive wardrobe.

- **The Style Seekers.** At the other end of the spectrum are the Style Seekers, also known as Maximalists. These personalities love fashion, trends, and expressing themselves through what they wear. Some people are Style Seekers by trade, like those in entertainment or fashion. Most Style Seekers would wither if their wardrobes weren't full of statement-making pieces and *lots* of change.

- **The Traditionalists.** The Traditionalists are the halfway point between the two fashion personality extremes. They don't crave fashion quite as much as a Style Seeker and prefer more novelty than a Minimalist; they want a stylish but versatile wardrobe and to update it each season with a few new looks.

What personality type speaks to you? I'm a Traditionalist with Style Seeker tendencies. Some of you might be Minimalists at the office and Style Seekers by night. Your personality type is also likely to change over time. Many of us are more trend-driven when we're young and get more traditional as we settle on a career and a personal style. Adjusting your Fashion Personality Type can be a fun exploration in fashion and a chance to embark on new conscious-closet strategies. So just revise and update your type as needed.

THE CONSCIOUS CLOSET'S SIX PARTS

You'll start to put together your conscious closet over the book's first five sections, starting with a closet cleanout and ending with learning how to care for and maintain your clothes. The sixth and final section of the book will teach you how to join a wider movement for change. It's important to read the entire book, as each section reveals something new about fashion's impacts and what we can each do about them. But some sections will be better suited to your Fashion Personality Type than others.

1. Part One: "Goodbye, Fast Fashion!" is your launching pad to a conscious-closet journey. It's dedicated to helping you reset your shopping and fashion habits by first paring down and clearing away clothes you don't like and that don't work. You'll learn to sustainably and ethically donate, swap, recycle, and sell your pieces to help tackle the problem of textile waste.

2. Part Two: "The Art of Less" digs into wardrobe building and the timeless art of buying less by buying better clothes. Minimalists and Traditionalists will be most inspired by the conscious-closet strategies laid out in this section, but all readers will get a lot out of Part Two's tips on investing in quality and shopping with savvy.

3. Part Three: "The Art of More" shares how to consume clothing and follow style consciously. If you're a Style Seeker, the chapters on resale and renting will be transformative, as they're all about how to keep up with trends and rotate your closet without harming the planet. All readers should pay close attention to the chapter on fashion finances and affording a conscious closet!

4. Part Four: "The Sustainable Fashion Handbook" shows exactly how to choose more eco-friendly fibers, kick toxic chemicals out of your wardrobe, and find and support brands on the cutting edge of sustainability. The materials we wear have a tremendous environmental impact, and all readers will benefit from learning more about our clothes on micro and macro levels.

5. Part Five: "Make It Last" is back-to-basics training on how to care for what you wear, including sustainable laundry habits that are dramatically better for your clothes, easy and satisfying mending

techniques, and advice on hiring professionals to make repairs and alterations.

6. In the book's final part, Part Six: "The Fashion Revolution," you'll link up with like-minded others and join the movement to collectively change the fashion industry. Here you'll learn about working conditions for garment workers, the fight for living wages, and how to hold brands accountable and join a fashion activism organization.

YOUR CONSCIOUS-CLOSET COMPONENTS

There are *many* ways to build a more conscious closet, from supporting conscious brands and choosing more sustainable fibers to rediscovering, reimagining, and mending the clothes you already own. How you build your conscious closet will be unique to you. Gabby, a twenty-five-year-old friend from Atlanta, is a Style Seeker. She has a small, interchangeable collection of high-quality core pieces at the heart of her wardrobe, what's known as a "capsule wardrobe" (more on this in Chapter 11). And her statement pieces are purchased vintage and secondhand. Blake Smith, founder of the wardrobe-organizing app Cladwell, is a Minimalist with a small but versatile wardrobe of just thirty-five items. You'll hear more from Blake at the end of Chapter 11. Emily, a close friend and Manhattan editor, is a Traditionalist who rents a stylish wardrobe for work. You'll hear more about Emily in Chapter 16. My own conscious-closet strategy is changing all the time, but I mostly shop for quality, buy my core pieces from Conscious Superstars (brands and retailers with the most sustainable and ethical business models), and fill in the gaps with lots of affordable secondhand pieces. Activism, community building, and social change, while not on the components list, are also a huge part of the conscious-closet equation, as we'll discuss in Part Six. I've watched conscious fashion help every single person it touches look and feel better, but one of conscious fashion's selling points is that it can and does look so many different ways.

THE COMPONENTS

While your outcome will be one-of-a-kind, we'll all use similar building blocks to create a better wardrobe. Here are the components of a conscious closet, boiled down to their essentials.

- For keeps: clothes you already own, love, and want to keep wearing

- New-to-you: swapped, borrowed, handmade, hand-me-downs, resale, secondhand, thrifted, and vintage

- Rentals: leased fashion

- Quality: timeless pieces built to last

- Better Big Brands: clothes by brands and retailers on the path to being green and ethical

- Conscious Superstars: pieces by the most pioneering, ethical, and sustainable brands

THE TIMELINE

The Conscious Closet will change your perspective and the way you shop and dress forever by the final chapters, but building a new wardrobe takes time. It no doubt took a while to build up your current wardrobe, and it'll take time to build the conscious closet you want. At first, you're going to have 100 percent of your existing clothes. They might in no way reflect your true fashion philosophy. That's perfectly fine. The vast majority of the conscious-closet journey is dedicated to the clothes already in your closet and your next purchase. The slower you take the process, the more informed choices you'll make and the more permanent and life-changing the results will be. In time, the wardrobe that reflects both your values and your style will start to emerge. I promise. Let's get going!

PART ONE

Goodbye, Fast Fashion!

I've found that many people are afraid of taking a hard look at what's in their closets, because fashion is scary to many people.

—TIM GUNN

The Conscious-Closet Cleanout

The conscious-closet journey begins with a cleanout. There's just no way around it. Our closets are meant to hold the beautiful things that we are excited to wear. But they've been hijacked and turned into dark recesses for our impulse buys and fashion regrets, and clothes that we don't like, that don't work, that don't fit, and that just need to go.

My formerly over-stuffed wardrobe contained hundreds of items, and yet I wore only a sliver of what I owned. Each morning, I would open the doors just far enough to grab the same tops and bottoms again and again. I'm not alone. Consumers buy twice as much clothing as they did twenty years ago, and most of it ends up as clutter.[1] A 2018 study of households in twenty countries, by moving company Movinga, confirmed that more than 70 percent of the average wardrobes is going unworn.[2] A Conscious Cleanout is the ideal opportunity to clear away all the excess and reconnect with the clothes you own!

A Conscious Cleanout is about more than just getting rid of stuff. You can find advice on how to clean out your closet anywhere, from TV shows and blogs to books. There is no shortage of tips. But most of it is wrong. The reigning advice on cleaning out a closet suggests that we strip our closets down to the hangers without any further consideration of where our clothes end up once we're done with them. Closet organizing gurus often instruct their clients to toss old clothes into the trash, even though *95 percent* of all clothes are reusable or recyclable! A Conscious Cleanout is different, and it is just the very first step in a more mindful and eco-friendly process of parting with clothes.

THE CLEANOUT GUIDELINES

Set aside a few hours, perhaps make yourself a drink or some tea, and fearlessly throw open those closet doors. Don't forget to go through any unworn clothes in storage under your bed or elsewhere. As you decide what to purge, put the rejects into one big pile for now, and we will divvy it up later. Do *not* throw anything away. I'll explain how to recycle worn-out pieces in a bit. As you consider what to keep or toss, there are a few simple rules to keep in mind:

- **Purge by season.** Focus on in-season clothes *only*. There are a few reasons for this. It's easier to make clear decisions about the items you're currently wearing. What's more, in-season used clothes are what's in demand, whether you're selling, swapping, or donating, which you will be. A Conscious Cleanout takes a bit more time and effort, and making decisions about a smaller volume will keep you from getting overwhelmed and give your clothes a better chance of finding a happy new home.

- **If you love it, keep it.** Keep the items that make you feel confident and look great. It's fine to keep pieces you suspect are "unethical," perhaps made in a sweatshop, or that might not be so eco-friendly. Building a conscious closet starts with greater awareness and the *next* garment you purchase, not by feeling guilty about the ones you already have. What's more, the most sustainable clothes are the clothes you already own and want to keep wearing.

- **Ignore money.** Try not to worry about the money spent. If it was pricey but you don't like it and aren't wearing it, there's no point in hanging on to it. In Chapter 5, I will show you how to sell your castoffs to recoup some of your money.

- **Put sentimental items into storage.** Reserve your closet as a sacred space for your wardrobe, meaning the clothes you are currently wearing. Put sentimental items into protective coverings and into storage. Grandma's wedding dress and your old concert T-shirts will be better preserved that way. There are also companies such as Campus Quilt, Project Repat, and Too Cool that will turn your T-shirts into memorabilia quilts if you'd rather those items be around every day.

- **Pay attention to what you wear most.** Use the cleanout to get reacquainted with what you've got and to sharpen your sense of personal style. Notice your favorite pieces and consider why they make you happy. Is it the color, the cut, the fabric, or something else? We're going to rebuild your wardrobe with clothes that make you feel this way all the time.

YOUR MAGIC WARDROBE NUMBER

Everyone has a Magic Wardrobe Number, the number at which his or her wardrobe works best and getting dressed becomes easier and more delightful, instead of a chore. How much clothing could you eliminate and still thrive? Perhaps that 70 percent of your wardrobe you're not wearing?[3] Not only do we own too much clothing, we are also *highly* deluded about how much of our clothes we actually wear. Americans *think* they wear 43 percent of their wardrobes, for example. In fact, we wear 18 percent.[4]

Not only do we overestimate how much of our closets we're using, we underestimate how far a smaller but better-chosen collection of clothes can take us. Consider that a coordinated wardrobe of thirty-one items can carry you through *the year* without repeating a look.[5]

By choosing well, it's possible to create enough outfits for *three months*—wearing something new every single day—with only ten tops and ten bottoms that all go together interchangeably. I'm not trying to dictate your Magic Wardrobe Number. My point is that more clothing can create clutter and chaos, and less clothing can go a long, long way.

Your Fashion Personality Type will influence your Magic Wardrobe Number. I know Minimalists who own 50 pieces or fewer and Style Seekers who own 250 or more, but it'll depend on your lifestyle, your career, whether you work from home, and so on. But even Style Seekers have lots of clothes they're not wearing and can benefit from cutting back to a smaller wardrobe and turning to renting and resale to keep their closets lean (much more on this in Parts Two and Three). As a Traditionalist, I've cut my wardrobe by well over half, from 354 to around 155 items. It's still a big number, but it provides enough novelty to ward off the urge to shop and I'm able to wear most of it throughout the year with careful management. I'll explain more about how I do it in Part Two.

WHAT NEEDS TO GO

Now that I've hopefully convinced you to size down your wardrobe, the next step is deciding *what* to cut. There are obvious things to get rid of, including items that are threadbare and those pieces that haven't fit in a decade. For the tougher choices, always think about how each piece works with your wardrobe as a whole. I recommend reading through Chapter 11 on wardrobe-building before making any permanent cuts to your closet. You're whacking the weeds to reveal the foundation of a functional wardrobe and personal style lurking underneath. Here's how to go about it:

- **Aim for balance.** A wardrobe functions best when you have an appropriate ratio between tops and bottoms and when your colors, cuts, and styles *go together.* Much more on this in Chapter 11. Prior to my cleanout, I owned sixty-one short-sleeved tops and only two pairs of dress pants. It was clear that I needed to cut back on tops and hang onto the pants. Cut where you have too much and bring your closet back into balance.

- **Cut the dead ends.** Wardrobe dead ends are those pieces that go with nothing else in your closet and are difficult to make work because of the color or style. If there's a dead-end piece that you love and *want* to keep, make note of what you need to make that happen—whether it's a matching pair of pants or a pair of shoes in a certain color.

- **Prune the trendy stuff.** Cut back on the number of trendy pieces (especially those that are wardrobe dead ends) and keep only those that reflect your personal style or that blend well with other items. If you're a Style Seeker, you might want to keep more of your trendy stuff, but if you've got stylish items you're no longer wearing, they might be good pieces to sell. More on this in Chapter 5.

- **Purge dingy underwear and basics.** Worn-out underwear, socks, and basics linger long past their expiration date and create clutter. Pare down. Keep what's in great condition. Buy fewer basics like tank tops, leggings, tights, and plain T-shirts moving forward. You really don't need so many, and they have no resale value, wear out quickly, and take up space that could be used for more dynamic clothes.

- **Learn from the never-worns.** Study those pieces you bought and never wore. It's okay to reject clothes over the smallest things: a sleeve that's too poufy, a print that's just too whimsical, a blue that's too blue. Make note of these little details that put you off and keep them in mind to help you shop smarter moving forward.

- **Kick out bad fabrics and poorly performing brands.** If a piece looks worn-out before its time, it needs to go, but notice both the brand *and* the fabric before you do so. This is where I started to get really fed up with certain discounters and fast-fashion brands. I was tired of pilled-up sweaters, faded colors, and shoes and accessories that broke after a few months of wear. At the same time, notice what fabrics make you feel comfortable and confident and what brands make the clothes in your closet that still look great after seasons of use.

GIVE EVERYTHING A SECOND AND THIRD TRY

Yes, I know that I told you to cut your wardrobe *way* back, but it's also just as important to give your clothes a chance whenever possible. Wearing what you've got for longer is one of the most effective ways to green your wardrobe. Figuring out ways to make your clothes work is not only better for the planet, it's key to staying happy and satisfied with the clothes you buy and the wardrobe you're building. Here are items you should consider sparing from the reject pile:

- **The maybes.** If you're on the fence about anything, keep it! "Give everything a second and even a third try," suggests Andrea Montali, a New York–based professional organizer from Dream Organization.[6] Could some of your maybes become go-tos with a little effort? Hang them at the front of your closet, make it your mission to find something to pair them with, and wear them within a month.

- **The benchwarmers.** If you've worn a piece to death but it falls out of rotation, it can be difficult to tell when its time has passed for good. You can hang these options in the front of your closet to inspire yourself to wear them. If the piece you're considering is a timeless wardrobe item, like a quality leather jacket or classic wool peacoat, put it in storage and give yourself some time off. If it's a really on-trend piece, it might be a great option to sell.

- **Worn-out versus repairable.** Minor damage is no reason to part with clothes. You can and should make all possible repairs, whether it's patching holey jeans, sewing on a loose button, or removing pills from a sweater. Or you can have a professional make repairs for you (much more on this in Part Five: "Make It Last"). If your items are faded, broken beyond repair, and worn-out, it's okay to get rid of them, but keep in mind that you might be washing or maintaining them incorrectly. See Chapter 22 for proper and sustainable laundry techniques.

- **Might fit again.** If you have garments you love that have fit issues, they might just need a tune-up from a local tailor. I'll talk more about how to find and hire one in Chapter 23. You can let out a waistband, shorten a hemline, or slim down a pant leg, for example. It's also okay to keep beloved clothes around to accommodate weight loss and gain. Our bodies are changing all the time, and it's expensive and wasteful to go out and buy a new wardrobe when it happens. But also be realistic: If you know your body has changed for good, try to let go.

THE WARDROBE IMPACT INVENTORY

While you're going through your clothes, take the time to do an Impact Inventory of your current wardrobe. This is a chance to document how you've been shopping and to take a snapshot of where you're at before you continue on your conscious-closet journey. To take an inventory, simply count up your total number of pieces, excluding socks and underwear, and tally the percentage of your wardrobe that you're wearing versus what you're not. A ballpark figure is fine. Keep this information handy for your Fashion Fast in Part Two and Chapter 17, which is about fashion finances and affording a conscious closet. Next, look at the inside labels on ten to twenty pieces of clothing—both those items you're keeping and getting rid of—and jot down the countries your garments and shoes are made in as well as what materials and fabrics they're made of. Finally, give yourself a rating from 1 to 10 on your awareness of environmental and social issues in fashion. Don't get discouraged; this isn't an exercise in guilt. Check out my before-and-after Impact Inventory to see how far I've come! Your number will climb as you read this book, and you'll notice how much more excited about and connected to your clothes you feel as your awareness increases.

Elizabeth's Wardrobe Impact Inventory

MY FAST-FASHION-CLOSET INVENTORY (2011)

Wardrobe Size: 354 items

Percentage of Wardrobe Worn: 14 percent

Conscious-Closet Components: hand-me-downs, vintage, thrift; the rest is conventional fashion

Fabrics: acrylic, polyester, rayon, and blends of synthetics and natural materials

Origins: Bangladesh, Vietnam, China, Turkey, Korea, Hong Kong, and one vintage item "Made in USA"

Knowledge of Environmental Issues in Fashion (on a scale of 1 to 10): 1

Knowledge of Social Issues in Fashion (on a scale of 1 to 10): 5

MY CONSCIOUS-CLOSET INVENTORY (2019)

Wardrobe Size: 155 items

Percentage of Wardrobe Worn: 85 percent

Conscious-Closet Components: hand-me-downs, handmade, thrifted, rented, quality, Conscious Superstars, Better Big Brands

Fabrics: cotton, polyester, rayon, organic silk, organic cotton, Tencel, recycled cotton, recycled nylon, recycled PET, leather and suede, linen, silk, merino wool, cashmere

Origins: United States, Italy, China, Vietnam, Pakistan, India, Bangladesh, Dominican Republic, Vietnam, Sri Lanka, Hong Kong

Knowledge of Environmental Issues in Fashion (on a scale of 1 to 10): 9

Knowledge of Social Issues in Fashion (on a scale of 1 to 10): 8

You've now finished phase one of your Conscious Cleanout! Your closet should be looking lean and trim and full of only those pieces that you're excited to keep wearing. You might even see a handful of bare hangers—space for your new conscious-fashion finds! I hope you're feeling a tad lighter and freer. After my Conscious Cleanout, I could see my closet floor for the first time in years. Now that you've got your own pile of castoffs, you're no doubt wondering how to get them out of your home as soon as possible and how to do so *consciously*. Over the next few chapters, I'll teach you everything you need to know to develop a Clothing Reuse Plan so you can properly send your castoffs to greener pastures. Over the course of the book, you'll learn how to never return to this place of chaos again.

Your Clothing Reuse Plan

A **closet cleanout is** a chance for a fresh start. After a gleeful closet purge comes the trip to the local charity or thrift shop, where our used clothing begins its new life in the closet of a fellow fashion lover or bargain hunter around town. Or so we think. We've been taught over the years that our used clothes are both virtuous and green. Nowadays, our closet castoffs rarely stay local, and they no longer have the clear-cut benefits we imagine.

Most consumers buy a large quantity of clothes and wear them for a short amount of time, producing staggering volumes of unwanted clothes. A growing percentage of our clothing ends up as waste. Across the United States, 23.8 billion pounds of clothes and shoes are thrown into the garbage each year, about 73 pounds per person.[1] Clothing donations to charities and thrift shops have shot up dramatically, too. In a single year, New York–New Jersey-area Goodwills collect 85.7 million pounds of clothes, the equivalent in weight of about 200 million T-shirts.[2] Savers, a US-based for-profit thrift chain, processes 265 million donated tops and 40 million pairs of shoes a year, according to its 2017 annual report.[3]

Owing to the profusion of used clothes in the world, it's hard to imagine how it could all get bought up at the local charity or thrift shop. And it doesn't. According to SMART, a trade association of used-clothing collectors, charities sell only 20 to 25 percent on average of what we donate through their thrift shops.[4] So, what *really* happens to the vast majority of what we donate, that other 80 percent? Charities and thrift shops pack it up and sell it by the pound to rag traders, who sort through it in giant warehouses and decide its fate based on trendiness, cleanliness, and condition. From there, most of it is exported overseas.

Used clothing at a sort-and-export facility in New Jersey. The majority of used clothing donated in the United States is sold to facilities such as this one.

Used clothing exports from the United States have more than tripled in the last fifteen years, from 537 million pounds to a staggering *1.7 billion pounds* of clothes annually.[5] For a visual, the average pair of women's skinny jeans weighs about one pound. Each year we export the equivalent in weight of enough old jeans to clothe the populations of China and the United States *combined*. Today, America is by far the largest exporter of unwanted clothes in a global trade worth almost 4 billion dollars annually.

At least used clothing sent abroad gets reused, right? It once was, but that's changing fast. Exporting clothes is no longer the tidy solution for clothing waste that we might imagine. Our clothes often take a circuitous route around the world, but most of it that's fit to be worn lands in sub-Saharan Africa. Oxfam estimates that as much as 70 percent of old clothes end up there.

In 2016, I traveled to Nairobi to get a more complete picture of how our castoffs impact Kenya, which imports almost 300 million pounds of them per year.[6] I found that many secondhand dealers (there are an estimated forty thousand of them in Nairobi alone) love the work but can't make a living off of it. As the volume of used-clothing imports goes up and the quality of our clothes goes down, the pay for many vendors is getting worse. Many used-clothing dealers in Africa are living in extreme poverty, meaning our disposable fashion makes for bad jobs both *during* its manufacture and *after* it's discarded and resold as secondhand goods.

There is a rising tide of poor-quality and soiled clothing that gets donated in affluent nations and then shipped abroad and dumped onto poorer countries. My research into New York City's clothing waste stream revealed that many people no longer bother to launder, repair, or remove pet hair or other detritus from their donations. African nations are increasingly the ones left to handle this garbage. In Ghana, a leading importer of used clothes from the United States and other Western countries, our old clothes are literally filling up the local landfills. According to the OR Foundation, a nonprofit studying the global secondhand trade, 40 percent of all used clothing imported into Ghana each year is now so low-value or damaged that it's immediately landfilled rather than worn or resold. A staggering 48 million pounds of used clothes went into the city of Accra's landfill in 2018.[7] The reasons? The clothing that arrives there is often worn-out, dirty, too big, or the wrong style. There's also just far too much of it.

There's a much better way forward. It starts with each of us taking greater responsibility for our used clothes by developing a

Clothing Reuse Plan, a list of four go-to strategies for consciously getting rid of closet castoffs, whether they're in pristine condition or have more in common with a dishrag than a garment. Get started by going back through your pile of closet castoffs and considering what might go into each category. In the following pages, you'll get a crystal-clear sense of what goes where.

1. **Donate or give away.** Items to donate are those that are in clean and wearable condition.

2. **Sell or swap.** Items to sell or swap are your highest-value, on-trend, and in-season pieces in pristine condition.

3. **Repairs.** Items with loose buttons, small tears, and removable stains should be cleaned and repaired (using tips in Part Five: "Make It Last") and then placed in one of your first two piles.

4. **Recycle.** Items to be recycled are worn-out beyond repair, like a sneaker with a worn-through sole, a stained and holey T-shirt, or, yes, your used underwear and socks. Depending on the textile recycling options near you, you might be able to combine this pile with your donation pile. More on that in the next few chapters!

How to Do Good
with Old Clothes

For generations, donating has been a generous way to support charities and give clothes and other household goods a second life. Some of us imagine our donations go directly to those in need in our local community. But most major charities don't work that way and haven't in a long time. Most charities *sell* clothing donations (rather than give them away) to raise money for their programming. This virtuous cycle has funded reuse and community building for years. Donating clothes to charity remains a popular and convenient way to part with old clothes, but it's time to do it more mindfully. Here's how.

- **Investigate before you donate.** If you want your clothing donations to have a positive impact, start by giving to a reputable charity that has a mission you believe in. Always investigate organizations *before* you donate. If you've never thought to look up what majority charities actually do, now's the time! Goodwill is dedicated to job placement for the disabled, for example. Watchdog websites like Charity Watch, Charity Navigator, or the Better Business Bureau's Give.org assess and rank charities and are a great resource for learning about a charity's mission and how it uses money raised through the sale of used clothes. US charities should be far more up front and transparent about how our donations are used and where they end up, but we can do our part by looking into the organizations we give to.

- **Vet the bins.** Clothing donation bins—those metal boxes that invite you to "donate here"—are run by a dizzying number of organizations. Some raise cash for charity, while others are purely for profit. Bins are an ultraconvenient way to part with old clothes or to help raise money for a good cause, but *a few* are run by disreputable organizations that masquerade as charities or place bins on private or public property without permission.

  To avoid bad actors, look for bins that are clearly marked with the organization's name, contact details, and any claims about what the donations are used for (if they're for charity versus for profit, for example). Double-check the claims online with a quick Google search, or by using Charity Watch or another watchdog website I mentioned previously. It's legal for bins to be run by a for-profit organization, as long as they're honest about where the money and donations end up. I personally have no problem donating to an aboveboard for-profit collector, as they do the important work of keeping clothes out of the landfill and are often more transparent about exporting clothes to the developing world than charities. You might prefer to donate only to organizations raising money for a local cause. Think it through, but the choice is up to you.

- **Donate directly to those in need.** It's possible to give some of your clothes directly to those in need. Check with local homeless shelters, crisis centers, or churches to see if they're hosting a clothing drive or accepting donations. Many charities run annual coat drives. The global nonprofit Dress for Success has locations across the United States and collects high-quality work wear, while more regional organizations like Becca's Closet and Operation Prom have collection points in many cities for formal wear. You might also have a local version of these programs. International aid organizations often collect clothes for disaster victims or refugees on an as-needed basis. Don't just drop off your donations! Always make sure that there's a need and find out *exactly* what items are needed, whether it's coats and boots or baby clothes. Aid organizations are often inundated with clothing donations, so don't be surprised if you and your items are turned away or you're asked to donate money instead.

HOW WE CAN BUILD AN ETHICAL, TRANSPARENT SECONDHAND CLOTHING TRADE

There are fantastic aspects to the global secondhand trade. Secondhand clothes create jobs around the world, provide an affordable supply of stylish clothes, and ensure that clothing gets reworn and reused. I look forward to a future where countries like Ghana and Kenya are driving innovations in textile recycling, setting the standards for upcycled fashion design, and partnering with reputable and ethical exporters that are committed to circulating high-quality clothes, rather than dumping beat-up items on developing nations. Progress is already happening. You might not be able to stop your top from going to Ghana, but you can ensure that the person *selling* your T-shirt earns a better livelihood, and the person who ends up *wearing* your T-shirt can wear it with pride. My best advice is to donate your clothes clean and in the best possible condition and to always follow proper "Used-Clothing Etiquette," which I've outlined on the following page.

Here's the most responsible way to get rid of old clothes: You can keep your clothes local by organizing a clothing swap with your friends or community or sell your items directly to another person through the resale market, using tips in Chapter 5. Donations should be thoughtful and seasonally appropriate. Ultimately, you'll need to create less clothing waste to begin with by buying less and choosing higher-quality clothes that have great resale value.

Used-Clothing Etiquette

Whether donating, selling, or recycling used clothes, give away your items clean and in the best possible condition. All of these efforts support better jobs, keep clothes out of landfills, and give your items the best chance of getting worn again.

- **Clean your clothes, no exceptions.** Clothes should *always*, with zero exceptions, be clean when you donate, sell, swap, or recycle them. Set-in stains are fine if you're recycling, but odors and unwashed dirt and grime are not. Do this out of respect for the dozens of people who will handle your clothes. Dirty clothes also might end up in the dump, as it takes secondhand clothing dealers precious time to wash them.

- **Remove personal belongings and detritus.** Inspect your pockets and the fabric and remove all pet hair, lint, dirty tissues, coins, receipts, and the like. Otherwise, you're leaving those tasks to be done by someone else.

- **Tie your shoes together.** Shoes should be donated in pairs (tie shoelaces together, buckle straps together, or tie shoes together with a piece of string or rubber band), so they don't get separated. There's an overseas market for single shoes, but those that are paired up are much more valuable and have a greater chance of finding a new home.

- **Mend and repair.** All donated clothing should be mended or repaired whenever possible to extend the item's life and keep it out of landfills. More on how to do basic repairs or hire someone to make them in Chapters 23 and 24.

- **Never leave your donations outside unattended.** If you're dropping your items at a clothing donation bin or outdoor donation point, and the collection point is full, do not leave your items outdoors unattended. Clothing left outside might get rained on or become damp and then mildew. From there, it will be landfilled.

Clothing Is Not Garbage

Perhaps it's a dingy bra with a broken strap, a lone sock, or a shoe with a worn-through sole. There are clothes from your Conscious Cleanout that have no doubt seen better days, and no amount of scrubbing or mending would redeem them. Many of us make an honest effort to donate our gently used clothes, but we're confused about what to do with the pieces that are worn-out or broken. *Isn't it disrespectful to donate these items?* Sometimes we get in a rush, or get frustrated because the donation point is so far away, and suddenly we find ourselves just throwing our clothes in the trash.

But landfills are no place for clothes.

By volume, clothing is the fastest-growing category of waste to US landfills. Just as the amount of clothing we ship overseas has accelerated, the amount of clothes going to our dumps has almost doubled in the last fifteen years and is increasing by 6 percent per year.[1] Globally, the news isn't much rosier: One garbage truck of textiles is landfilled or incinerated every single second around the world.[2]

Trashing clothes is as pricey as it is horribly wasteful. The vast majority of clothes are thrown out before their useful life is over, which amounts to lost value, resources, and landfilling fees. The British throw out as much as 16 billion dollars' worth of old clothes each year,[3] while New York City pays more than 20 million dollars per year to landfill and burn textile waste.[4] At least textiles break down in the landfill, right? Some do, and it's a major problem. Natural fibers, such as cotton, wool, and linen, slowly decompose. That cotton T-shirt, when trapped in a landfill, releases methane, a greenhouse gas twenty-five times more potent than CO_2.[5] According to the EPA, landfills are the third-largest human-caused source of methane emissions in the United States.[6] Meanwhile, synthetic clothing (made of plastics) doesn't readily biodegrade and might take hundreds of years or more to decompose. Some synthetics, like polyester and man-made rubber, are created out of hazardous chemicals that can be released into the air or ground as they slowly break down.[7]

On the other hand, keeping clothes out of the landfill by donating, rewearing, or recycling them has tremendous environmental benefits. According to the EPA, for every 2 million tons of textiles we keep in circulation and out of landfills, we can reduce carbon emissions equivalent to taking 1 million cars off the road.[8] In fact, reusing a ton of textiles saves twice as much carbon as recycling a ton of plastic, one of the most commonly recycled materials.[9]

WHERE TO RECYCLE CLOTHING

When we think of recycling, we think of paper and plastic, not clothes. And, in fact, textile recycling has a broad meaning, which I'll explain after this section. So where does this supersecret textile-recycling service take place? The options are often hiding in plain sight. You are likely *already* recycling some apparel without realizing it. Many charities, national thrift store chains (and many local ones), and a growing number of brands are set up to pass on our used clothes to recyclers. Here are the options, at the time of this writing, for organizations that accept worn garments, accessories, and shoes in *any condition*:

- **Major charities and thrift shops.** Check to see if your local charity or thrift store takes items in any condition to be recycled. Many do. Charity policies vary from community to community (partially because charities like Goodwill are run independently, by region), so it's wise to either look online at the acceptance policies or, better yet, call your location and ask. Savers, a national thrift store chain that collects clothing on behalf of nonprofits, takes worn clothing in any condition and passes it on to recyclers.[10] If you live in or near a big city or on the coasts in the United States, you'll have an easier time finding a charity or thrift store willing to take worn clothes and shoes. For those of you in small towns, the good news is that you produce far less fashion waste than us city slickers, but you might have a harder time finding a place to recycle textiles. I'll cover some alternatives shortly.

- **Clothing donation bins.** Many clothing donation bins are run by organizations that accept worn clothes and will pass them on to recyclers. Check for the organization's name and contact information on the side of the bin and look up their acceptance policies online. Planet Aid and USAgain are major operators of collection bins, for example, and both accept clothing in any condition.

- **In-store garment collecting.** A growing number of clothing brands and retailers have in-store collection boxes where you can donate used clothes by any brand and in any condition. At the time of this writing, Levi's, Reformation, Columbia, H&M, & Other Stories, Forever 21, and the North Face have in-store recycling bins. Nike's Reuse-A-Shoe program accepts athletic shoes by any brand for recycling in most of its retail stores. I'll keep an updated list of stores offering this service on my website, TheConsciousClosetBook.com, but it's best to call ahead and confirm that your location offers these services.

- **Brand take-back programs.** In the future, clothing companies will take full responsibility for the reuse and recycling of their own products via take-back programs. A few brands are leading the way. Eileen Fisher collects, repairs, and resells its own gently used merchandise at a discount through its Eileen Fisher Renew stores and website (you'll hear from the director of Renew in Part Three: "The Art of More"). And Patagonia runs a successful national repair and resale program called Worn Wear.

- **City textile recycling.** A growing number of cities collect used clothes for reuse and recycling or coordinate a network of clothing drop-off points for citizens. Austin, Texas, and Raleigh, North Carolina offer curbside pickup for used clothes, while New York City's refashionNYC program runs collection bins in large apartment buildings and coordinates collections in weekly farmers' markets, which are picked up by Wearable Collections. Google "textile recycling options near me" to find out what's available.

NO RECYCLING OPTIONS NEAR YOU? HERE'S WHAT TO DO

You have options. You might encourage a local retailer, grocer, or other business to host a clothing donation and recycling bin. If you're a business owner or school administrator, you might host a bin on your property or campus. You can also lobby your city to start a municipal textile-recycling program. SMART, the US trade group for clothing recyclers and bulk collectors, has a number of online resources for those interested in bringing textile recycling to communities, including fact sheets and videos you can share with local government and media. You might also ask around and see if there are creative ways to dispose of worn-out items in your community. Are there local organizations that might need scrap material and fabric? Artists, fashion students, or schools might be able to use your clothes for craft or design projects. Some animal shelters can utilize worn clothes as stuffing for dog beds or toys for pets.

Last but not least, you can and should reuse clothes for repair projects and, if you're so inclined, refashion worn pieces. As I mentioned, worn-out and damaged items are not always sorted out for recycling (though this *must* change), so why not try to find a use for them around the house? This is the way humans "recycled" worn clothes for ages. Scrap denim is ideal for mending and patching, which you'll learn how to do in Chapter 24. Cotton T-shirts make great cleaning cloths and rags. And worn or stained items and scuffed-up shoes are great to wear for yard work or other outdoor activities.

THE FUTURE OF TEXTILE RECYCLING

In the future, fashion might use its waste as a resource, by designing clothes that are easy to recycle back into new clothes. For now, textile recycling has a broad meaning that encompasses any type of clothing reuse, including rewearing clothes as secondhand (the most sustainable option) or downcycling clothes into lower-value products like rags or insulation. For example, T-shirts and flannels can be turned into industrial rags used by factories, car washes, or salons; old denim can be shredded to insulate new homes. Many types of clothing and footwear can be shredded and downcycled—with some shredding companies turning everything from shoes, handbags, baby clothes, and jackets into fibers. To be clear: No matter whether you donate to a charity, collection bin, thrift store, garment collection program, or most anywhere else, your clothes are likely going to end up in the global secondhand clothing trade or will be downcycled rather than recycled in the traditional sense.

Less than 1 percent of clothing is recycled in the truest sense of the word, meaning broken down and turned *back into new clothes.*[11] This desperately needs to change to make fashion more sustainable and to solve the clothing waste crisis. Luckily, there is progress being made to make fashion more "circular," meaning using waste from the industry as the raw materials for new clothes. There are massive investments in textile-to-textile recycling at the time of this writing, which will enable more old clothes to be transformed into new ones, saving tremendous amounts of energy, resources, and waste. Evrnu and Worn Again are two startups working on chemical recycling technology for cotton and blends of synthetic and natural fibers. There are a number of recycled textiles already on the market, including recycled wool and cashmere as well as recycled polyester and nylon, and we should demand more of these materials from brands. I'll talk more about recycled fibers in Chapter 18, but keep an eye out for recycled content on your fabric labels.

We can also ask our favorite brands to take responsibility for their used products by offering take-back programs and spearheading solutions to waste! Legislation can help. France is one of a handful of countries whose governments are looking at laws that require clothing companies to reuse or recycle their own products.[12] In the United Kingdom, Parliament is considering a penny-per-garment "fast fashion tax" to fund a national clothing recycling plan.[13] The United States, home to some of the world's largest clothing brands and the most waste, needs to step up with its own legislation to rein in the waste and pollution caused by the fashion industry. You can help by spreading the word that clothing is not garbage!

Turn Castoffs into Cash

I'**ve made a** lot of spare cash selling secondhand fashion. It's my side business, and I absolutely love it. I get a rush every time I hear the eBay *cha-ching* sound notifying me of a sale or get a five-star rating from a satisfied buyer on a resale app like Poshmark. Selling your closet castoffs is a satisfying and sustainable way to give your very best used clothes the second life they deserve, all while raising funds for your conscious closet. Selling worn clothing is as green as donating it, and it often means your clothes stay closer to home to boot. What's more, it feels good just knowing, really *knowing,* where your clothes end up and knowing that they are making someone else happy.

Back when eBay was the only online option and local consignment shops mostly traded in luxury goods, selling used clothes was a bit of a slog. That's all changed. A profusion of slick, easy-to-use online resale services, like thredUP, Poshmark, and the RealReal, have made it ultra convenient to buy and sell secondhand fashion. There are also more brick-and-mortar resale shops in the United States (and around the world) than ever before, ready and waiting to buy your very best castoffs.

By following a few tips and tricks, you can sell your clothes and potentially make some serious cash. Globally, consumers toss out more than $460 billion worth of clothes that could be worn again![1] If you can't imagine yourself as a resale guru just yet, you will after this chapter. Now it's time to survey your closet castoffs and get ready to sell!

WHAT YOUR CASTOFFS ARE WORTH

Most clothes are like cars—drive them off the lot and they start to lose their value. Don't get discouraged; get informed. Look up the value of your items *before* you set out to sell them, by doing a little research on resale websites like thredUP and the RealReal, where resale experts and sophisticated algorithms price items based on extensive knowledge of the secondhand clothing market. You can do this by searching for similar items using terms like "ASOS printed dress, size small" or "Balenciaga sneakers, size 8." If you use eBay as a tool to look up resale value, make sure to research the price of *sold* listings. Those new to the resale game often overestimate the worth of their clothes, and many items ultimately sell for much less than what they're first listed at. Look around on a few resale sites and compare prices. The results will give you a ballpark idea of what your items will fetch, and if they're worth selling at all.

What do you do if your clothes aren't worth very much? You have options! You can of course donate, recycle, or use them around the house. If you're intrepid, you can sell them in bulk to a website like thredUP, which might pay you a little bit of money and will recycle anything that doesn't have resale value. Moving forward, always look up resale value *before* you shop and buy better brands that are worth more in the resale economy! To afford these better brands, I highly recommend that you also *shop* resale (more on this in Chapter 14).

What's Valuable?

Not all used clothes are fit to sell. Here are types of clothing that do well in the resale market:

- **On trend and recent.** Items that are on trend and from a recent season (less than three to five years old) sell best. If you have a funky vintage piece to sell, it might be valuable. Advice about the vintage market abounds online.

- **Luxury and designer.** Luxury and designer brands are, as a rule, many times more valuable than mass-market brands. Luxury handbags are some of the most valuable items in the resale market.

- **In season.** Secondhand shoppers tend to buy what they can wear right now. If you have a valuable piece (like a coat or pair of designer sandals), but it's not the right time of year, hold on to it and sell it next season. Handbags, denim, and accessories are seasonless and always sell well.

What's Not?

These types of clothing, on the other hand, don't do as well in the resale market and are better-suited to either swap, donate, or recycle:

- **Damaged items.** Resale shoppers and buyers will overlook signs of wear and discreet stains on high-end designer pieces but not on much else. Consider if it's worth fixing your items before selling. I resoled a pair of Rachel Comey boots and sold them for 110 dollars (with a worn sole they would have been worth about 30 dollars). Can you remove that stain? Can you work the snag back into the fabric? It could be well worth your time or small investment.

- **Basics.** Simple, low-cost clothes like tank tops, leggings, and plain T-shirts are a tough sell unless they're new with tags. Most buyers are looking for pricier items that they can get for a bargain by buying used.

- **Kids' clothes, menswear, work wear.** Most children's clothing doesn't fetch much money secondhand. It might be better to swap or trade locally. The same is true of a lot of mass-market menswear. The exceptions are premium denim and street wear, brand-name outdoor gear and designer suits, or designer *anything*. Work-places are getting more casual, and there's an oversupply of suiting and conservative work wear in the secondhand marketplace as well. Professional clothing, whether it's men's or women's, is a tough category to sell but a great category to donate.

TIME VERSUS MONEY: CHOOSING A RESALE STRATEGY THAT'S RIGHT FOR YOU

You've done the research and identified your most valuable pieces to sell. Now it's time to cash in. Your options for selling secondhand clothes grow by the day. At the time of this writing, just a few leading online resale companies in the United States are thredUP, the Real-Real, Tradesy, Rebag, and Grailed. There are websites like dePop and Poshmark, which double as social media platforms; popular brick-and-mortar resale chains, including Buffalo Exchange, Crossroads Trading, and Plato's Closet, as well as many fantastic locally owned, independent buy-sell-trade and consignment shops to choose from. In New York, we are blessed with many iconic buy-sell-trade and consignment shops, from Beacon's Closet and INA to Tokio 7.

With so many apps, websites, and consignment stores vying for your castoffs, how do you choose a selling method that's right for you? It's easier than it sounds: Decide how much time and effort you want to put into selling your clothes versus how much money you want to make back on what you've purchased. In resale, more time and effort equal more money. Is it cold, hard cash or a convenient way to clear out your clutter that's most important to you? Read on to find the answer and the best option for you.

- **I want to try an online service that does *all* the work.** There are online resale companies that will take on the process of selling your clothes for you, including photographing, describing, pricing, and shipping your pieces. At the time of this writing, thredUP takes women's, kids', and designer clothes, and the RealReal and Rebag focus on designer clothes and luxury handbags, respectively. Getting started is easy. Create an account, send in your stuff (either in a prepaid bag or box or in your own packaging), and wait for a payout. These companies take a higher commission for their services (for example, thredUP pays the seller 5 to 25 percent of the list price on items listed below $50). The pros of full-service resale sites are the *tremendous* convenience. If you're busy, or the idea of photographing and listing your clothes simply doesn't appeal to you, I highly recommend a full-service website!

- **I want to sell my clothes myself, online!** If you'd really like to try to squeeze every last dollar out of your castoffs (as I often do), and the idea of taking pretty pictures of your clothes and connecting with buyers around the world sounds like fun (it's great fun, if you ask me), list your pieces yourself through a do-it-yourself resale app. The most popular ones in the United States at the time of this writing are Poshmark, Tradesy, dePop, Vinted, and Grailed. And there is of course eBay, the granddaddy of resale. Each of these apps has a slightly differently community, so look around. Tradesy skews toward bridal and luxe handbags, dePop is younger and trendier, and Grailed is for designer menswear, for example. Feel free to cross-list your item on a number of relevant sites. It'll sell faster!

The benefits of the do-it-yourself websites are that it's free to list and these sites take a much lower fee (Tradesy and Poshmark both let you keep up to 80 percent of the selling price on most items, for example). It's fast and easy to list, too. These apps all have easy-to-use interfaces that let you photograph and list your items from your phone in a few minutes flat. The downsides are dealing with shipping and customer service on your own, which adds to the time spent

DIY selling. My advice: Take clear, well-lit, attractive photos, so your buyers know exactly what they're getting, be completely honest about any flaws, and make sure you do your homework on resale value before setting your price. An item priced too high simply won't sell.

- **Get me off the Internet. I want to sell in person.** The fastest and most time-tested way to sell your clothes is to pop them into a bag and take them to the nearest buy-sell-trade or consignment store in town. A buy-sell-trade store will pay you on the spot for your clothes, whereas a consignment shop will pay you a commission once your items sell. In general, buy-sell-trade stores tend to peddle in trendier, mass-market brands, while most consignment shops focus on higher-end name brands and luxury pieces. But there are exceptions. The benefits of selling at a buy-sell-trade store are the instant payouts, and you can shop immediately with your cash! Consigning locally can be the best way to get the *most* money for your designer pieces. Keep in mind that brick-and-mortar stores are far more selective than online shops. They only have so much space for inventory, so don't be surprised if they're quite picky. You'll have much better luck by calling ahead or checking online to find out the season they're buying for as well as the specific styles they're after.

Secrets of a Resale Guru

If your clothes and shoes are looking a little worn, you can get them into selling shape with a few tricks. The more store fresh your clothes appear, the higher their resale value and the better the chance they'll find an interested buyer!

- **Remove fuzz:** Use packing tape or a lint roller to remove *all* traces of fuzz, pet hair, and lint, no matter how small. These particles add a distinct worn-out look to items.

- **Press out wrinkles:** Pressed clothes look nicer and are an easier sell. Take the time to iron or steam your pieces, and reshape areas that have become warped from wear, such as bent pocket edges, cuffs, or hems.

- **Banish odors:** Launder washable items in cold water and air-dry to avoid any additional fading or pilling. If you have dry-clean-only items that smell a bit musty, spritz them with a mixture of one-part vodka to four parts water and air-dry. You might be able to skip the cleaners.

- **Shave pills:** Sweaters and knits often form pills in the armpits or on the sides from friction and machine washing. Many pills can be banished by "shaving" them off using a cheap disposable razor or battery-operated fabric shaver. Just skim the fabric; pressing down too hard will create holes.

- **Clean soles:** Use an old toothbrush to remove traces of dirt from the treads of your shoes. For dingy insoles, try placing a damp paper towel inside your shoes to loosen dirt, then wipe away. Touch up scuffs with shoe polish or even a black or brown Sharpie for small spots.

- **Perfect your presentation:** If you're selling in person, keep in mind that most resale shops will put your clothes straight out onto the sales floor. Make the effort to clean, press, and fold your clothes and place them neatly into a nice shopping bag. It can help to wear a chic outfit, too. It primes the buyer to take you and your clothes more seriously.

Clothing Swaps Can Save the World

There is a hyperlocal, supersocial way to part with old clothes and freshen your wardrobe at the same time: Swap them! Clothing swaps are gatherings where people meet and mingle and exchange their closet castoffs, and they've gone from local pastime to planet-wide phenomenon in recent years. Through the beautifully simple act of exchanging used clothes, swappers save the planet another landfilled garment and the water and resources needed to make new textiles.

At a swap, you just might walk in with a collectible concert T-shirt and walk out with a red Hermès suit. It happened to Patrick Duffy, the founder of Global Fashion Exchange (GFX), a New York–based organization that's coordinated megaswaps in thirty-six countries around the world and extended the life of a whopping 1.2 million pounds of clothes. "Swaps are opening people's eyes to a completely new way of doing things," says Duffy. "The old way was shop and buy. The new model is swap and borrow."[1]

If you love the sound of swapping, check around to see where the next one is happening in your community. Or, better yet, organize your own! Here are a few ground rules to putting on a successful swap in your area or among your best-dressed pals. The Global Fashion Exchange website has additional tips and resources for those looking to organize a larger swap.

1. **Choose your space and gather supplies.** You can host a swap in your living room, a classroom at the local college, or even a convention center, if you want to think big. Find a spacious spot and gather some supplies, such as tables, racks, and hangers on which to display the clothes and facilitate the swapping. Have some full-length mirrors on hand. Set up some makeshift fitting rooms if need be. To get swappers mingling and talking to one another, put together a playlist of great music and set a good vibe. "It does make a big difference for swappers to walk into a place that feels good, that looks good, that's got great lighting, and that's got great music," says Duffy.[2]

2. **Set your acceptance policies.** Convey to all swappers that they should *only* bring stylish items in tip-top condition. Duffy defines acceptable swap items as "something you'd be excited to gift to your friend."[3] Think cute dress that you wore once to a party versus old, ratty sweatpants. Decide if you'll limit how many items swappers can bring (lest someone show up with their entire wardrobe). Is it two pieces, ten, or unlimited? Many swaps establish a currency for swapping, using tickets or tokens that are then exchanged for swapped items. Consider assigning extra tickets for valuable items like designer labels or quality leather jackets. And don't forget to advertise your swap well, so that you get a good selection of inventory.

3. **Swap 'til you drop.** Presentation is key to a successful swap. Organizers should sort and put out a selection of items as fast as possible after swappers arrive or ahead of time, if you can. Items should be folded or hung neatly and organized by style and category (shoes with shoes, tops with tops), so swappers can easily find what they're interested in. Swaps can get messy fast, so it helps to have a point person, or a few, to reorganize clothes throughout the swap.

4. **Donate extra clothes.** There *will be* leftover clothes. Have a strategy lined up to responsibly donate them ahead of time. Donate to a local charity or textile recycler of your choosing. Or, if it's a small swap, you can require swappers to take their leftovers home.

5. **Add a take-home message.** Swaps can and should double as a space to raise awareness about the importance of sustainability in fashion. You could print out and hang up statistics you discover in this book: "For every T-shirt we swap, we save the planet 2,168 gallons of water!" or "For every garment worn twice as long, its carbon footprint is reduced by 44%!"[4] At Kennesaw State University in Georgia, clothing swaps feature posters with quotes from Bangladeshi garment workers about sweatshop conditions in the fashion industry. You'll hear more about KSU students in Chapter 28. You might create a unique hashtag for your swap to help spread the message about clothing exchanges. And don't forget to collect contact information so you can invite everyone back to your next swap!

A WORLD WITHOUT CLOTHING WASTE

You now have the skills you need to mindfully clean out your closet and reuse, rewear, recycle, and resell what you're no longer wearing. You've learned how to do your part to reduce the amount of clothing waste in the world and keep fashion in use for as long as possible. Moving forward, it's a great idea to do mini-cleanouts every time you're flipping through your closet, considering on a regular basis what should stay and what needs to go. Don't let your castoffs pile up. Make your Clothing Reuse Plan part of your routine. Sell your valuable clothes and shoes as *soon* as you're tired of wearing them and before they become dated. You'll make more money that way. You can keep a small bag in the bottom of your closet (I keep mine in a hall closet) to hold garments or shoes you plan to donate or recycle. Make it a goal to make the trip to the charity or recycler of your choice once a season. It'll keep you from getting overwhelmed and clutter from piling up. Plan that swap you've been meaning to organize with your friends! Repair or reuse everything else. By following these steps, you'll find that it's possible to operate an almost zero-waste closet with ease. In the coming chapters, we'll learn how to *prevent* so much clothing waste and wardrobe clutter from happening in the first place by buying better and buying less. This is our mission as we head into Part Two: "The Art of Less."

PART TWO

The Art of Less

**Buy less. Choose well.
Make it last.**

–VIVIENNE WESTWOOD

The Stylish, Sustainable Power of Less

The Art of Less is a philosophy based on the thoughtful, intentional consumption of fewer items of clothing. The Art of Less isn't anti-fashion. It's anti-clutter, anti-waste, and anti–mindless consumption. Far too much clothing ends up in landfills and incinerators or just sitting in the back of our closets, unloved and collecting dust. Buying less and wearing our clothes more is a simple and sustainable solution.

But if less were really all that easy to put into practice, we'd be doing it already! To truly unleash the power of less, we need to cultivate strategies in our everyday lives that help us to consume less and to consume better. We need to know *how much less* and *less of what*.

The Art of Less has tremendous personal benefits. It is the secret to building a functioning wardrobe, affording better-quality clothes, and staying sane amid a swirl of fashion discounts, deals, and changing trends. Buying less might sound daunting, but it doesn't have to be. We can choose to think of it as wearing what we love more. Most of the chapters in Part Two are dedicated to the timeless arts of buying well and, from there, dressing well with what you've got.

Less is a boon for the planet. It is the single most effective way we can reduce our fashion footprint. The vast majority of the clothing industry's environmental toll happens while manufacturing new clothes, specifically in the process of turning fiber into fabrics. According to the sustainability consulting firm Quantis, *93 percent* of the carbon emissions and water used in making fashion happens while creating the textiles that become our clothes.[1] That's why I've dedicated several chapters in Part Four to an in-depth look at sustainable, nontoxic fibers and the companies that use them.

Just by doing our part to buy carefully and wear our clothes for longer, we can help make fashion more sustainable. We can reduce the per capita demand for more new clothes, and stretch out the water, energy, and chemicals used to make what we wear. Less is so simple, but the impacts are huge: One study by Wrap UK found that wearing a garment just nine months longer reduces that garment's carbon, water, and waste footprints by 20 to 30 percent.[2] That is the sustainable power of less.

Brands also need to do their part to make less clothing. There is a glut of fashion manufactured each season, far in excess of what consumers can buy. It's trashed or burned instead. An estimated 2.2 billion pounds of overstock and unsold clothing are landfilled or incinerated around the world every year, according to a 2018 report by the Ellen MacArthur Foundation, a UK charity that promotes sustainability. Two billion pounds of clothes is the equivalent in weight of 5 billion T-shirts, enough leftover stock to dress the adult population of the planet. In 2018, H&M announced that the brand was stuck with 4.3 *billion* dollars' worth of unsold goods. And a few months later, luxury brand Burberry was caught destroying 24 million dollars' worth of excess clothing and accessories (they later agreed to ban the practice), proving that it's not just fast-fashion brands whose production methods have gone off the rails.[3]

Incredible progress is being made to make the manufacture of new clothes sustainable. And there are easy ways to keep up with trends that have a much smaller environmental impact. And yet, neither negates the equally urgent need for less.

The Fashion Fast

I **can't stop thinking** about this one pair of beautiful cowboy boots made in Mexico of black-and-white cowhide. I saw them on Instagram, and now they're bouncing around inside my head, whispering, *Buy me,* and tussling with the half-dozen pairs of other boots I already own for a spot in my closet. We're constantly bombarded with the latest trends and gorgeous products on social media, on TV, or while walking around the world. How do we resist the allure of the new and just appreciate what we've got? How do we learn to *leave space* in our wardrobes for the right things, things we actually love and want to wear?

Enter the fashion fast! You can also call it a clothing diet, a shopping diet, a fast-fashion ban, or a no-shopping challenge. Call it what you will, a fashion fast is the opposite of fast fashion. It is a full and intentional break from buying new clothes and the perfect way to kick off the Art of Less. There are a number of fantastic reasons to go on a fashion fast—and to repeat the fast on the regular. You'll free up a shocking amount of money and time and gain a razor-sharp understanding of what motivates your purchases. I took a fashion fast while writing my first book, *Overdressed,* and I imposed one on myself while writing this book, as I started to justify my addiction to vintage Escada under the guise of "research." Here's how to make the most of your own fashion fast.

THE FASHION FAST RULES

1. **Survey the situation.** Before you start, tally up how much clothing you've been buying and what you've been spending. A quick way to arrive at an estimate is to count the hangers of the pieces you think you purchased in the past year and multiply it by an estimated price paid (so, forty items times 40 dollars each equals 1,600 dollars—ouch). Download an app that tallies your screen-time use or use iPhone's Screen Time function to look up time spent browsing online shops as well. These figures can be startling but are important motivation to take the fast and change your shopping habits once the fast is over.

2. **Set your parameters.** You could fast for a few weeks, a month, one season, or a full year. Choose a length of time that is challenging but is something you can realistically stick to. Make rules ahead of time about what you can and can't buy. Are you including shoes and accessories? If you simply *have* to buy an outfit for work or a special event, use your fast as an opportunity to borrow an item from a friend, attend a clothing swap, or shop your own closet.

3. **Find your allies.** Whether you need the moral support or simply want to take the challenge with friends, fashion fasting with others can be great fun. Tell friends when you start so that they can either join in or help hold you accountable. Social media fashion fasting has been popular for more than a decade, so consider finding fellow fasters with hashtags such as #fashionfast, #clothing diet, #shoppingban, and #noshoppingchallenge.

4. **Free your time.** Fully take back your time spent shopping! Recycle your catalogues and cut out all browsing online. If necessary, use a browser extension like Icebox for Chrome to "Put It on Ice"—in other words, to stop you from making purchases. Consider

unsubscribing from emails and promotions from clothing brands. To block ads from clothing companies on Instagram, select "Hide Ad" on a few ads, and you'll start to see less of this sort of content. Or just limit your time on social media in general. Next, dedicate some of those reclaimed hours to your existing wardrobe. Here are some ideas of how to fill your time.

- **Tackle wardrobe repairs.** If you've been putting off getting your shoes resoled or sewing that button back on, now is a great time to get it done! Part Five: "Make It Last" is full of tips on how to mend and repair or hire someone to fix your clothes and shoes.

- **Shop your closet.** Social media has made wear-it-once culture cool. Buck the trend and show off the pieces you love to wear again and again. Pair them up in fresh ways and restyle and accessorize outfits to give them new life. You can post your results to social media using hashtags like #shopyourcloset or #30wears, a movement to rewear each item in your closet *at least* thirty times. If you're looking for inspiration, Duchess of Cambridge Kate Middleton is well-known for repeating looks, as is Tiffany Haddish, who has worn her white Alexander McQueen gown to four high-profile events. Actress Emma Watson is another famous outfit repeater (not to mention all-around sustainable fashion champion). Her outfits often meet the #30wears test, too!

- **Take a capsule wardrobe challenge.** Really push yourself to get creative with the clothes you already own by taking a capsule wardrobe challenge! Capsule challenges require that you only wear a small number of clothes over a set amount of time and try to come up with new outfits each day out of your limited stock. There are several challenges to choose from.

Project 333, started by *Be More with Less* blogger Courtney Carver, inspires participants to choose thirty-three items for their wardrobe and wear them for three months. The 10x10 Style Challenge, created by blogger Lee Vosburgh, permits just ten items over ten days. Participate on social media with the hashtags #project333 #10by10challenge or #capsuleward robechallenge. Or make up your own capsule wardrobe rules! Fellow conscious fashionista Benita Robledo and I started #glamcapsule, a wardrobe capsule challenge based around our brightest, boldest pieces. You'll be surprised at how far a few items of clothing can go, not to mention the wardrobe-building chops you'll gain from pairing the same clothes a different way each day. I now know how to style my all-red pantsuit into five different outfits—some chic and glam, and others casual and rock 'n' roll—as a result!

HOW TO HOLD ON TO THE LESSONS OF THE FASHION FAST

Some fashion fasters use their diet to save up for a dream wardrobe item, perhaps by a pioneering conscious brand. Others identify and overcome their shopping triggers that lead to buying regrets. The fast can help you figure out if you tend to buy impulsively when you're happy, sad, or bored, for example. Set goals to be a smarter, more discerning shopper. After a fast, I try to hold on to how it *feels* to not buy anything, which is simply like a person in control. I'm usually relieved at the money I've saved and the clutter I've prevented. I'm rarely sad that I've skipped a pair of boots. Fashion fasting can help cultivate the discipline to be in a store without buying, hold out for better purchases, and treasure what you already own, all useful skills in building a conscious closet.

Upping Your Quality Game

My work in the secondhand industry gives me rare access to all kinds of brands in a wide range of makes and models, from boohoo to Balenciaga. I've wrapped myself in stunning camel-hair coats that could last generations and slithered out of disintegrating faux-leather jackets destined for the landfill. I've experienced quality clothing so awe-inspiring it made me misty-eyed, and it's taught me this: There are *vast* differences in the quality of clothing made today, from disposable to passable to transcendent. And we should all know these differences.

Everything in our wardrobes needn't be exquisitely made. It's not realistic. I have 2-dollar polyester yard-sale finds hanging next to Italian wool blazers. But as you depart from your fashion fast and start to build a more satisfying conscious closet, you should strive to own quality clothes and learn to recognize them. This chapter will help you choose better, longer-lasting, more beautifully made apparel, no matter your budget or where you shop. Good-quality clothing is good for the planet because it lasts. But quality also lasts because it's so damn compelling. It's that essence that draws you to a garment again and again.

WHERE TO PRACTICE SHOPPING FOR QUALITY

Good-quality clothing is clothing made with care and intention from start to finish, from the overall design to the type of fabric, thread, buttons, and seams used to create it. Quality clothing is made to last, wear well, and look good over time. Learning to spot quality requires exposure to well-made clothes and attention to detail, but anyone can master it. Here are several places to practice shopping for quality:

- **Your own clothes.** Which pieces in your closet have stood the test of time? Which pieces *seem* like good quality to you? Study the fabric and the way the garment is put together to start to better understand why.

- **Grandma's closet.** Scour the wardrobes of friends and loved ones who own finer pieces. I've spent hours in my ninety-two-year-old grandmother's closet, examining and trying on her coats and dresses. Clothes made fifty years ago were not made to throw away.

- **A wide range of stores.** Go on a try-on trip and touch and try on the best *and* the worst clothing, from the softest merino wool to the coarsest polyester in shops as wide-ranging as luxury chains to dollar stores. It's through comparison that differences in quality become clear.

- **The men's department.** Men's clothes are still on the whole better made than women's, as the styles change more slowly and more durable design is expected. Study the way men's suiting and dress shirts in particular are constructed and how the fabric feels.

- **Thrift and vintage stores.** Thrift stores are full of pre-fast-fashion clothes made with more thought and intention (and of course full of plenty of awful clothes as well!), and these well-constructed pieces provide a great education.

THE QUALITY RECIPE: FABRIC, CONSTRUCTION, FIT, AND DETAILS

Now that you've gotten a little real-world education in quality, it's time to dig deeper into what makes a fine piece of clothing. Quality is a recipe in which the ingredients are fabric, construction, fit, and details. Here's an in-depth review of what to look for in each ingredient as you shop.

The Basics of Great Fabric

Fabric is the most important ingredient in the quality recipe. It determines so much about the appearance, comfort, durability, care, and cost of your clothes. Fabric comprises as much as half of the cost of a garment, which is why you'll often see brands and retailers cutting corners here.[1] Here's how to tell if you're buying a quality material:

- **Is the fabric ideal for the garment?** When shopping for quality, start by looking at the fabric label, which can be found at the neck, side seam, or waistband. The very first thing to consider is if the fabric is right for the garment. You can answer this question by thinking about where you plan to wear the piece. Are you wearing it outside on a hot day or in an air-conditioned office? Are you going running in it or going to a party in it? Choose the fabric that has the appropriate features, whether it's comfort, warmth, beauty, or performance. Some examples: Many high-tech synthetics are ideal for activewear, swimwear, and outerwear, as they're lightweight, they resist abrasion, and they dry fast. They can also offer performance features like waterproofing. Wool and cashmere are ideal for sweaters, as they're insulating but breathable. Cotton is an ideal all-weather material because it can be either cozy or airy, while silk is often used in eveningwear because of its unmatchable luster and beauty. The cheaper you shop, the more wrong fabrics you'll see, like clammy polyester summer dresses or nylon blended into denim shorts just to lower the price.

- **Does it breathe?** Breathability is a fabric's ability to absorb moisture from your skin and the environment, which is key to feeling cool, dry, and comfortable in your clothes. Breathability is very important when it comes to everyday clothes that you wear next to your body, such as tops, jeans, pants, and intimates like underwear and socks. Natural fibers, like cotton, linen, and wool, are all very breathable, as is viscose rayon. Most synthetics used in everyday, low-cost clothing, such as acrylic, polyester, and nylon, are not breathable and trap moisture next to the skin, especially woven or non-stretchy synthetic garments. Polyester and nylon can be manufactured and finished in ways that make them more breathable, by changing their molecular structure or the weave of the material to help these fibers pull moisture to the surface of the fabric. To shop for more comfortable synthetics, look for clothing labeled as "moisture wicking" and that feels soft and smooth to the touch. But you won't find these airier types of synthetics in low-cost stores. When in doubt, choose natural fibers or viscose rayon for your everyday clothing and intimates, as they're sure to keep you comfortable. If you're buying a garment made out of a blend of fibers, make sure that at least 50 percent of the fiber content is a natural material or viscose rayon.

- **Is it beautiful?** If you're buying a garment for mountain climbing, beauty won't be top of mind as you shop. For everyday clothing and formal wear, the aesthetics of your fibers matter *a lot*. Look beyond print and color and consider if the weave and finish of your fiber is, yes, beautiful. Low-cost, low-quality fabrics, especially cheaper polyesters and viscose rayon, can be very flat and dull, for example, have a limp or stiff drape or boast an unflattering sheen. Good-quality materials have a beautiful texture and finish that reflect light in a more natural-looking and pleasing way. For example, the natural crimp and loft of fine wool, the nubby variations found in high-quality cotton and linen, and the rich sheen of silk can be quite handsome. There are of course beautiful synthetics, too. I own a gorgeous rust-colored blouse in acetate, a more rarified type of viscose rayon that mimics silk. Some of the most beautiful fabrics have a nap or raised surface, like velvet, bouclé, flannel, or suede. Consider how the fabric drapes, as well. Does the fabric hang and move in a beautiful way? Avoid materials that are clingy and staticky.

- **Consider the hand feel.** Rub the fabric between your fingers and thumb. This is known as a fabric's "hand feel," or the way the textile feels to the touch. Hand feel is most important in everyday clothing and formal wear, as it enriches the experience and pleasure of wearing your clothes and can be the feature that draws you to a garment. In my own wardrobe, for example, I have a merino wool cardigan with leather elbow patches that has a polished softness to it that I love. I also have 100 percent cotton T-shirts that are divinely smooth and soft to the touch. Good-quality merino wool, cashmere, cotton, and silk are all known for their exceptional hand feel. The quality of a fabric is determined by the weave and the fineness and length of the fibers, and there are lower-quality versions of both natural and synthetic material. Avoid fabrics that feel stiff, cold, dry, or rough. Keep in mind that fabrics can also be too soft (the softer the cashmere, for example, the more prone it is to pilling[2]). Use your hands as a guide, and no matter the price, choose a fabric that is pleasing to the touch.

- **Thin versus sturdy.** Fabrics are getting thinner, as retailers try to shave costs. To give two examples, my vintage cotton T-shirts from the 1990s weigh about three to five ounces more than my modern T-shirts, and my vintage 100 percent cotton jeans weigh almost *a pound* more than my modern denim. Ultra-thin materials are popular, especially in casual knitted items like T-shirts and summer dresses, but they rarely last. Try to choose a more densely woven fabric that feels substantial, is slightly weighty, and isn't sheer (unless it's supposed to be). This indicates a longer-lasting, higher-quality piece. A fabric's weight is also key to giving a garment proper drape.

- **Is it durable?** You want your clothes to look good for as long as possible. How do you avoid materials that pill, stretch out, wear thin, fade, or break from regular wear and washing? A lot of factors contribute to clothing's durability, including the weave and thickness of the material, which we've already discussed, and the sewing, which we'll get to later in this chapter. Let's start with pilling. How do you avoid materials that pill, which are those little balls of fabric that form due to friction or machine washing? Some fabrics, like fleece, flannel, and knitwear, are bound to pill, but if they're good quality, they will pill less and—just as important— will return to their original appearance once the pills are removed. You can remove pills with a razor or fabric shaver (refer back to the tips in Chapter 5). How do you avoid materials that pill up and won't return to their original appearance? Materials that are prone to pilling include low-grade viscose rayon knits (its lesser varieties also lose their shape when washed), synthetic fleece, as well as some blended fibers. When materials with different competing properties like polyester, cotton, and spandex are mixed together, they can pill and shrink at different rates when washed.[3] If you do buy a blended fiber (it's getting hard to avoid them), look for a ratio of 75 percent or higher of one material, such as 75 percent wool, 20 percent nylon, and 5 percent elastane.

Brands and retailers have a tremendous amount of control over durability, as they can add finishes that make clothing resistant to pilling, fading, and abrasion and test their products for longevity. The cheaper the price, the less likely it is that manufacturers have gone to the necessary lengths to add these features. If you've shopped a brand and had performance failures in the past or your clothes start to look worn-out fast, it's time to shop elsewhere. As consumers, we also have a lot of influence over the longevity of our clothes; it's possible to make even lower-quality fabrics last by changing the way you wash and maintain your clothes (more on that in Part Five: "Make It Last").

- **How do you clean it?** One last thing to consider when choosing a fabric is the laundering instructions, found on the inside label of your clothes. Make sure you're willing to follow any care instructions, including suggestions to hand wash or air-dry, when choosing a garment. Don't confuse easy-care garments with quality. As you'll learn in the chapter on laundry (Chapter 22), Americans in particular overwash their clothing and rely on machine washing instead of steaming and airing out their clothes, which shortens the life span of what we wear. In turn, retailers are making more and more of our clothes out of synthetics that can better endure incessant washing. Ironically, polyester, nylon, and blended fibers with a heavy percentage of synthetics attract odors, meaning so-called easy-care synthetics have to be washed more often.[4] You might also avoid low-cost synthetics and viscose rayons that are hand-wash only or dry-clean only. "Often the cheapest clothing is synthetics that cannot tolerate machine washing and drying," says Karuna Scheinfeld, a product designer. "These materials put the burden on the consumer to pay as much or more in cleaning as they paid for the garment."[5] Read my Q&A with Scheinfeld at the end of this chapter to learn more about the relationship between quality and the materials that brands and retailers use. Many quality garments and delicate natural materials, like those that are tailored and those made of silk and cashmere, tend to be dry-clean only or need to be hand-washed. The good news is that natural materials and tailored garments don't trap odors as easily as clingy clothing and synthetics and can be washed far less often as a result.

Naturals versus Synthetics

In the late nineteenth and early twentieth centuries, synthetic materials like polyester, nylon, spandex, and viscose rayon were debuted to great fanfare. Man-made materials were and still are celebrated as modern miracles for saving women countless hours scrubbing, ironing, and laundering more delicate natural fibers. Fast-forward to the 1980s, and synthetics were looked down on for being clammy, tacky, and flammable.

How things have changed! Incredible innovations in synthetic fibers have created more sophisticated, better-looking, and more comfortable man-made fibers. Most consumers buy synthetics without even noticing. Polyester and nylon together make up almost 60 percent of all textiles manufactured globally, while cotton has shrunk to a quarter of the fiber market.[6] Has this new reality made the age-old debate between naturals and synthetics obsolete?

Yes and no. Synthetics are undoubtedly better than they once were, and most people would consider them indispensable for working out or being outdoors. But polyester and viscose rayon are found in abundance in our everyday clothing simply because these materials are easier to make and cheaper—often *much* cheaper—than natural fibers. Most clothing today is designed to cost below a certain price point (let's call it the Impulse Threshold) to entice consumers into buying clothes at a disposable clip. Synthetics are integral to the Impulse Threshold, as they allow brands to meet that low price.

For your reference, the prices of common fibers from cheap to expensive are as follows: Polyester, nylon, acrylic, and conventional viscose rayon are cheapest to produce. Cotton and higher-performing viscose rayon like modal and lyocell are in the middle, in terms of cost to make. Leather, silk, linen, very-high-quality cotton, cashmere, and wool are many times more expensive than synthetics to manufacture and as a result are in a shrinking percentage of what we wear.

You can use this information to know when you're paying a fair price for fabric: Flip through the fabric labels whenever you're out shopping. If you spot the overuse of synthetics and viscose rayon by a brand in everything from T-shirts and jeans to blazers and dresses, it's a reliable indicator that low price is king over quality. On the other hand, if you find a range of materials on offer, from cotton and wool to viscose rayon and polyester, that's a clue that the brand is choosing the fabrics that *best* serve their garments. The one exception is activewear, swimwear, and outdoor clothing, which rely on synthetics for performance reasons.

Despite my understanding of synthetics and their place in the world, I have a deep affinity for natural materials in everyday clothing. Their cultivation supports farmers and farming communities around the world, and they have been a part of human culture for thousands of years. Synthetics often set out to re-create properties at a lower price point that natural fibers already possess, and fall short. Adding odor control or antimicrobial features to synthetics can come with certain health and environmental risks, for example, which I'll discuss in Chapter 19. Cotton, silk, linen, and wool have dimension and personality in the weave of the fabrics that lab-made synthetics often fail to replicate. What's more, many quality natural materials break in and age beautifully, rather than wear out or break apart. My wool sweaters, sturdy cotton T-shirts, leather jacket and shoes, and silk shirts look gorgeous after many years of wear. By contrast, in my years of sorting used clothes, it's almost without exception synthetic faux leather, synthetic and viscose rayon knitwear, and blended fibers combining synthetic and natural materials that look worn-out, pilled, and misshapen after regular wear and use.

Another issue that muddles the synthetic versus natural materials debate is the fact that a lot of clothing today is made out of blended materials of natural and synthetic fibers. Sometimes, blends are used to nudge the price down a bit while adding strength or wrinkle-resistant properties to a natural fiber that's more prone to these issues. But blends can also diminish quality by combining competing materials together that don't age or wash well. How can you tell if a blend is used to reduce price in a way that compromises quality? My rule of thumb is to choose clothing that is at least two-thirds of one single material. Scheinfeld recommends avoiding clothes that are a mix of more than three materials, as that's a sign of cost-cutting.[7]

Whether you're firmly in the natural-fiber camp or choose synthetics or blends for price, performance, or even ethical reasons, select the best quality you can afford and choose materials that *you* value and that work for your lifestyle. As I'll explain in Chapter 18, it's possible to buy more sustainable versions of whatever fiber suits your fancy.

THE ART AND SCIENCE OF GOOD CONSTRUCTION

Now that we've addressed good fabric, it's time to move on to construction. Construction is the way your garment is put together. Good-quality garments feature careful construction, from proper proportions and fit to strong sewing and expert placement of seams, which all combine to create a garment that can endure stress and strain, all while enhancing your appearance. To shop for good construction, start by inspecting the sewing.

Superior Sewing

You don't have to be an expert seamstress to notice good sewing. Start by examining the visible stitching on the outside of the garment and then turn the garment inside out and examine the stitching on the inside in good light. Here's what you're looking for:

- **Strong thread in a matching color.** The thread should match and blend into the garment, unless it's in a contrasting color for design reasons (like the gold or yellow topstitching on jeans). This is also an opportunity to tug on the seams; if the thread breaks, put the garment back, as it's an indication that low-quality thread was used throughout.

- **Neat, even stitches.** Look for stitches that are straight and evenly spaced and a consistent distance from the edge of the garment. An exception: If your garment is handmade or couture, the stitches will show more variation.

- **Lots of stitches per inch.** Generally, the more stitches per inch, the greater the seam strength and the more durable the garment. A stiches-per-inch (SPI) factor of 8 to 10 is typical in ready-to-wear fashion and is a sign of good strength. There are a few exceptions. "Heavier thread with a longer stitch length looks better on heavy materials like wool and coats, and I suggest looking for that," says Timo Rissanen, associate dean and professor of fashion design and sustainability at Parsons School of Design.[8]

- **Reinforced stitching in high-stress areas.** Look for strong and dense stitching in areas that will be pulled and stretched repeatedly during wear, such as around buttonholes, armholes, the back seams, belt loops, and where pockets and straps connect to the garment.

- **Strong, high-quality fasteners.** Fasteners refer to buttons, zippers, snaps, buckles, or anything that helps you into and out of your clothes. Tug on fasteners and test them out to make sure they don't feel thin or brittle—I often run a nail across them to make sure any paint or finish won't chip. Zip and unzip the zipper or snap and unsnap the snaps. They should work smoothly, without catching or slipping, and feel very sturdy. Buttons should also be sewn on securely. Tug on them to make sure.

- **What to skip.** Avoid garments with crooked sewing and loose, unclipped threads poking out (see Figure 1). Skip garments with broken or skipped stitches or puckered seams. These are signs of a garment made in haste with no basic quality control.

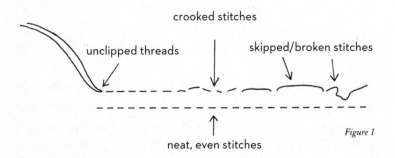

Figure 1

Sturdy Seams and Tidy Hems

Now that you've looked at the overall stitching, take a closer look at the seams and hems. Seams are the joints on your clothes where two pieces of fabric are sewn together. They are there to prevent the fabric from unraveling, to neaten the inside of the garment, and—most important—to keep your clothes together as you wear them. Here's how to check seams and hems for quality:

- **Check the strength.** To test the strength, gently try to pull the fabric apart at the side seams. You shouldn't be able to see daylight between the stitches, and the seams should return to their original appearance when you let go of the fabric.

- **Do the seams lie flat?** Seams should be sewn closed to lie flat against the garment and your body, so that they don't irritate your skin or add bulk. A generous seam allowance, where there's extra fabric left in the seam, is another sign of quality. It means you can let the garment out and alter it.

- **Inspect the finishing.** There are a variety of ways to finish or close seams. In mass-market clothes, the seams are often finished with a serger, which creates a noticeable tightly looped pattern (see Figure 2 on the next page). Serged seams are cheap and fast to create and relatively strong; just make sure there aren't any loose threads or broken stitches. In a higher-quality piece, you will find a more labor-intensive and visually appealing seam. The seams and inside sewing will be as neat and tidy as those on the outside. A Hong Kong seam, also known as a bias bound seam, and a French seam (see Figures 3 and 4 on the following pages) are two examples of high-quality seams to keep an eye out for.

- **How are the hems finished?** Hems are the finished edges of your garment, such as the bottom edge of a skirt or pair of pants. The sewing on any hemline should be tidy and straight. There are *many* ways to hem a garment, just as there are to make seams. A cheap hem will be closed with loose, crooked, or sloppy stitching

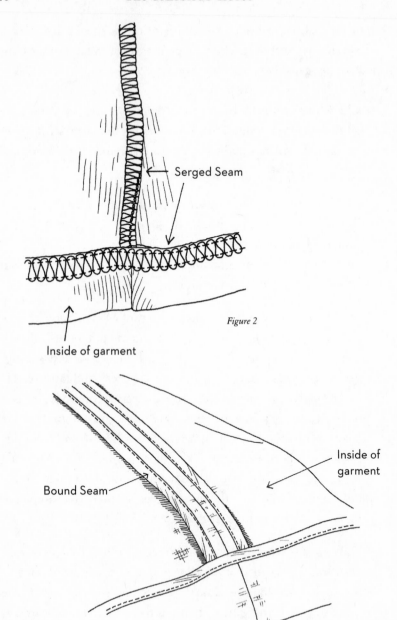

Serged Seam

Inside of garment

Figure 2

Bound Seam

Inside of garment

Figure 3

and the hem will be too flimsy to give the garment proper drape. The highest-quality garments are hemmed so that very little or no stitching is visible from the outside, creating a streamlined look. Look for extra material in the hem so that the garment can be easily altered.

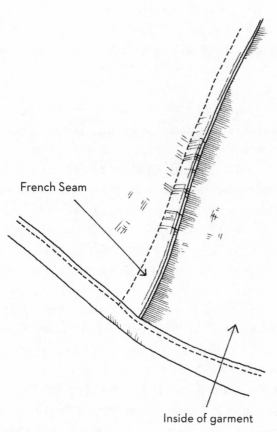

French Seam

Inside of garment

Figure 4

Divine Construction Details

We've covered the basics of stitching, seams, and hems. But very-good-quality garments are packed with all sorts of design and construction touches that elevate them to another level and make the piece more functional, flattering, and pleasurable to wear. If you've ever bought a garment and felt like something was lacking in the fit or design, you're not alone. Construction is often simplified and skimped on in order to meet the Impulse Threshold. Here are the divine construction details to keep a close eye out for when shopping for quality:

- **Generous construction.** With low-cost, low-quality clothing something has to be compromised to hit a price point, whether it's in the fabric, sewing, or construction. Perhaps a lining is foregone, an elastic waistband is used in place of a fitted waist, or a dress is designed to be sleeveless and short rather than cap-sleeved and knee-length to cut down on material costs. You can think of this as stingy construction. Good-quality garments are generous, using the fabric, sewing, and construction that makes for the best piece. "The proportion is based on design rather than cost savings, and each detail is considered," says Scheinfeld of generous construction.[9] Functional buttons and pockets, rather than the use of mock ones, are another reliable indicator of quality and generous construction, says Rissanen. "These are details that cost more to manufacture but speak of a heightened level of attention to detail that likely permeates the whole garment," he says.[10] I'll provide an example of stingy and generous construction from my own wardrobe. I have two knit T-shirt dresses, one of passable quality and one of good quality. The first, made by a fast-fashion brand, is unlined, a tad too short, and made out of a paper-thin cotton that clings and rides up. The high-quality T-shirt dress by contrast is fully lined and ruched on the sides for a more flattering silhouette and drape, the sleeves and hemline hit at the right length, and the piece is finished with an invisible hem. These seemingly small differences make a dramatic difference in the appearance and performance of these garments.

- **Discovery details.** Good-quality clothes are often a process of discovery, where the designer or brand has embedded features into the piece for the wearer to find and enjoy over time. Scheinfeld, who calls these "discovery details," says, "These are details so thoughtfully considered that they make you love the garment and appreciate the brand and designer."[11] An example of a discovery detail in my closet: I have a vintage Donna Karan leather trench coat finished with unimaginably supple leather-lined pockets. It's not something I would have noticed in the store, but it's become one of my favorite things about wearing this piece.

- **The beauty of tailoring.** Tailored garments are "molded to the body through cutting and sewing shaped pieces of fabric," explains Rissanen.[12] Low-quality clothing favors clothes that are fitted through stretch or that have no tailoring details because they're cheaper to make. Most of them can't touch the beauty of a tailored garment. In general, tailored garments like coats, suiting, and well-made dress shirts are very durable, as they are sewn to frame the body, rather than rub against it, and are often made out of thicker, loftier fabrics like wool. In my own closet, shopping for quality has meant adding more woven (nonstretchy) and tailored pieces. One very basic tailoring detail to look for is darts, triangular folds of fabric sewn into garments that give clothing shape and form. Let me give an example of what a difference tailoring makes: In my wardrobe, I have two bustiers, one knitted and one tailored. The first, from a fast-fashion chain, is made out of a low-quality acrylic knit that is stretching out and pilling and is finished with serged seams that irritate my skin. The second bustier is a vintage Dolce & Gabbana, which is crafted in a pinstripe wool and tailored with molded bra cups, hook-and-eye closures, and bound seams that are both comfortable and beautiful. The second garment has lasted decades and is one of my favorite wardrobe pieces both to wear and to study.

The Fundamentals of Fine Fit

It's important to make sure your clothes are neither too tight nor too loose, but good fit involves much more than sizing. A well-fitting garment will match your proportions and allow you to move with ease, all without exposing parts of your body that you're not intending to.

Quality brands go out of their way to ensure proper fit and to keep the fit consistent from garment to garment, explains Scheinfeld. "The highest-quality manufacturers are rigorous about fit consistency, so if you find that a certain brand often fits you well and is made well, it's generally an element you can count on."[13] On the other hand, if you never know what size you are in a given brand, and some garments fit and others don't, that's an indicator of a low-quality brand that is skimping on fit testing or skipping it entirely.

To examine fit, you'll have to try the garment on and spend some time in the fitting room. "It's worth the pain of the fitting room to determine which brands you can count on and return to season after season," says Scheinfeld.[14] The first thing to consider is if the garment allows you to move freely and comfortably. Can you sit down without the waistband gaping or falling down? Likewise, your shirt shouldn't open and show your bra or chest when you breathe or stretch. In a well-fitting garment, the shoulder seam will sit right on the outer tip of your shoulder and not extend past it, the torso and legs will be fitted but not tight, and the sleeves will stop just below your wrist and not hang over your hand. Ask yourself: Are the seams sitting in the right spot? Is everything the appropriate length? Are the straps, pockets, and other details in the correct position? If you've said yes to all of the above, you're on the road to good fit.

When you're trying on a garment, it's important to look past the surface details like print, color, or embellishments to how a garment feels and fits on your body. Close your eyes and pay attention to how the fabric feels next to your skin. Mentally scan down your body and ask yourself if the garment is comfortable and not clingy or restrictive. Walk and spin around to test the drape and motion of the fabric. Is the fabric moving as it's supposed to, without riding up or bunching? Next, sit down—make sure the piece is still comfortable, that the hem isn't riding up too high, and that you like the way the garment looks when you're sitting as well as standing. Last but not least, look in the mirror and ask yourself if this is something you're truly excited to wear! Put the piece back if you've got any doubts.

A Note on Warranties

Quality is a recipe that includes good fabric, construction, fit, details, *and a warranty*. When shopping for quality, look for a brand that stands behind its product. Look to see what kind of warranty is offered, what returns are accepted, and what type of repair and replacement services are provided. "The better the guarantee, warrantee, or return policy, the better the quality typically is," says Scheinfeld.[15] Nudie Jeans, a sustainable denim brand, offers free repairs on jeans for life, for example. Patagonia offers repairs, replacements, or refunds for damaged products or if the product simply doesn't live up to expectations. Céline, Givenchy, and Chanel are just a few of the high-end brands that offer repairs within one to two years of purchase.[16]

Quality Cheat Sheet

HIGH-QUALITY GARMENT

- The garment is made of sturdy, beautifully woven fabric with a pleasing hand feel and that drapes and moves properly.

- If you're shopping for activewear or performance garments, the garment is made from a material that wicks moisture, dries fast, cleans easily, prevents chafing, and so on.

- A garment other than performance or activewear is made from natural fabrics, such as cotton, linen, wool, leather, or cashmere; they are more expensive but tend to wear better and last longer and are easier to repair.

- The sewing is straight and strong and the construction is generous. Seams and hems are as tidy and appealing-looking as the outside of the garment.

- The thread and notions, like buttons or zippers, are durable, thoughtfully chosen, and matching in design or color.

- The garment comes with extra buttons and in some cases extra thread. This indicates the garment is designed to be kept and cared for.

- The garment comes backed with a warranty or repair service.

LOW-QUALITY GARMENT

- The fabric is stiff, dull, thin, staticky, clammy, or otherwise unappealing looking or feeling.

- The fabric choice is improper for the garment, such as synthetics used in warm-weather garments or heavily blended fabrics that wash and wear poorly.

- The stitching is crooked or loose, with lots of unclipped threads. Hems and seams are finished in the cheapest, weakest, and least visually appealing way.

- The construction details are stingy, such as lack of functional pockets and tailoring, elastic where there should be a fitted waist, or awkward or too-short designs.

- Notions and fasteners are cheap or flimsy and break or chip easily.

- A warranty or repair policy is nonexistent or very limited.

HOW TO USE PRICE TO JUDGE QUALITY

Quality costs more because it requires more time and labor to design, fit, and sew and is made with better, more costly materials. Quality is always worth the money because it lasts far longer and looks much better. But using price to gauge quality will only get you so far; it all depends on what kind of garment you're buying and the garment's level of complexity. While a good-quality T-shirt can and should be affordable, it's hard to imagine a quality winter coat or more formal dress that's cheap. And, yes, a couture runway or red carpet gown, sometimes made with the contributions of dozens of skilled artisans, might really cost as much as a car to make. High price is a more reliable guide for quality if you're buying something complex, like coats, tailored dresses, dress pants, and blazers. It's less trustworthy if you're buying something basic like a T-shirt or simple summer dress. Always use your Quality Cheat Sheet and be your own sleuth.

How Much Does Quality Cost?

Well-made garments start to emerge in the mid-market, where clothes are priced from around 30 dollars for a simple top in a good fabric to around 150 to 500 dollars for more formal dresses, coats, or tailored pieces. These are the prices at which the full quality checklist can be met: good fabrics, construction, fit, and details. If this is out of your current budget, don't fret. See Chapters 14 and 17 on shopping resale and fashion finances, respectively. I assure you it's possible to scale up and own *very* fine garments on a tight budget. But always keep in mind that quality lasts longer and will pay for itself over time.

If you are shopping cheap—down below the Impulse Threshold—always put your purchases through the ringer before you buy them. Use the Quality Cheat Sheet. Some low-cost clothes will last and look great for a long time; many others won't. Tug on the seams, run zippers up and down, and stretch and scrunch the fabric to make sure it doesn't crease too easily or stretch out. Wash these pieces very carefully. Just because it's cheap doesn't mean it should fall apart after a few wears.

You should also be somewhat cautious of clothes that advertise themselves as vaguely "designer." Authentic designer clothing is more expensive and that price should always be backed up by good materials, inspired design, and expert craftsmanship. Advertising low-quality clothes as "designer" just to overcharge for a name is a problem in some off-price and outlet stores, lower-end department stores, and boutiques in the United States. "Designer" sometimes is a genuine indication of good design, materials, and sewing, but it can also be an excuse to slap on a high markup that doesn't equate to better craftsmanship. Don't be fooled. Use your Quality Cheat Sheet and follow the recipe.

When shopping for fine clothing, we don't always get what we want. Ask yourself which part of the quality recipe you're able to live without. I always prioritize fine fabrics, with rare exception, and prefer to wear a simple design made out of a good material. But I know a lot of Style Seekers who use the opposite approach and prioritize an interesting design and are willing to overlook a cheaper, synthetic material as a trade-off. Make decisions about quality based on your budget, priorities, and Fashion Personality Type.

Five Wardrobe Staples to Buy for Quality

Your entire wardrobe will look more polished, and you'll look and feel more put together, by buying high-quality versions of these five wardrobe staples. If buying for quality feels out of reach, refer to the resale and secondhand shopping chapters (14 and 15, respectively), and scale up slowly, piece by piece, over time.

1. **Winter coats.** Coats are complex garments that need to be sturdy enough to be worn on the daily and taken on and off repeatedly for months on end. Buy the best you can afford. Choose something very well made, functional, and timeless. Likewise, a good leather jacket should last a lifetime. Pick a classic cut instead of something trendy. Choose leather that feels supple but durable. Double-check for very strong stitching, a heavy-duty zipper, a full lining, and functional pockets.

2. **Sweaters.** A good wool or cashmere sweater can last an eternity. A crewneck, turtleneck, or cable-knit sweater always looks classic and chic. Good wool will feel substantial, lofty, and filled out, not thin. Ultrasoft knits can be a sign of poor quality.[17] Good wools will soften with time and wear.

3. **Handbags.** Resist the temptation to buy a cheap knockoff and get a good, high-quality genuine leather handbag by a trusted brand name. Very-high-quality designer handbags can be had at affordable prices on resale websites like Tradesy, the RealReal, thredUP, and Rebag. High-quality faux leather bags are also increasingly easy to find (Stella McCartney and Matt & Nat are two popular brands making chic and durable synthetic leather products). More on leather and its alternatives in Chapter 18.

4. **Jeans.** Most of us live in our denim, so it pays to buy the best you can afford. Skip paper-thin jeans in favor of denim with a bit of heft and weight to it. Jeans in 100 percent cotton last an

> eternity and are easy to mend. If you want a little stretch, opt for no more than 2 percent spandex. Blended fabrics of polyester, viscose rayon, and spandex are almost always a sign of cost cutting and can lead to your denim quickly pilling and stretching out.
>
> 5. **Shoes.** As I'll describe in full in Chapter 10, if there's one item in your wardrobe you should always buy for quality, it's shoes. I usually have one pair of canvas sneakers and synthetic running shoes that I burn through in a year to eighteen months, but the rest of my footwear is leather dress shoes that are built to last for years.

From Big-Box Stores to Conscious Brands: Where to Find Well-Made Clothes You'll Love for Years

I can't possibly list all the brands and retailers manufacturing well-made clothes, but that's good news! There are still a lot of gorgeous, thoughtfully made garments out there in the world. I've found perfect cotton T-shirts in big-box chains, supple leather flats and cashmere sweaters in fast-fashion stores, and my favorite wool winter hat in the clearance bin of an off-price store. You can find quality *almost* anywhere now that you know what to look for. I encourage you to read through to Chapter 20, on shopping consciously, so you can choose quality brands that are doing their part to be more ethical and sustainable, and scour the chapters on resale shopping to land the very best deals (I afford quality by shopping secondhand). Here is how to look for quality no matter where you shop:

- **Dollar stores.** Proceed with caution. You might have some luck buying passable basics like socks and T-shirts, but the sewing tends to be loose and sloppy and the fabrics have a tendency to be subpar and quickly pill and lose their shape.

- **Fast-fashion chains** (H&M, Zara, Fashion Nova, Missguided, Forever 21, etc.). Fast-fashion chains make ultrastylish clothes. But they also make gobs of product, so the quality is hit-or-miss from item to item and from company to company. Skip the really cheap online fast-fashion chains where prices start at a dollar. It's not possible to make much of anything of quality at that price. Use your Quality Cheat Sheet and switch to brands with more consistent quality.

- **Big-box stores** (Walmart, Kohl's, etc.). Big-box chains tend to test their products well and churn out the same basic styles over and over again. This means T-shirts, tanks, underwear, kids' clothes, and activewear can be quite reliable. Skip the handbags and shoes and anything trendy or more complex and designer-looking, as big-box stores rarely deliver good quality on these items.

- **Mid-tier and high-end department stores** (Dillard's, Macy's, Saks, Bloomingdale's, Nordstrom, etc.). Department stores aren't as popular as they used to be, and that's too bad because they're one of the most reliable places to find a range of name brands, from mid to high quality. Support your local department stores, and ask a sales assistant to help in your search for quality.

- **Branded retailers** (J.Crew, Levi's, Gap, Anthropologie, etc.). Branded retailers in general have to uphold a certain standard of quality to maintain their reputation and justify the higher prices they charge (higher compared to fast fashion, that is). Brands often have strong product testing, but like many chain stores, the quality is more hit-and-miss than it once was. Follow the quality recipe!

- **Brand-name outdoor and athletic apparel** (The North Face, Athleta, Patagonia, Nike, Adidas, etc.). This is a great category for finding long-lasting clothes. That's good news since so many people wear activewear as fashion. Most major outdoor and athletic brands have rigorous testing standards and are constantly innovating better designs and materials.

- **Off-price stores** (T.J.Maxx, Ross Dress for Less, Marshalls, etc.) **and outlet malls.** Off-prices stores and outlets were once a reliable way to land well-made and name-brand products at a discount, but no longer. Today, many sell a lot of factory rejects or canceled orders—the products that should have never made it to a store in the first place.[18] But much of the merchandise is lower-quality product manufactured *exclusively* for these stores and is intentionally mislabeled as discounted. There are occasionally good-quality items in outlets and off-price stores, but proceed with great caution and use your Quality Cheat Sheet to find them. Wherever you shop, beware of the manufacturer's suggested retail price, where the price is shown as deeply discounted from the list price. With MSRP, the lower price is the real price and the discount is faked to lure shoppers into thinking they're getting a deal.[19]

- **Designer boutiques.** Locally owned boutiques can be the ideal place to shop for high-quality independent designers and land one-of-a-kind pieces that are worth every penny. But beware the cute little boutique that carries overpriced polyester frocks and faux leather boots that are no better than what the fast-fashion or big-box stores are selling. Boutiques are locally owned, which is important, but make sure the quality matches the price. Use your Quality Cheat Sheet!

- **Luxury brands** (Versace, Gucci, Balenciaga, Prada, etc.). Yes, most luxury fashion, particularly the clothing, exists on an otherworldly plane of exquisite fabrics and craftsmanship. If the exclusivity, hype, and logos bother you, you're not alone. But don't shun luxury brands without first experiencing the craftsmanship. I am blessed with a hand-me-down Armani suit and Versace blazer that are the most gorgeous pieces in my wardrobe. Luxury quality can be transcendent. It's possible to snag luxury clothing through end-of-season sales or on liquidator websites like the Outnet or Gilt. But you'll find the biggest savings in the resale market, where luxury pieces can be snagged for hundreds and even thousands of dollars off the retail price.

- **Conscious-fashion brands.** *Most* conscious-fashion brands (you'll learn what defines a conscious brand and how to seek them out in Chapter 20) make good-quality products as part of their ethos to combat fast fashion and to be more sustainable. Here are just a very few examples (there are many amazing conscious brands to choose from): Eileen Fisher uses exquisite and long-lasting natural materials, PACT organic makes long-lasting and soft intimates in 100 percent organic cotton, and Brother Vellies and Mara Hoffman make smartly designed and stunning high-end clothes and shoes in eco-friendly fibers.

You now have the tools to find well-made clothes wherever you shop and no matter your budget. Quality is essential to the Art of Less. The magic of quality clothing is that you often automatically buy less. You don't want to buy more because you're perfectly content to wear what you've got. Quality is a joyful way to cut back consumption, save the planet, *and* tame your wardrobe, all at the same time.

How Apparel Designers Create Clothes That Last

Q&A with Karuna Scheinfeld,
Vice President of Design at Canada Goose

ELIZABETH: You're known in the clothing industry for quality product design and you have a passion and expertise for designing clothes that truly stand the test of time. What goes into a good-quality garment that will last forever?

KARUNA: To some degree, it depends how it's used and how it's cared for. Here's a great example from when I was working at Woolrich: We made an iconic wool check shirt that had been in the line in one form or another for over fifty years. Sometimes people would have it for generations, since they were just using it to be warmer in the winter and to chop wood. Whereas we had a whole business of fishermen in Alaska who would buy the shirt for one fishing season. They would just destroy it while they were working and have to throw it out. There alone, you have an example of a product that could last sixty years or it could last six months, depending on who's using and how they're using it. Here at Canada Goose, we offer a warranty program where we repair jackets if something is faulty. We see twenty-five-year-old jackets come through that just need a minor repair and are still going strong. They are designed to last that long because we know we will hear about it if they don't, and we like it that way.

ELIZABETH: Aside from consumer care, how does the way a garment is made determine its quality?

KARUNA: A huge portion of quality is about the attention paid at every level of manufacture by the people making it and how much they personally care about what they're making. Are they actually thinking about the intention of what this is for and trying to create the best version of that? Do they see the long-term value and investment of making it great instead of making it fast?

ELIZABETH: It's hard to imagine a large discounter or fast-fashion chain having that kind of thorough attention to detail in place.

KARUNA: It would be impossible. Those brands are just too big and it's too fast. The minute you get into that level of quantity and supply chain where you don't have control over consistency, you sacrifice a level of quality.

ELIZABETH: What's the minimum level of quality testing that brands do?

KARUNA: There will be some minimum of testing on everything, just because brands don't want all of their product to be returned. Depending on the brand and depending on the product, and under normal testing, shrinkage, pilling, and colorfastness are all common tests. They would test washing and care instructions. Abrasion is a common test for active or outdoor brands.

ELIZABETH: Natural versus synthetic fibers. Are natural fibers always higher quality?

KARUNA: No, you really have to be more specific about what you're measuring. But there's something important about having lived as a species with natural fibers for so long that is meaningful. There are sustainability issues with plastics that we still don't totally understand. And we're inventing new versions of fibers every day, and we have no idea what the effect of them will be. We know how natural fibers decompose. We know how they wear.

ELIZABETH: Fabric blends are now in the majority of the clothing we buy. Is that about price, or can blends improve quality or performance?

KARUNA: It's almost always a cost thing, but here are some exceptions. One exception is in the world of functional clothing, whether it's intimates or yoga or outdoor brands. Blends can be an ideal marriage of complementary fibers or they can be a dilution of function. For example, in extreme cold weather environments, some percentage of cotton and wool mixed with a highly durable nylon will ensure that the fabric doesn't freeze, so it might last longer than those natural fibers alone.

ELIZABETH: Is there a way to look at a blend of fibers and know if it's going to negatively impact the quality?

KARUNA: The more ingredients are in it, the less likely it will be blended for function or higher quality and the more likely it's blended for price or duty advantage. I think that's fair to say. If I see a fabric has more than three ingredients, I'm generally suspicious.

ELIZABETH: I've noticed that cheaper stores and brands use polyester in almost everything now. Why is that?

KARUNA: It's a combination of two things. Cheap synthetic fibers are way cheaper than cheap natural fibers. A cheap polyester is maybe 50 cents a yard. It's just dirt cheap, whereas a cheap cotton might start at 2 dollars a yard. But it also has to do with care. Polyesters don't shrink, and consumers like that. With polyester, you can make a cheap garment, and it'll look the same as when it was purchased for longer.

ELIZABETH: How much can we trust price and our own hands and eyes to guide us when we're shopping for quality?

KARUNA: In general, with fabrics, the nicer it feels and the better it looks, the more expensive it is, because the mills and designers have had to make an effort to achieve all of those features.

Buying Better Footwear

I still have my feet on the ground,
I just wear better shoes.

—OPRAH WINFREY

I'm the woman who once bought seven pairs of 7-dollar shoes in a fit of impulse-buying fury, a moment I describe in the opening pages of *Overdressed*. I'm not proud of it. I knew my shoes would fall apart, so I bought myself a fleet of backups and threw them in the garbage one by one as they did just that.

The footwear industry has massive environmental impacts. It's responsible for 700 million tons of carbon emissions per year, the equivalent of burning more than 765,000 pounds of coal.[1] Many of the components in our shoes, from synthetic rubber to chrome-tanned leather, don't biodegrade and are difficult or impossible to recycle; some are made of toxic building blocks. Shoes, even cheap ones, can and should be made with more sustainable, nontoxic, and recyclable or biodegradable materials. But consumers can do their part by buying more durable shoes whenever possible. High-quality shoes really do look and feel so much better and will help you spend less money over time. Here's how to shop for better shoes:

- **Feel the weight of the shoe.** A quality shoe will feel sturdy and the weight will be equally distributed. Clunky, stiff, inflexible, or even very light components are a sign of poor quality and can make a shoe uncomfortable or prone to breaking. Many sneakers are designed to be lightweight, but a dress shoe or casual shoe should feel a bit substantial.

- **Consider the materials.** Your foot needs to breathe. Leather, cotton and other types of canvas and some knitted synthetics are all examples of breathable materials. The materials also need to be very durable, resilient, and able to resist a variety of indignities (dirt, water, salt, snow, etc.). While knitted synthetic materials are the standard for most lightweight running shoes, leather is a popular shoe material for many other types of footwear because it's moldable, durable, resilient, repairable, and retains its appearance well. Leather footwear is often much longer lasting than many faux leather products, which are typically made by bonding polyurethane to a canvas backing that chips and cracks very easily and can't be repaired. Good leather dress shoes with a replaceable sole can last five to fifteen years. The life of a quality running shoe is three hundred to five hundred miles.[2] For athletic shoes, I recommend going to a shoe store and talking to an employee or looking online to find the most durable shoe for your workout routine.

  If you're looking for an animal-free footwear option, skip polyvinyl chloride faux leather, also known as PVC, as it often contains phthalates and emits dioxins during its manufacture that are linked to endocrine disruption.[3] Joshua Katcher, designer of vegan menswear line Brave GentleMan, recommends looking for a high-quality polyurethane (called PU) by examining the material the faux leather is bonded to on the inside of the shoe. "The most durable, long-lasting vegan leathers outperform conventional leather in tensile and abrasion tests, and they are set on a nonwoven backing that mimics skin," says Katcher.[4] Skip backings that look like liquid-coated canvas, as those are more likely to fail he says. In Chapter 18, I cover faux leather innovations that are natural and biodegradable, rather than plastic-based.

- **Look for expert assembly.** Any stitching on the uppers should be straight and tight. Check that all components are neatly cut out and sewn together evenly. If you're looking at a high-end dress shoe, the sole will be stitched to the uppers and the insole will sometimes be stitched down as well. This is a marker of very good quality. That said, most mass-market shoes are glued together, and those glues can vary from weak to solid and secure. Skip buying shoes that have visible dribbles of glue or places where the glue is showing, as these are signs of haste and low quality. Tug on the tip of the sole, pulling it away from the upper, to make sure it's firmly cemented. Keep shoe glue (I use a brand called Shoe Goo) on hand to fix split soles, to reattach loose pieces and insoles, and to fill in holes in the soles of your sneakers.

- **Check fasteners.** Any fasteners, including zippers, buckles, shoelaces, and elastic, should feel substantial and high quality as well. Test the fasteners, as the fasteners on a cheap shoe are often the first things to break, long before the sole wears out, and can be expensive or impossible to repair.

- **Inspect the inside.** The inside of the shoe, including the shaft and the insole, should look as finished as the exterior. Make sure all seams and components on the inside are sewn flat so they won't irritate your foot or ankle. Press down on the insole to ensure it's springy and well padded, as this is key to making the shoe comfortable to wear.

- **Scrutinize the sole.** In general, a thick leather or rubber sole and stacked heel are going to last the longest. When shopping for quality, check to make sure you can replace the sole; it can mean the difference between your shoes lasting six months and your shoes lasting six years. If you're buying a heel or women's flat that has thin soles by design, a cobbler can add a protective half or full sole to make it last longer.

- **Try it on.** A good-quality shoe will be very supportive and flex correctly when you step. Cheaper shoes often have very thin soles that are stiff, so make sure the sole flexes properly (at the correct part of your foot). Think about comfort, too. A good shoe won't irritate or pinch your foot. Keep in mind that quality-leather dress shoes will mold to your foot or break in over time. No matter what price point you're shopping at, walk around and make sure there aren't components of the shoe that are pinching or jabbing into your foot. Obviously many high heels will be less than comfortable whether the shoe fits or not, but supportive, high-quality construction can help you prevent long-term damage to your feet. Always take the time to buy the right size (shoes, unlike clothes, really don't work if they're too tight or too loose). A cobbler can stretch a leather shoe about a half size, at most.

HOW MUCH DO GOOD SHOES COST?

I'll save you the suspense—you don't need to spend anywhere close to a thousand dollars to get a good shoe. Luxury brands, the ones that make shoes that cost more than your rent, sell products crafted out of top-notch materials, but they also overcharge for the brand name. The price on a really good leather dress shoe, the kind that will last you years, starts at around a hundred dollars and goes up from there. These shoes can be repaired again and again and more than pay for themselves. Casual street shoes and athletic shoes can be found more affordably. If you know how to shop smart, you can get quality shoes inexpensively.

No one said you had to pay full price or shop retail. I have multiple pairs of fine-crafted leather boots from thrift stores that I bought for less than 20 dollars apiece. After a proper resole, they're ready to wear for seasons to come. For the same price that I paid for my bag of disposable 7-dollar shoes, which fell apart and are now sitting in a landfill, I have quality shoes that will last for years.

How Footwear Designers Create Shoes That Last

Q&A with Carl Blakeslee, Creative Director at Sorel

ELIZABETH: You've designed for a number of brands that make long-lasting footwear. As a shoe designer, are you still seeing a range of quality being made?

CARL: I see plenty of well-made footwear out there in the market, designed and built to last many years and in some cases many decades. But I also see an overabundance on the more disposable side. In the end, the consumer makes the decision to spend twice the amount for quality or half the amount for disposable, and the brands react and adjust to those needs.

ELIZABETH: Making a shoe is more complicated and probably more expensive than making clothes, right?

CARL: Yes, I think so, because it's more like equipment. It's like making a bike or other hard goods because there are so many different components. Each one of those components has to interact with the others, so it's a more complex process and requires more investment up front.

ELIZABETH: What decisions are made in the design process that can lower the quality?

CARL: "De-specing" is the term used when looking at lowering the costs in order to hit a more competitive price point. I've worked on making shoes like this before, where you're sitting around a table with twenty-five people trying to figure out how to lower the cost. Those are very difficult conversations. Most designers don't like this sort of process. We tend to lean toward creating higher-quality, more interesting designs that we can be proud of and that consumers will covet and develop an emotional connection with.

ELIZABETH: Who is responsible for disposable footwear? Is it the brands in the way they design product, or is it the way consumers use products?

CARL: It's both, and it's a symbiotic relationship. Consumers are responsible because they make the final decision to buy cheaper products, demanding more value and on-trend designs. To answer these consumer needs, brands are producing products so quickly and so fast, endlessly trying to stay in front of these consumer trends.

ELIZABETH: What kind of quality testing do you do in footwear?

CARL: There are lots of different tests that happen throughout the process, from abrasion to strength to wear and fit and colorfastness, and then we give our shoes to human wear-testers and we ask them to do certain activities or put a given number of miles or hours in the product.

ELIZABETH: Soles are probably the most important part of the shoe. What are our shoe soles made out of?

CARL: Synthetic rubbers are very prominent now compared to the old days. Rubber used to come from a natural resource and that's changing. Most soles are either 100 percent petroleum-based rubber, natural gum rubber, or a combination of natural and synthetic.

ELIZABETH: Is there a quality difference between using natural versus synthetic rubber soles?

CARL: Whether you use natural rubber or totally synthetic, you can make either one of those last longer just by the way you engineer the sole in the molding process. Neither one really by itself is less disposable than the other in my opinion.

ELIZABETH: Italy used to be the best place to produce shoes. Are there other countries known for good-quality shoes, too?

CARL: Vietnam is one that's emerging as a step up from the norm. Asia, in general, has embraced the concept and demand of shoe-making in the traditional sense. Portugal, Spain, and even some of the old American footwear producers are making exceptional product and carry the reputation and higher cost associated with it.

ELIZABETH: If I'm out shopping for shoes, is there an easy way to tell if I'm buying something disposable versus better quality?

CARL: With shoes, you get what you pay for (usually). If you're buying a 20-dollar shoe, you can be sure that whatever materials that were put into that product are the cheapest available and probably produced by a factory that cares less about quality and more about volume. The best way to *know* that you are buying something disposable is to look at the design itself. If it's more of a "trendy" design versus more "classic," it's a good indicator that it may be a little more disposable.

Secrets of a Well-Built Wardrobe

Now that you've learned how to buy gorgeous and well-made clothes and shoes, it's time to put them into a cohesive collection known as a wardrobe. A wardrobe is a highly strategic ensemble of clothing that works in tandem. Each piece elevates the whole. When every garment has a purpose and every color and cut goes with something else, your wardrobe can carry you through life in style, no matter the occasion.

My fast-fashion closet was *not* a wardrobe. It was a screaming match of colors, prints, and trends. Once I learned the fundamentals of wardrobe building, the process of getting dressed became joyful and easy instead of stressful. Nowadays, whether I'm dressing for a television interview, a fashion conference, or drinks with friends, I know I can reach into my closet and build a look that I feel confident in without hesitation. Building a wardrobe is the pinnacle of the Art of Less because it ends in closet contentment (an actual thing), lets you shut off that pressure to keep up with the new and the next, and allows you to just wear and enjoy your clothes. I've found that a well-built wardrobe is one of life's greatest pleasures.

THE FOUR FUNDAMENTALS OF WARDROBE BUILDING

You picked up a few basics of building a wardrobe during your Conscious Cleanout, as you cut pieces by season, purged your dead ends, and pruned your trendy items and anything you had in excess. Next, you'll pick up the Four Fundamentals of Wardrobe Building, which are as follows:

1. **Identify your colors.** Like many shoppers, I was like a human magpie in my fast-fashion days, attracted to anything eye-catching and shiny. I had more than two dozen hues in my old wardrobe, few of which complemented one another or complimented *me.* A good wardrobe is built around a select number of colors that really pop with your unique skin tone and hair color and mix and match with ease. You will be amazed at how easy it is to build appealing outfits once your wardrobe abides by some basic color theory. Unlike trendy colors, *your* colors are timeless and personal. Look past what the fashion industry is peddling as the color of the season to find those hues that flatter you.

    There are tons of quizzes and sample color palettes online to help you choose your colors down to the shade and hue. For example, you might look lackluster in navy but amazing in baby blue, which looks great with white and coral or richer reds. Anuschka Rees's modern and tasteful wardrobe-building book, *The Curated Closet,* is a tremendous resource for choosing a color palette. I'm also a fan of Carole Jackson's *Color Me Beautiful,* a bestseller from the 1980s. If you can endure the scourge of blue eye shadow, the color theory advice still holds up. As for how many colors to choose, Rees recommends a nine-shade color palette, though you might settle on a wider or narrower range. The trick is to choose colors that go well together. My wardrobe rotates around just five main colors. My neutrals are black, cream, and camel, which all go well with my accent colors, which are bright, bold shades of yellow and red. I also have a few pieces in royal blue and hunter green. While I'm sure I'll expand on and mix up my colors over time, I won't return to wearing colors that clash and don't look great on me.

2. **Settle on your cuts and silhouettes.** It's not ruffles or bold prints that make our clothes really stand out; it's cuts and silhouettes. Having a closet full of clothes that fit and complement your body will help you to feel and look fantastic in your clothes. It can also make you impervious to buying trendy clothes that look better on the rack.

   This is the most difficult of the four fundamentals (I admit, it can take a while to get right), but here are some shortcuts: Most modern clothes are just variations of a set of cuts and silhouettes. They are an assemblage of a neckline, sleeve length and shape, waist height (mid, low, high), and hem length. From there, there is the overall outline or silhouette of the garment, meaning whether something is body skimming, straight fitting, flared, drapey, and so on. Hop onto the home page of virtually any clothing brand's website, and you'll start to see what I mean.

   Your cuts and silhouettes can really be boiled down to knowing the necklines, sleeve lengths, waist height, and hem lengths that flatter you, and from there determining the overall silhouettes that *best* suit your body. Ignore everything else. Examples from my wardrobe: For necklines, I look best in a boat neck, crewneck, or a turtleneck versus a V-neck or scoop. For sleeves, I look best in long, sleeveless, or capped, and I skip three-quarter-length. For silhouettes, I look good in boxy, structural shapes over something form-fitting, and I rarely wear a head-to-toe drapey outfit. Some of my favorite books that address cuts and silhouettes and go into far more detail than I can here are *A Guide to Quality, Taste and Style* by Tim Gunn and *How to Get Dressed* by Alison Freer.

3. **Say "no" more than "yes."** There is an avalanche of fashion out in the marketplace. Most isn't right for you or for me. Stay true to your colors, cuts, silhouette, and personal style and only let those perfect pieces into your wardrobe. That means saying no far more than yes to clothes. Moving forward, as you shop for your wardrobe, you'll find it liberating to just ignore certain types of clothing that don't flatter or—just as important—simply flatter *less* than others. On my list of silhouettes and colors I say no to, simply because they aren't as flattering as others, are wrap dresses, cropped jeans, empire waistlines, eggplant purple, anything with skinny straps. I could go on and on. By eliminating extraneous choice, you'll have an easier time choosing well for your wardrobe.

4. **Hone your personal style.** Personal style simply means knowing what little corner of the fashion universe makes you feel most confident and comfortable. It's the overall aesthetic that you just feel like yourself in. Are you classic or trendy? Feminine or more androgynous? Put together or laid-back? Edgy or preppy? If you aren't quite sure, ask a few close friends to describe your style. You'll quickly realize that you have a strong sense of style, even if it's currently buried under a closet of clothes that aren't quite working for you. Knowing your personal style will allow you to sift smartly through trends, shop without getting overwhelmed, and zero in on only those looks that work really well just for you.

Here are a few secrets about personal style: Most people who have great style prioritize it and put time into cultivating it. It's not something they're just born with. Make time for your personal style and it'll start to emerge. Your personal style is also strongly determined by your colors, cuts, and silhouettes, and that's work you've already done. Last, personal style is a journey. You'll get better at recognizing and honing it as you spend more time putting thought and intention into choosing well for your wardrobe, so don't feel pressured to have this figured out right now.

Here are some other fun and effective ways to explore style that have worked for me: Sign up for a clothing rental subscription service for a month or two, like Le Tote, Gwynnie Bee, or Rent the Runway (or those on offer in your country), and try on many different looks at home and send them all back when you're done (more on rentals in Chapter 16). Or, spend a few afternoons trying on clothes in a wide range of stores, snapping photos of yourself in different looks. These photos can help give you some distance to see what works and what doesn't, objectively. Last but not least, you can and should read about the art of personal style, whether it's in magazines, blogs, or books. Just a few of my favorite books on style that go into far more detail and with more savoir faire than I can here are *Harper's Bazaar Fashion: Your Guide to Personal Style,* Tim Gunn's *A Guide to Quality, Taste and Style,* Andrea Linett's *The Cool Factor,* and Stacy London's *The Truth About Style.*

CHOOSING CORE PIECES

Now that you've learned the fundamentals, you can use these principles to choose your core and accent pieces. A wardrobe is built around a foundation of core pieces, versatile go-tos that can create outfits with almost everything else in your wardrobe. Your cores will reflect your color palette, personal style, and shapes and silhouettes. Cores tend to be in neutral, versatile, solid colors (or very versatile prints, such as stripes) that are easy to mix and match. Cores are also made in versatile cuts (think classic white button-down shirt versus ruffled purple top) that can easily be layered with other pieces in your wardrobe. However, there are few rules in modern fashion, and I'm sure there are many of you out there who will successfully build your cores around bold colors and prints.

- **What counts as a core?** A core could be a good pair of blue jeans, a trusty pair of ankle boots, or a classic boyfriend cardigan. But there are no hard-and-fast rules about what counts as a core. Choose timeless pieces that excite you and reflect your personal style. They should be the pieces that *you* find versatile and want to wear again and again. My cores are anything but traditional. They include a croc-print leather pencil skirt, a vintage black bodysuit, a spandex crop top, and a pair of snakeskin ankle boots. I also have a range of core pieces in red, proving again that what counts as a core doesn't have to be boring or safe.

- **Expand your range.** One common wardrobe-building pitfall, particularly when choosing core pieces, is to fall into an outfit rut, like the jeans-with-top look. No matter how many cute tops and skinny jeans you own, jeans with a top is really just *one* look. Choosing core pieces in a wide range of cuts and silhouettes will make your wardrobe *far* more versatile. For example, try wide-leg or cropped jeans instead of just skinny. If you're in a rut wearing separates, look for some dresses or jumpsuits in a color that's easy to mix-and-match. If you only wear miniskirts, branch out with a midi or maxi. Get creative with your colors, too. Many people believe that cores have to be in bland hues of gray or brown. Not true. Why not try a pair of pants or shoes in a bold but easy-to-match-up color? My red trousers are surprisingly versatile.

- **Scale up your cores.** It's common to feel like your cores are falling flat or look a little boring. If this happens, scale up with better fabrics and subtle design twists. It's important to keep them *versatile,* so resist the urge to grab something that won't coordinate with other pieces in your closet. This is where it really pays to shop for quality, which you're now an expert at. Instead of a basic tank top for layering, consider a classic silk shell or camisole in silk or linen. You can also choose textured fabrics to make your cores (and your entire wardrobe) more dynamic. Look for materials like corduroy, tweed, suede, linen, flannel, or chunky knits. Pairing different textures can create new looks, as well. While traditional pencil skirts look too stuffy on me, a leather pencil skirt is just my speed. I'm constantly scaling up my core pieces, finding ever-more-perfect versions of what I like.

ADDING ACCENTS AND ACCESSORIES

Accent pieces are clothes, shoes, and accessories that have more color, print, shine, and flare than your cores, and they add the sizzle to your wardrobe. Accent pieces should fall within your color palette, personal style, and cuts and silhouettes. Accents are pieces that drive away boredom from the practicalities of wardrobe building and keep things fun. Accents are a little less versatile and worn less frequently than the cores, but they are no less essential.

One way to choose great accent pieces is to look for items that are eye-catching but that don't make a complete statement on their own. For example, in my old wardrobe I owned a purple ruffled top festooned with a confetti print. It was a typical fast-fashion garment that had too much going on and went with only one pair of pants I owned. Try choosing accents with a pop of color *or* an interesting print *or* a compelling design, rather than going for garments that are a mash-up of all three. You'll create a more versatile and personal wardrobe as a result. This doesn't mean you have to choose boring clothes. For example, I now have a purple mohair blazer in a classic cut that can be surprisingly muted or wild, depending on my mood and what I pair it with.

Another idea for choosing fantastic accents is to use prevailing trends to your advantage. Sift through what's in style and find trends that reflect *your* personal style. By carefully choosing trendy pieces that are right for you and fit into your personal style, you can create a wardrobe staple out of an otherwise passing fad. For example, the current loafer trend fits right into my somewhat androgynous style. I bought two pairs this season—one in black patent leather and one in orange—and will happily wear them once the loafer trend is long gone.

THE MEAT-AND-POTATOES RULE

Fashion designer Michael Kors said it best: "Seventy percent of the clothes you own should be meat and potatoes. Thirty percent should be icing and fluff—that's color, pattern, shine, and accessories." For your wardrobe to work well, you need the proper ratio between your core and accent pieces. It is really tempting to build a dessert-heavy wardrobe. Resist the urge. If you want to actually wear the clothes you own, the bulk of your wardrobe should be core pieces that are highly versatile and a smaller ratio should go toward accents. The classic wardrobe ratio is two-thirds cores and one-third accents, or about 70 percent to 30 percent. As a Traditionalist, it's a ratio that works well for me. If you're a Minimalist, your ratio might be more heavily weighted toward core pieces, so something more like 90 percent cores to 10 percent accents. If you are a Style Seeker, you might imagine that your wardrobe ratio will look nothing like the ratios of the other Fashion Personality Types. But even Style Seekers need a well-balanced ratio of cores and accents at the heart of their wardrobe. From there, you might rent or shop resale for your trendiest items (more on how in Part Three: "The Art of More").

HOW TO BUILD A CAPSULE WARDROBE

A capsule wardrobe is a small, perfectly planned-out, tightly edited wardrobe of versatile clothes. It's a wardrobe distilled to its essence, with no extraneous pieces. A capsule wardrobe can have as few as ten items or as many as thirty or more. What defines a capsule wardrobe is not its smallness but the versatility and intentionality of its contents. A sample twenty-six-piece capsule wardrobe for fall might contain the following: one cardigan; two sweaters; eight tops; five bottoms; three dresses/jumpsuits; two lightweight jackets; one coat; two pairs of casual shoes; one pair of dress shoes; and one pair of heels, all in coordinating colors. Every single piece goes with something else, and the outfits are thoughtfully considered and planned ahead of time.

If you're looking to get far away from the nonstop churn of fast fashion, capsule dressing and its timesaving, life-altering simplicity might be just the thing for you. Although the principles have been around for decades, capsule wardrobes are enjoying a massive resurgence. Eileen Fisher, a brand that got its start by designing pieces for capsule wardrobes, offers an eight-piece capsule collection called the System, for example. But there's a widespread movement of capsule enthusiasts who carefully build their own capsule wardrobes each season (either by shopping for it or by selecting items they already own) and then wear only those items. Here's where to get inspiration to build your own capsule wardrobe.

- **Blogs and social media.** I mentioned a few capsule wardrobe blogs earlier in the book, but there are many. Search "capsule closet" on YouTube to watch others put together their capsules or hop onto Instagram and search the #capsulecloset or #capsulewardrobe hashtags to find endless inspiration. You can also check out

Pinterest for sample capsule wardrobes, wardrobe color palettes, detailed shopping lists, and related advice.

- **Cladwell and other wardrobe-organizing apps.** There are apps that can help you organize your wardrobe, and they can help you plan your capsule as well. The one I use is called the Cladwell app, and you'll hear from Cladwell's founder, Blake Smith, at the end of this chapter. There are other apps, including Stylebook, Closet-Space, and Pureple that offer similar wardrobe-building tools as of this writing. You can use them to plan and add items to your capsule using either stock images or photos of your own clothes. Using an app is *much* faster and easier than trying to pair up everything in your closet in real life.

CREATIVE WAYS TO USE CAPSULING

If capsule dressing sounds a bit too strict for your everyday life, it can be wonderfully beneficial in many other ways. Here are a few.

- **Build a capsule at the heart of your wardrobe.** You can use capsule wardrobe techniques to build a small capsule at the heart of your wardrobe that pairs up with most of your other garments. I use this strategy myself.

- **Capsule dressing for Style Seekers.** For Style Seekers, building a capsule wardrobe and renting or seasonally thrifting and reselling the rest of your wardrobe is a great way to keep up with fashion while keeping your closet streamlined and tidy.

- **For work and travel.** You can also use capsule principles to build out a separate work wardrobe and to pack for vacations or professional trips. I have a travel capsule for lectures, which I store on the

Cladwell app. My outfits are planned out and can go straight into my suitcase when I'm packing, saving time and stress.

- **To practice wardrobe building.** Building a capsule wardrobe is also perfect practice for learning the fundamentals of wardrobe building, as it challenges you to think through how your clothes go together and reveals how your colors, silhouettes, and cuts work together. If you didn't take a capsule wardrobe challenge during your Fashion Fast, I highly recommend that you take one either for ten days, a month, or for a full season. For inspiration, look on social media using hashtags like #capsulewardrobe challenge.

ORGANIZATION AND PLANNING: HOW TO GET THE MOST OUT OF YOUR WARDROBE AND WEAR WHAT YOU'VE GOT

Now that you have the fundamentals of wardrobe building down, you're ready to learn how to put your wardrobe to work. It might sound obvious, but a wardrobe's most powerful feature is its wearability. Wardrobes are workhorses, built and designed to get better and sharper over time and with repeated use. Granted, it may be some time before you have a fully built-out wardrobe and a fully realized conscious closet, but I want to give you the tools you need to keep your wardrobe in order and to maximize its potential. Modern wardrobes are large, which makes them an organizational and creative challenge. Proper management is key. Here is how to get the most out of your clothes.

- **Gather your closet-organizing supplies.** To use your wardrobe, you need to be able to clearly see your clothes and get to them with ease. Unfortunately, many closets were not built with the modern wardrobe in mind and are dark and quite small. Assess whether you need additional shelving, hangers, hooks, or coat racks. Have you considered whether having your clothes out in the open might work better—on a rolling rack, for example? I use a rolling rack in addition to my closet space and have a shelving unit for my shoes and bags. It's my DIY version of a walk-in closet. Do you need additional lighting to see your clothes? You can buy all these supplies secondhand. Craigslist and swapping apps have tons of free and gently used storage solutions on offer.

- **Put your clothes in order.** No two people organize their closets exactly the same, but the goal is to make your closet clean and inviting and to order your items so that you can assemble outfits with ease. Organize your closet so that it's as enticing as your favorite store. Here are some suggestions: Keep like items with like (tops with tops, dresses with dresses, sweaters with sweaters), and within large categories, such as tops, create subcategories based on color and sleeve length and organize from casual to dressy. I organize my closet by sections of my life as well—my everyday clothes are in the front and my event- and fashion-related wardrobe is in the back. Once a week, put your closet back in order. If anything is going unworn, pull it to the front, where you can see it. When the season turns over, put your out-of-season clothes in storage or in the back of your closet, and get organized again.

- **Plan an outfit-building day.** You can continue to stare into your closet each morning, hoping for inspiration. But a more successful and timesaving strategy is to set aside an outfit-building day once a season (I try to do it once a month) and reconnect with what's in your closet and build fresh outfits. Put on some music and get creative. For those pieces you haven't been wearing, your bench-warmers, pull them out and figure out how to make them work. I recently bought a pink leather miniskirt (not in my color scheme!) and forced myself to make four outfits out of it before I put it back in my closet. You can use the hashtag #outfitbuilding day to post your results or for inspiration.

- **Make a look book.** Invite a friend over to photograph you in your outfits or take some mirror selfies. Print them out and keep them in a folder—your own personal look book. My friend Felicia Jocus, a wildly talented creative director and personal stylist, taught me this trick. These photos do *not* have to look perfect or Instagram-ready; they are just to capture the general gist of outfits that work. Make notes on each outfit to remember what type of occasion it works best for, such as work, social media, or a formal event. This might sound like a lot of work, *and it is,* but you'll be amazed at the time it will save you down the road. I was on a panel recently and waited until the day of to choose an outfit. Thanks to my look book, I threw on a preplanned head-to-toe outfit (down to the handbag) in minutes that looked polished and gained me compliments. The only things I had to consider were my makeup and hair.

- **Use an app.** We can all benefit from extra help keeping track of our wardrobes and coming up with outfit inspiration. I highly recommend, for any Fashion Personality Type, that you use a wardrobe-organizing app like Cladwell, Stylebook, and Closet-Space to log everything in your wardrobe, keep track of what you're wearing (and what you aren't), and find outfit inspiration. Most of these apps generate outfit suggestions from your own wardrobe and can inspire you to wear pieces you haven't worn in a while. I've used Cladwell countless times for last-minute style inspiration, whether I'm hanging out with friends or have a business meeting, but I also use it to figure out how to work a challenging piece into a chic outfit. You can use stock photos to populate your virtual wardrobe, but if you take the time to add photographs of your actual clothes, the apps are that much more effective.

- **Hire a pro.** Yes, you can build and execute a well-tuned wardrobe all on your own. But a talented closet organizer or personal stylist can put you on the right track and even give you better results. Prices vary depending on location and experience level. Find a pro who meets your budget and needs. They'll save you loads of money in the long run by showing you creative ways to wear what you have.

How to Be Happy in Your Clothes

Q&A with Cladwell Founder Blake Smith

ELIZABETH: What exactly is Cladwell, and what does the app do?

BLAKE: Cladwell is an app that focuses on what most of us focus on when it comes to our clothes: what to wear each day, managing your closet, and honing your personal style. Users enter their wardrobe into the app piece by piece, using either stock images or pictures of their own clothes. And then, every morning, we show you different possibilities of how to get dressed. We use the feedback of what you wear each day to get better at dressing you and to help highlight which clothes to buy or get rid of. The fun part is that we do this as a community, so you can see influencers or your friends' wardrobes as well. Or you can choose to keep your wardrobe private.

ELIZABETH: So many of us are struggling to dress well with the clothes we've got. Why has it taken the fashion industry so long to pick up on this and offer a solution?

BLAKE: Brands focus on what you're going to buy next—because that's how they make money. Most humans are more focused on what we're going to *wear* next. There's a fundamental misalignment between the clothing industry and how we all experience our clothing. That's what we want to fix.

ELIZABETH: You've got a lot of data now on wardrobe building. Can you tell us the secret to building a functioning wardrobe?

BLAKE: Our thesis is that a happy closet contains only things that you actually love and wear all the time. If that's what's in your closet, you will have much better moments of getting dressed each morning. We show you that you have enough, and you're free to just be more creative on the other side and enjoy your clothes rather than feel discontent.

ELIZABETH: According to Cladwell, my 155-piece wardrobe creates 130,000 outfit combinations. Were you surprised at just how much variety our closets create?

BLAKE: I don't think we realized how the math would work until we actually launched the app. We put in all the inputs, like color and silhouette, and the number ended up breaking the server. It was surprising. But the point of this feature is to show users that they have a plethora of options. People have way too much clothing and they think they have nothing to wear, so we try to show the opposite. We show them that actually you have more than enough clothing and you have tons to wear.

ELIZABETH: Is there an ideal wardrobe size?

BLAKE: We've found that our average customer has about 150 items in their wardrobe and uploads about 60 of those pieces into the app. Everyone is different. You need to look at your life and figure out what are the scenes of your life, like are you going to the office or working from coffee shops or staying at home? You have to think, *How often am I doing that?* And then the more personal part is thinking, *How comfortable am I with repeating things within those themes?* It's just looking at those factors and doing the math.

ELIZABETH: What changes do people experience when they use Cladwell and finally get to a place where they're happy with their wardrobes?

BLAKE: People spend less time in the morning thinking about what they need to get dressed. They're going to the cash register less. Our average customer says they save about 600 dollars a year in purchases they are not making. And there's a general sense of knowing oneself that I think permeates everything you do. There's something really powerful about knowing your own style.

Buying Less by Buying Better

Buy what is truly fantastic.

—NINA GARCÍA

I t might be a surprise to see a chapter on shopping in the Art of Less. But, as you'll learn, buying better will help you to consume less and choose well for your wardrobe. When I sort secondhand clothes, I am astonished at how much clothing is tossed out either new with tags or never or barely worn. My sorting partner and I estimate that these never-worns and rarely-worns are *at least* a third of the one thousand pounds of donated clothes we go through each week.

The data backs up our experience. A 2015 survey showed that a third of British consumers were inclined to stop wearing a garment after just three wears.[1] Just as shocking, a survey of American consumers found that a third of our wardrobes are dedicated to clothes we've *never* worn or haven't worn in a year.[2] It makes me wonder: How much better would we feel and look and how much money would we save if we cut out all those wasted buys? What if we *only* bought those perfect pieces we couldn't wait to wear? Would our closets be empty? No. They would be leaner and better. Let's slow down and make smarter, more careful, and more satisfying clothing choices when we shop. We'll buy less without even trying. Here's how to put the Art of Less into practice when you shop:

- **View deals with a side-eye.** The number one reason we buy what we don't wear is because it's on sale or it's so cheap that we're willing to overlook flaws.[3] We all know that we're manipulated by discounts and low prices, and we need to take this far more seriously. Marketers design prices to cue our primitive brain and block our "cognitive assessment" of what we're buying.[4] And we're very easily thrown off our mission to buy a perfect piece by the price tag. When you shop, avoid looking at the price tag for as long as possible, until after you assess the basics: fabric, color, design, quality, fit, and so on. Once you do peek at the price, ask yourself: Would I want this item if it were twice as expensive or if I was paying full price?

- **Be wary of cheap.** Yes, a very low price is a surefire way to save, but it can also change how you *feel* about what you buy. According to journalist Ellen Ruppel Shell in her book *Cheap,* we perceive things bought on sale as less desirable, less efficacious, and even less durable than things for which we paid full price.[5] The less we pay for something, the less we value it and the less likely we are to take care of it! If you're buying something on sale or low-priced, take a good look at it and ask yourself if you can find a way to *value* and care for this item anyway. An example: I recently bought a 5-dollar bralette that broke the first time I wore it (and again, the second time). I overrode my temptation to chuck it in the trash and sat down and sewed the broken straps back on. Now I like it quite a bit.

- **Try everything on, no exceptions.** This is especially true if something is cheap. It's not in our rational interest to use our time or money to take or ship something back to the store if it's inexpensive.

- **Buy less at a time.** Try limiting your purchases to one or two items *per shopping trip.* There's a powerful motivation for this. First, our brain's capacity to closely analyze objects plummets the more we have to consider. Too much choice often overwhelms the human brain.[6] Nowhere is this more true than when you're trying to shop in the bowels of a giant fast-fashion store or off-price chain that's packed wall to wall with clothes. Buying one or two items at a time gives you the opportunity to successfully add new items into your life. Promise yourself you won't buy anything else until you've figured out where your new pieces fit into your wardrobe and you've worn them multiple times.

- **Plan your purchases.** Most of our clothes are bought on impulse; we're buying items without wider thought of how they fit into our lives or our wardrobes—and it doesn't end well. Regret is the most common experience following an impulse buy, with 44 percent of people reporting this unfortunate feeling.[7] The process of discovery is part of the fun of shopping, but if you can stick to a general shopping list and choose items that fit into a clearly defined place in your wardrobe, you'll have more success.

- **Hold out for great clothes.** Good clothes don't always show up on command. Instead of buying something that's just *okay* in their stead, be prepared to leave a shopping session with nothing in tow. Hold out for those pieces that make your heart stop. Learning how to be in a store without buying is a wonderful superpower that can keep your closet lean and full of only those pieces you love and want to wear.

WARDROBE-SHOPPING CHECKLIST

Now that you're impervious to deals and bad buys, let's turn to a few more strategies for shopping well for your wardrobe. Before choosing a new piece, flip through your closet and look for gaps and weak links. It might not be a color you're missing, but a shape or cut. You're picking members of a team, so look for items that shine best in combination with everything else and unlock lots of new combinations. Resist the temptation to buy what you already have—and branch out! Here is a shopping checklist to keep you on track:

- Does this fit my personal style? Or is this in fact someone else's personal style and I just appreciate it?

- Is this part of my color scheme? If it's outside of my color scheme, am I prepared to bring new pieces into my wardrobe to match it?

- Is this on my personal list of approved cuts and silhouettes?

- What does this go with, and how many new outfits can I create with this piece?

- Do I already have something like this?

- Do I need to buy anything else—shoes, accessories—to make this work?

- Where will I wear it and how often? If it's not a lot, I will consider renting, borrowing, or buying secondhand.

REACHING CLOSET CONTENTMENT

In the process of building a wardrobe, you might experience a strange sensation called closet contentment, where your clothes go together, suit your life, and leave you feeling happy and confident. Bask in it! Closet contentment is that rare moment of equilibrium where you're satisfied with your wardrobe. You've truly mastered the Art of Less when you reach closet contentment. Enjoy it because it is rarely permanent. Our wardrobes are in a constant state of evolution, just like we are. When is it time to overhaul your wardrobe? Body changes, career changes, or big moves might call for it. And, of course, fashion is constantly changing, and you might soon feel the pull to take your wardrobe in new directions, and now you have the skills and the savvy to build on what you've got. Now that we've mastered the Art of Less, we'll completely switch gears and talk about how to consciously and sustainably keep up with fashion and trends without harming the planet. This is no doubt the part of the book that Style Seekers have been waiting for.

PART THREE

The Art of More

Style is not a privilege, it's a right.

–STACY LONDON

Keeping Up with Style, *Consciously*

I've traveled the world from the garment factories of southern China to the vast secondhand markets of Kenya and found a love of style wherever I go. In Guangdong, I met young garment factory girls who spend their one day off a week shopping for cute jeans. In Nairobi, I discovered young fashion designers and secondhand dealers reinventing America's old T-shirts into custom street wear. In Biella, Italy, I met textile tycoons in the centuries-old wool industry who can describe a fluffy ball of sheep's hair with the passion of a skilled sommelier characterizing a fine wine. Style has connected me to people and places in ways I never imagined. It is a worthy, beautiful, and deeply human pastime.

But we've got to change the way we go about it.

In just fifteen short years, global consumption of clothing has doubled, and the environmental impacts of fashion have climbed in tandem.[1] I've already described how current modes of consumption create catastrophic waste. But the way we manufacture new clothes is truly unsustainable, commanding a staggering level of resources, especially water, chemicals, and fossil fuels, that can't continue. Each year, clothing production requires 24 trillion gallons of water, enough to fill 37 million Olympic-size pools.[2] And the fashion industry spews more globe-warming carbon dioxide annually than all international flights and maritime shipping combined.³ And that's nothing compared to how big fashion is on track to get: Consumption of clothing is set to triple by 2050, as world incomes climb and a taste for fashion and disposable consumption spreads.⁴ In thirty years, if nothing changes, fashion will command a quarter of the world's *entire carbon budget* (the budget that would keep us under two degrees of global warming), warns the Ellen MacArthur Foundation.

It's so important for us to buy less and buy carefully, whenever we can, but the planet depends on our figuring out how to produce and consume fashion and style sustainably. It's simpler than you might imagine, but it will take the will of brands, citizens, and governments coming together to drive change, and fast. Making fashion sustainable starts by greening the materials we wear, as textile making is where the biggest environmental impacts happen. Brands must simply use less water and land and fewer toxic chemicals and fossil fuels to craft new clothes, all while using more renewable, recycled, recyclable, and sustainable resources. Part Four: "The Sustainable Fashion Handbook" will delve into these efforts in full.

Before we get to that, Part Three: "The Art of More" will lay out a plan of how we can consume fashion sustainably on an individual, everyday level. The Art of More is dedicated to strategies for sharing fashion and viewing it as a service we lease, access, and enjoy, rather than a product we buy. Sharing fashion is now possible thanks to the meteoric rise of resale websites like thredUP and rental companies like Rent the Runway. By shopping secondhand and renting, we can greatly extend the life of clothes and protect the precious resources that go into making them. I'll also talk about thrifting and vintage shopping as key to the Art of More before delving into fashion finances. Shopping cheap while shopping often is not a bargain, and I'll share my strategies for how to invest better in your clothes and afford the conscious closet you want, whether you're saving up to buy a high-quality piece or constantly turning over your closet with new trends. Style is about change. In a way it's all about more, and Part Three will show you how to enjoy the ever-changing churn of fashion, *consciously.*

The Rise of Resale Not Retail

I **love old-school thrift** store shopping and will dig for hours to find a treasure at a roadside garage sale. But if you haven't tried resale shopping, I must explain how little it has in common with secondhand stores of the past. It's *so* different that it justifies having a newfangled name: resale. Resale apps and stores have re-created the traditional retail shopping experience: The clothes are stylish and in pristine condition. They're barely worn. Many are even new with tags. Resale websites, like thredUP and the RealReal, offer returns and product authenticity. There are no moth holes or dusty, dated fashion for sale. Think of it like having your most stylish friend cherry-pick from the world's closets and gather all the good stuff that's going unworn in one place. The resale market is possible because of the surplus of unwanted clothes in the world, but it offers a creative solution to this problem, too.

WHY RESALE RULES

Well over half my wardrobe is purchased secondhand from the resale market, mostly from websites like the RealReal, thredUP, or eBay, or from curated consignment stores around the world. I'm not alone in shopping this way. Fifty-six million American women shopped secondhand in 2017, up from 44 million, with resale websites responsible for the bulk of that growth.[1] The resale market is growing much faster than traditional retail, which is on the whole struggling, and is on track to overtake fast fashion by sales volume within the decade.[2] And while you might have a certain preconceived notion of a secondhand bargain hunter, perhaps a devoted coupon-cutter or an eccentric college kid, 13 percent of all resale shoppers are in fact millionaires. And while you might imagine that anyone raised on fast fashion would turn their noses up at wearing used clothes, think again: Gen Z are the largest shoppers of secondhand of any generation. The truth is, *everyone* loves a good value and an increasing number of people want to shop sustainably. Resale has become the best place to have it both ways. Here are just a few reasons more consumers are choosing to buy used:

- **It's jaw-droppingly cheap.** Really, the deals can be unbelievable. Shopping secondhand is anywhere from 10 percent to 90 percent less than paying retail, every day. No waiting for a sale. Just to give you a flavor, I purchased a never-worn 189-dollar silk top by Equipment off thredUP for 34 dollars (80 percent off retail) and my trusty pair of Vans canvas sneakers brand-new off Poshmark for 37 dollars (30 percent off). Still not impressed? I snagged a genuine leather skirt on Swap.com for 4 dollars. But my best scores are undoubtedly my patent leather Prada loafers, purchased on the RealReal for 700 dollars off the retail price, and a Phoebe Philo for Céline cropped turtleneck for 100 dollars from Material World, some 80 percent off the retail price.

  These savings add up dramatically over the course of building a conscious closet. Buying used is the main reason I can afford higher-quality and conscious brands and can pay full price, when I have to, because the other half of my wardrobe is bought at such a steep discount.

- **Puts the treasure hunt back in shopping.** Fast fashion is cheap and trendy, but it's taken the process of discovery out of shopping.

Everything kind of looks the same, and everyone seems to be wearing the same trends at the same time. On resale websites, there are all sorts of brands and styles, sitting side by side. As of this writing, Poshmark has 25 million items for sale by 5,000 different brands.[3] What retail store can top that kind of variety? If you shop resale websites and stores with an open mind, the vast selection almost guarantees that you'll find something you like. I find it to be a far more dynamic way to shop than retail.

- **Creates savvier shoppers.** Resale shoppers are savvy shoppers. They know which brands hold their value and know how to invest well in their wardrobes. For the same price or less than they'd spend shopping at discounters or at fast-fashion chains, they can build a higher-end wardrobe at an accessible price. Resale shoppers can spot quality a mile away, because the secondhand clothing market values quality brands. And resale shoppers take very good care of what they wear, so that items hold their value. They're on the front lines of making clothes last, which makes them doubly sustainable consumers.

WHY RESALE IS A CONSCIOUS CHOICE

By making it easier and more accessible to shop used, resale is helping to reduce the water, chemicals, and energy we need to make new clothes. Imagine if half of everyone's closets were purchased secondhand? According to the Ellen MacArthur Foundation, for every garment worn twice as long, its carbon footprint is reduced by 44 percent![4] And based on research conducted by thredUP, shopping secondhand extends the average life of a garment by 2.2 years. We all need to work to share and buy more clothes secondhand, and the resale market is making it easier and more popular than ever before.

Fast fashion has been described as the democratization of fashion.

But the title has passed to the resale market, by allowing anyone, on any budget, to afford high-end, quality clothes by designers that were once out of reach to the average person. Shopping this way incentivizes people to invest in longer-lasting, higher-quality brands, because they can afford to! What's more, the existence of an efficient second-hand marketplace could incentivize brands to make more durable clothes, because they could sell their own merchandise multiple times in the resale (and rental) economy, opening up new streams of profit. Eileen Fisher is already doing this. The company sells its pristine-condition used clothes at a discount through their highly successful Renew website and retail stores. I own a Renew silk jacket that's flawless and that cost a third of the retail price.

Resale could eventually help reduce the culture of fast fashion and lead people away from disposable clothes. It's already started. Fifty percent of thredUP's shoppers shifted their purchases from off-priced stores like T.J.Maxx to shopping resale in 2018.[5] You'll hear more from thredUP's founder, James Reinhart, at the end of this chapter about how the site's shoppers are scaling up their wardrobes. Many companies are racing to figure out how to recycle textiles or cut down on fashion's impacts. This is incredibly important, but there's also a simpler solution: Brands can make high-quality clothes in smaller volumes, and we can circulate it on resale sites where everyone can afford and enjoy it.

HOW TO LAND BIG SCORES AND UNBELIEVABLE DEALS ON RESALE SITES

You can snag something luxe for a flea market price on resale websites. But there are a few tricks to help you find exactly what you're looking for. You're already familiar with the major resale sites from Chapter 5, including thredUP, the RealReal, Tradesy, Grailed, Poshmark, and Vinted. Buffalo Exchange, Crossroads Trading, and Plato's Closet are the well-known brick-and-mortar chains, which I'll touch on. I'll also talk about how to get the most out of shopping on eBay and in consignment shops.

- **Use the filters.** If you're shopping on a resale website, you can filter everything from color, style, and fabric to brand, occasion, and price to help narrow down your search. It might sound counterintuitive, but if you set the price filter between, say, 30 or 40 dollars and then cap the price at your upper limit (say, 200 dollars), you'll weed out the low-quality brands and will start to see brands that are a better value. In other words, that's where you'll see the real deals, like a 400-dollar Diane von Furstenberg dress marked down to 40 dollars. Tradesy even lets you sort by discount, so you can filter for items marked 90 percent off retail price!

- **Don't fear the luxury sections.** If you're considering skipping the high-end brands because you think they're out of reach, think again. This is where the best deals are, and the prices can be surprisingly inexpensive. There are items on the RealReal, which exclusively sells high-end brands, starting at 20 dollars. On do-it-yourself selling apps like Poshmark and Tradesy, you can often catch a buyer eager to unload a designer piece for a steal. For example, I bought a vintage Escada silk bomber jacket off of Poshmark for around 100 dollars, a piece I could sell for twice as much—although I can't imagine I'll be getting rid of it anytime soon.

- **Go for guilt-free fast fashion.** If you love the style and design of fast fashion but want to cut out the environmental impact, buy it on a resale site! You're doing the planet a favor by giving these pieces a much-needed second life, all while saving money. Buy-sell-trade chains like Buffalo Exchange, Plato's Closet, and Crossroads Trading specialize in young and trendy brands and styles.

They are a great place to both buy and sell your fast-fashion pieces in a never-ending sustainable circle.

- **Shop sales and clearance.** Yes, resale sites have sale and clearance sections, too. And the markdowns and selection can be epic. At the time of this writing, just the sales section on thredUP has more than fifty thousand items, starting at 99 cents. If you're not exactly sure what you're on the hunt for, you can view markdowns in your size and price range and just look around. If a piece you like isn't on sale, add it to your "Likes" or "Favorites," and wait for the price to drop.

- **Shop by fabric or material.** If your closet lacks luxurious fibers like silk or cashmere because you think you can't afford them, you can on resale sites. Search by material and style, such as linen dresses, silk shirts, genuine leather jackets, and cashmere sweaters, and you'll be delighted at the low prices.

- **Snap up new with tags.** There is a huge amount of brand-new, never-worn inventory on resale sites, at steep discounts. I often buy my jeans and sneakers new instead of gently worn on resale sites since I put so many miles on them.

How to Buy, Sell, and Flip Your Closet Every Season

No matter your Fashion Personality Type, resale can put an end to the financial drain that is the modern wardrobe. We're all guilty of buying something, wearing it twice, and pushing it to the back of our closets. Resale has made it possible to continuously buy, wear, and sell fashion in an affordable and sustainable loop. Here's how to put the virtuous circle of resale shopping to work in your own life!

- **Check the resale value before you buy.** I discussed resale value in Chapter 5, but here's some additional advice: Retail price doesn't determine resale value. Some brands just aren't worth much in the resale market. You have to do your homework and check to see that the brands and styles you're buying are both in demand and will sell for a high percentage of their retail value. For example, at the time of this writing, brands like Frye, Helmut Lang, Rag & Bone, Gucci, Louis Vuitton, and Vince are in high demand and sell for closer to their retail price than other brands. This makes them good investments. Many Conscious Superstars have great resale value too, including Reformation, Eileen Fisher, Everlane, Veja, and Elizabeth Suzann. Resale value is constantly changing, however, so make sure you do your homework before you shop.

- **Take meticulous care of your clothes.** If you plan to sell your fashion, you have to keep your clothes in absolutely pristine, tip-top condition. There are endless tips for this in Part Five: "Make It Last," or you can refer to "Secrets of a Resale Guru" in Chapter 5.

- **Keep all labels, boxes, and dust bags.** Keep all labels (size, fabrication, brand, and care labels) affixed to the inside of your clothes. If they're itchy and you need to remove them, keep them and sew them back on before you sell. Resale buyers rely on labels to authenticate what they're buying. Keep shoeboxes and dust bags for high-end items, as they bump up the items' resale value and add to the buyer's feeling of getting something new to them.

- **Don't wait to sell!** Time is of the essence in resale. If you have a current style by a hot name brand, sell your piece while it's at the height of its trendiness and desirability. Fashion is fickle, and nothing cool lasts. Sell your piece as soon as you've grown tired of it and while someone else will get maximum enjoyment out of it.

FINDING GOLD ON EBAY

eBay is the best-known, longest-running resale website, and it's still a great place to find designer and brand-name clothing and footwear at bargain prices. One of the main misconceptions about eBay is that it's only for auctions. There are just as many listings that are set at a fixed price. This is where those new to eBay will find the best treasures without the risk. One of my favorite eBay scores is a Pendleton blanket coat in like-new condition for 380 dollars off retail. You can also buy overstock items new in the box or with tags. I often buy my Keds off eBay, for a touch less than retail. Look for listings set on "Best Offer," which means that you can suggest your own price to the buyer. A good rule of thumb is to come in with an offer no lower than 30 percent below the asking price. And don't worry about fakes: eBay always sides with the buyer and will give you a full refund if you suspect you've purchased a counterfeit. There's a lot of inventory on eBay, so it's best to shop here if you know exactly what you're after (e.g., vintage Yves Saint Laurent, Patagonia windbreaker, Everlane puffer jacket, etc.).

TREASURE HUNTING IN CONSIGNMENT SHOPS

Owing to the profusion of fabulous designer clothes out in the world (and a heightened interest in fashion everywhere, thanks to social media), consignment shops are having a moment. I've shopped incredible consignment stores in rather obscure places, like Tyler, Texas, where the owner of the fabulous My Sister's Room aptly told me, "It's a small town with really great stuff." I walked out with a patent leather Escada skirt for 100 dollars. (I told you I'm obsessed with vintage Escada.)

Consignment shops tend to focus on selling higher-end brand-name or luxury items in pristine condition, but you can often find better deals in brick-and-mortar stores than on the Internet. In Munich, I landed a 600-dollar Rebecca Taylor tulle gown for the equivalent of 80 dollars with the tags still on. If this is still more than you'd like to pay, check the clearance rack or shop for out-of-season garments. Real-world stores have limited space and have to move inventory quickly, which means the discounts can be very good. My strategies for getting lucky in these stores are similar to my thrifting strategies, which you'll read about in the next chapter: Look outside of your size and the brands you're familiar with, and always try things on. If your town has a well-curated consignment shop, make it one of your go-tos! Support it and help it thrive.

Inspiring Shoppers to Think Secondhand First

Q&A with thredUP Founder and CEO James Reinhart

ELIZABETH: For those new to thredUP, tell us about your company.

JAMES: thredUP is a marketplace that connects buyers and sellers of secondhand clothing. We do all the work to facilitate the process. We send customers our cleanout kit, they fill it with all the things they are no longer wearing, we pick it up at their house, and we process it and make the clothes available online. We are essentially the largest thrift store on the Internet.

ELIZABETH: What gave you the idea for the company?

JAMES: I got the idea as I was getting dressed one morning. I had a closet full of clothes I didn't wear, and I had no money. I tried to take them to the local consignment store, and they said, "We just do luxury." Americans have closets full of nonluxury brands, but that doesn't mean that they're not valuable. They may have zero value in one person's closet, but they are worth money to someone else. So how do we unlock that value? I've always believed that the best businesses in the world figure out how to create a whole bunch of value that had previously not been unlocked. That's what Airbnb has done and that's what Uber has done. And it's what we set out to solve for our closets as well.

ELIZABETH: For those who've yet to experience online resale shopping, how does shopping on thredUP differ from, say, digging through the racks at a charity thrift shop?

JAMES: By putting the thrifting experience online, we've brought a level of curation and simplicity to it that works for the modern woman. I think that the traditional thrifter was somebody who was willing to hunt and do the work. The modern consumer is a busy woman, but she still loves the idea of the treasure hunt. She also loves the idea of finding quality brands for less.

ELIZABETH: Who is the thredUP shopper or the resale shopper? Is he or she a different person than the traditional secondhand shopper?

JAMES: People who shop on thredUP are just really smart shoppers. They tend to be tech savvy, but they're from all over the country. I'm very happy about the fact that what we've built has very broad appeal.

ELIZABETH: Why is secondhand sustainable?

JAMES: I think it's by definition sustainable. It's about taking clothes that have already consumed the planet's resources and giving them a chance to be used again.

ELIZABETH: Resale has completely changed the way I shop. I buy better brands and take exacting care of my clothes. Does this happen to other people?

JAMES: No question. Resale has allowed people at every clothing budget level to step up. So if you were a customer who used to buy essentially disposable fashion, you can buy secondhand name brands that are better quality. We hear time and again from customers that they now can find better brands and things that they feel better about wearing but at a lower price.

ELIZABETH: Many resale shoppers also turn over their closets more. What does this mean, and how does it not end up being really expensive?

JAMES: One of the powerful things about the resale economy is that it allows a woman to transition her closet much faster than previously. She's putting more units through there for the same price or in some cases she's spending more, but she's getting better value for her money. The way we used to spend on clothes is we'd buy a whole bunch of stuff and then a few years later just give it away. That all adds up. The new model is to buy more resale, rent a few statement pieces a year, and then sell your clothes for, say, 30 or 40 percent of what you paid. You're able to refresh your closet and feel better about the whole thing and actually pay less money over time.

ELIZABETH: It's like sustainable fast fashion.

JAMES: Yeah! It's like closet velocity. You could turn over your whole closet two or three times a year for the same price as what you used to be doing by buying everything new.

ELIZABETH: How can people maximize the amount of money they make selling on thredUP? Or is the service more about convenience?

JAMES: thredUP is the place to maximize convenience and make a little bit of money. If you really want to profit maximize, you have to sell your old clothes yourself. You just can't have it both ways. For people who are looking to maximize the dollar, unequivocally that also means buying higher-quality brands.

ELIZABETH: The resale market is growing really fast. How are conventional brands responding to what's happening in the resale market?

JAMES: Yes, it just keeps getting bigger and bigger. Estimates are that it will be worth 50 billion dollars in ten years. My dream was always that we would put a big enough dent in the universe and the consumer mindshare that retailers would start to understand that resale is here to stay. Every industry has come to terms with making sure that if something is produced, it has a useful second life to a different customer. Brands now know that their customer is shopping secondhand and they want to figure out how to make money off of it. But they're also waking up to the fact that they should be better environmental citizens.

ELIZABETH: More and more people are shopping resale. How do we get everyone thinking secondhand first?

JAMES: We need consumers to evangelize what's happening and why it's so great, and then I think we need companies like thredUP to keep growing and selling more and more high-quality product that allows more people to participate in the resale economy.

Thrift (and Vintage) Shop Like a Pro

I love a good charity shop.

—HELEN MIRREN

I'**ve thrifted and** shopped vintage everywhere from Berlin to Wichita. I have gone elbow to elbow with the competitive thrifters at the Goodwill Outlet bins, where piles of used clothes sell for pennies on the pound. When I was growing up, thrifting was still something of a well-kept secret. Now, everyone knows that it's the absolute cheapest way to build a sustainable, stylish, and one-of-a-kind wardrobe. Among my proudest thrift store scores are my 35-dollar vintage Gucci bag from a junk shop in Arkansas and a vintage 1970s patchwork coat plucked from a flea market in Georgia for a quarter.

It takes patience, a little luck, and a good eye to find thrift-store treasures. That, of course, is the fun of it. Anyone can become a pro thrifter with a little practice (and admittedly some free time). Here are my tips to get the most out of your thrifting adventures.

- **Make time.** Thrift stores are a jumble of fashion decades, sizes, and brands. Thrifting takes more of a commitment than regular shopping. Set aside a bare minimum of half an hour to look around and try things on. I usually spend an hour in a good thrift store.

- **Choose well-stocked stores.** Not all thrift shops yield the same quality of finds. Inventory is determined by the demographic the donations are coming from. I'm not ashamed to go straight to the thrift shop in the most affluent neighborhoods. Likewise, I love thrifting in small southern towns because I often find ostentatious 1980s designer clothes that look like they were worn by the cast of *Dallas*. The inventory is also determined by how the shop owners sort and curate the store. For example, some thrift shops sort out all the vintage items, a tragedy if you ask me. Hop onto Yelp or Google Maps and read online reviews of the thrift shops in the area (search for terms like "secondhand," "vintage," "used clothing," and "consignment"). Look to see if other reviewers have found good name-brand, vintage, or high-end and luxury pieces. Line up a handful of stores to visit, in case you strike out in one. This is an easy task: Thrift, consignment, and resale shops often cluster near one another.

- **Look outside of your usual brands.** Don't just stick to the brands you're familiar with. You'll miss out on too many great finds. Instead of looking at the label, look at the cut, shape, fabric, and color of what's on the racks. And don't be afraid to try a vintage or secondhand version of a brand you don't usually buy. I love vintage Chico's, White Stag, and Express, for example.

- **Shop on both sides of your size.** Items are very often returned to the rack or the shelf in the wrong spot. What's more, sizing has changed a lot over time.

- **See the potential.** Your thrifted treasures are raw material for a one-of-a-kind wardrobe. Here are a few of my favorite "thrift flips," meaning easy alterations to transform your thrifted diamonds-in-the-rough into wardrobe staples.

- Dated details like shoulder pads, buttons, and embellishments can be switched out or removed.

- Baggy eighties and nineties styles can be slimmed down through the leg or sleeve at the tailor.

- Long, billowy skirts or dresses can be turned into minis by simply lopping off the extra fabric and sewing or gluing the hem shut.

- The classic thrift flip is to take a cheap pair of vintage "mom jeans" and cut them into the perfect pair of cutoffs. Use tweezers to fray the edges.

- **Check for condition issues.** Most thrift stores do a presort for rips and stains, but plenty of defective items get through. And quite unlike the resale market, thrift shops often have a policy of "all sales final," meaning no returns. Check the armpits and collars of shirts for odors and stains and check for broken zippers, yellowing, and holes. Split linings and small holes are easy fixes. You'll learn more mending and repair tricks in Part Five: "Make It Last." While some condition issues are a no-go (yellowing is hard to reverse), you might be able to land a so-called damaged piece at very low cost if you're willing to fix it up. I nabbed a 600-dollar Isabel Marant coat covered in pills for 40 dollars at Beacon's Closet, a buy-sell-trade shop in New York. After ten minutes with a fabric shaver, it looked like new.

- **Just try it on!** Without modern branding and sizing to guide you, you'll never know if something works until you try it on. I sometimes wear a bodysuit and tights so I can change in the aisles, instead of waiting for a fitting room.

Thrifting for Core Pieces

Thrift stores are chock-full of pre-fast-fashion finds, when luxurious natural materials were go-to fabrics and structured, tailored pieces were the norm. They are the perfect place to build your core wardrobe pieces inexpensively. Keep your eye out for the following high-quality items for your conscious closet.

- Suede rancher coats (usually in the men's section).
- Denim jackets. Look for ones that are 100 percent cotton in a classic cut and built like a tank.
- Leather jackets. Check the men's section for the classic motorcycle style.
- Timeless, unfussy silk button-down shirts and linen shells.
- Classic wool coats and blazers. I have wool and cashmere coats dating back to the 1940s that look as chic as ever today.
- Cable-knit and crewneck sweaters in wool and cashmere.
- Vintage handbags. Department store brands like Liz Claiborne and Dooney & Bourke made great timeless leather bags in the 1990s. Classic Coach bags are equally timeless. Also keep an eye out for crocodile- or alligator-skin bags from the sixties.

SHOPPING VINTAGE: TIPS AND TRICKS

What's the difference between a good vintage shop and a store full of old clothes? It's a shop owner with a good eye and exceptional taste. Good vintage dealers spend their waking moments scouring the world for sartorial treasures, just to lay them at our feet. As loads of low-quality fast fashion gets churned out each year, vintage has become a sanctuary for high-quality and unique clothes from past eras. Vintage will only get more valuable (read: expensive) if the world continues on its current course. Still, it's possible to find reasonably priced vintage, and there are many occasions when a good vintage piece is worth every penny. Here are my tips for shopping smart in the vintage market and finding exceptional pieces.

- **Are you contemporary or retro?** If your plan is to blend your vintage pieces with contemporary pieces to look on trend, opt for more timeless cuts, prints, and fabrics or those that are back in style at the moment. You can also tweak details like buttons or a long hemline if they're dating a piece. For inspiration on how to work vintage into your wardrobe, follow vintage shops on social media. They often model their inventory and show how to wear retro styles in an updated way.

- **Know your decades.** Most vintage shops specialize in certain eras and styles, whether it's fifties pinup, sixties hippie, seventies rocker, or high-end European designer looks. One of the best vintage shops I've ever been to, Decades in Salt Lake City, has the best vintage from, yes, *every* decade, but this is a rare occurrence. Seek out stores where you're drawn to the aesthetic, and if you find one where you appreciate the buyer's eye, return to that store again and again.

- **Try on larger sizes.** In general, all pre-1990s vintage runs *much* smaller than modern sizes, so try on larger sizes than your norm in both garments and shoes. My dress size is an 8 in modern mass-manufactured clothes and a 14 or larger in vintage. If you're tall, have big feet, or are full-figured, you'll have better luck finding the right size in more recent pieces from the 1980s and 1990s, for example. That's my sweet spot.

- **Damaged or not?** Vintage quality varies wildly, from unworn and pristine to brittle and threadbare. Some strange things can happen to decades-old clothes. Keep in mind that some damages and odors, like deep-seated cigarette smells, can't be reversed. Decide if you can live with the condition problems and if you want to take on alterations and repairs, which can be expensive. I have a 1960s cropped cowhide jacket that is beyond gorgeous. It also deposits fur wherever I go. For me, it's a small price to pay to wear such a sui generis piece.

- **Don't skip the accessories.** Good accessories and handbags are overpriced nowadays, and vintage can be the way to owning distinct pieces for less. I scored a pair of 1980s collectible Christian Dior visor shades in a Munich vintage shop for the equivalent of 80 dollars. And my favorite handbag is a 1970s Bottega Veneta velvet clutch from Brooklyn's Amarcord, another one of my favorite vintage stores. While pricey, it was about 5,000 dollars less than a modern Bottega bag.

- **Shop designer.** All designers and brands have great decades, and many are in the past. It's really fun to explore what luxury houses were up to before fashion got so corporate and serious. For example, I love eighties Givenchy and Christian Dior. These fashion houses still make great clothes, of course, but I actually prefer the earlier looks, and they're vastly cheaper than current designer prices. It can help to have some basic knowledge of brands and designers, but you'll also pick this knowledge up the more you shop vintage!

Rent Your Next Wardrobe

Fashion is moving at a breakneck pace. What's new is considered old in the blink of an eye, and completely over if it's been on Instagram. Fashion's appeal is growing and spreading to every corner of the world, and it's impossible to imagine fashion slowing back down now. But it's time to answer the call of new styles more sustainably. We *can* fully enjoy trend-driven fashion, all without so much waste, guilt, and environmental impact. And we can do it by renting our fashion.

Maybe we won't lease our favorite pair of jeans, but statement-making pieces like a cocktail dress worn for one night, a designer "it" bag, or a trendy top that makes you feel fresh and cutting-edge until the fashion winds change are all perfect candidates for renting. For *those* pieces, renting just makes too much good sense for it to not get really huge. And that's exactly what's happening.

For years, renting on websites like Rent the Runway has been the secret to outdressing your friends at a wedding. But rental services are expanding beyond formal events to offering trend-driven clothes for everyday life. Rent the Runway kicked off the craze, with the 2016 launch of its Unlimited service, and fashion rental services are now cropping up around the world. In China, there's YCloset. In the UK, there's Girl Meets Dress and Chic by Choice. Other fashion rental companies in the United States include Gwynnie Bee, which features extended sizing; Le Tote, which pairs rentals with personal styling;

and Armarium, which leases ultra-high-end luxury fashion. American Eagle, Ann Taylor, and New York & Company are among the first clothing brands experimenting with renting a selection of their own merchandise. This is a new and evolving space, so I'll keep an updated list on my website, TheConsciousClosetBook.com.

Here's why renting is revolutionary: We're only utilizing a tiny fraction of the useful life of much of our clothing. Instead of a designer dress getting worn a few times and pushed to the back of the closet or thrown into the trash, that same dress can now be circulated and shared among a pool of renters. A rented piece of clothing is worn as many as thirty times, according to *Fast Company*.[1] Earlier in the book, I mentioned that some consumers only wear an item of clothing three times before considering it old.[2] If we assume that the average trendy piece of clothing is worn three times, that means renting can increase a fashionable garment's life span by as much as 900 percent! What's more, rental websites such as Rent the Runway and Le Tote retire clothing long before it's worn-out by selling it at a deep discount, giving rented garments *yet another life*. This is all music to the ears of a Style Seeker. Renting is a way we can have it all: We can follow trends and be more sustainable at the same time.

Renting has the potential to all but eliminate certain categories of clothes that are most commonly trashed or worn just a few times. For example, dresses are one item we're most likely to buy for an event and never wear again. Unsurprisingly, beautiful dresses are rental websites' bread and butter! Our work wardrobes, as well, tend to have surprisingly high environmental and financial costs, as they're often purchased just for the office, don't reflect our personal style, and are chucked when we no longer need them. I can't tell you how many bags full of drab dress shirts, suits, and sensible pencil skirts I see tossed out when I sort clothes. It's no surprise, then, that many women are using rental sites to lease clothes for work. At the end of this chapter, you'll hear from my friend, Emily K., about why she loves renting for the office.

HOW RENTING FASHION WORKS

If you're considering renting your fashion and you're not quite sure what to expect, here are a few features to know about:

- **Onetime rentals.** The most common way to rent clothes is for one-off occasions, such as a wedding or other formal event. Each rental service works a little bit differently, so shop around. Rent the Runway offers onetime dress rentals, as do peer-to-peer websites like Style Lend, where you're renting directly from another member's closet. Armarium offers rentals for luxury-label looks for red carpet events and the like. Onetime rentals are great for wearing a glamorous gown at an affordable price and for keeping your closet clear of wear-it-once outfits.

- **Monthly subscription plans.** Monthly subscription services offer rentals for everyday fashionable clothing and accessories, allowing members to rent a certain number of pieces at a time and swap them out throughout the month. Le Tote, Gwynnie Bee, and Rent the Runway Unlimited are a few sites that offer rental subscriptions in the United States. A monthly subscription is a perfect option if you're a Style Seeker and want to follow trends and wear something new as often as possible, or are simply tired of investing in clothes, only to have to replace them every few years when fashion changes or you grow tired of them.

- **Pricing and style.** Each rental service is a little bit different, in terms of pricing and the brands and quality on offer. If you're renting for a one-off event, the price of the garment is determined by the retail price. So, a 400-dollar designer gown will be more affordable to rent than a 4,000-dollar dress. If you decide to go with a monthly subscription service, shop around and find one that fits both your budget and your style. Rent the Runway

Unlimited has mid- to high-end designer brands and is 159 dollars a month at the time of this writing (they also have a more affordable plan for fewer outfits per month). Le Tote, which focuses on trendier, mid-market styles, is cheaper at 69 dollars per month. These prices do change, so you'll need to do your own research. Look around for conscious brands on rental sites as well! Rent the Runway carries Reformation, Mara Hoffman, and Stella McCartney, and we should ask all rental services to keep expanding the conscious options to make renting that much more sustainable!

- **Cleaning and repairs.** It's one thing to share a car or rent a room in someone's apartment, but isn't renting clothes gross? Not at all! All rental companies professionally clean, inspect, and repair clothes after every wear, which saves *you* time and money on laundry. What about the impact of dry cleaning? It's an important question, and one we have to assess closely as renting gains in popularity. While traditional dry cleaning has a high energy cost and relies on toxic chemicals, there are greener alternatives. Rent the Runway owns the nation's largest dry cleaner, for example, and they use an army of spot cleaners whose job it is to extend the life of clothes. The company also eschews the toxic solvent perchloroethylene often used in the cleaning process (more on green dry cleaning in Chapter 22).

THE ADVANTAGES OF RENTING *ALL* YOUR FASHION

Here are just a few of the benefits of a monthly subscription service for clothing rentals.

- **Price is out of the picture.** A subscription service is a flat fee, meaning you can rent an 800-dollar or 80-dollar dress without stressing about the price tag. In fact, you don't have to think about the price of the clothes at all. You can pick clothes based on the purest standard possible: what you're excited to wear. If you don't like something, you don't have to wear it. You can just send it back. If you love something, you can purchase it at a discount or just rent it again.

- **Fashion experimentation.** Renting allows you to experiment with your look and try completely out-there styles risk-free. This can help to sharpen your personal style. When I rent, I don't shy away from sequins, bold prints, and dramatic cuts. I'm not alone. Fifty percent of rentals on Rent the Runway have some sort of embellishment on them.[3]

- **It saves time on shopping and outfit planning.** You might find yourself addicted to scrolling rental websites for your next fashion fix, but renting can save you time planning outfits, doing laundry, and accomplishing the not-so-easy task of choosing well for yourself when you shop for clothes. I know parents and busy working-women whose time has been freed and style has been elevated by the low-stakes freedom of just renting what they wear.

BUT IS IT AFFORDABLE?

Subscription rental services are not exactly *cheap,* but they can be a fantastic value for the money. Whether or not they're worth the price will depend on your budget and your Fashion Personality Type. I personally prefer to invest my money in quality brands and buy pieces I want to wear for a long time. But that's because I'm a Traditionalist. If you're a Style Seeker, renting your fashion can be a better use of money, as it allows you to wear more clothes and better, higher-quality clothes at an affordable price. Stephanie, a thirty-one-year-old Style Seeker and an avid renter, spends 159 dollars a month on Rent the

Runway Unlimited. It might sound steep until you consider that she rented 116,000 dollars' worth of designer fashion in 2018. Emily K., whom you'll hear from next, is a Traditionalist, and yet she feels like renting is a wise use of her money since so much mass-market clothing today quickly becomes dated or falls apart. The price of renting is worth it to her, too. In both cases, these women are able to wear as much new-to-them clothing as they want, at a price they can afford.

When to Rent

Renting for really special occasions is a no-brainer (you get to wear gorgeous dresses at a sliver of the retail price), but here are some less obvious areas of your life where rentals can be transformative.

- **Any and all wear-it-once occasions.** Whether it's to feed your Instagram or dress for a music festival or holiday party, if it's an occasion where you know you're shopping for a one-time-only outfit, it should be rented.

- **Work.** See my pal Emily's interview at the end of this chapter. If you're tired of cluttering your closet with a separate work wardrobe, or you want to cut dry cleaning and laundry from your weekly routine, renting can be your secret weapon.

- **Vacations.** Renting for vacations is hugely popular. It makes sense. Sharing drool-inducing vacation photos is major currency on social media sites. Plus, why buy island garb or Vegas-worthy going-out clothes that you'll never wear again? Rent them!

- **Maternity and Kids.** Buying clothes for each stage of a pregnancy can get pricey and wasteful. Not surprisingly, maternity clothes are a big hit on both resale and rental sites. Rent the Runway and Le Tote are two companies offering stylish maternity clothes at the time of this writing. I predict that renting for kids clothes will be the next category to take off! Rent the Runway is one company offering rentals for children's clothing, as of this writing.

- **Weddings.** Buying, wearing, and then storing a wedding dress for decades is becoming a thing of the past. More bridesmaids and brides are opting to just rent their looks. It can be dramatically cheaper. Rent the Runway offers 1,500-dollar wedding-worthy designer gowns for 200 dollars. Resale websites like Tradesy are another great way to land deals on wedding gowns, and you can sell your gown on the same platform after your big day. Think beyond the day of the wedding, too. Consider renting outfits for your engagement photos, rehearsal dinners, and honeymoon.

HOW TO MAKE RENTING AND RESALE ULTRA GREEN

Can renting and shopping resale be truly green if we're mailing clothes back and forth all month, ratcheting up fuel expenditures and packaging? Isn't it just encouraging more consumption? These are important questions. I'm not suggesting that renting and resale have *no* environmental impact, but they are greener than the current paradigm of buying and tossing barely worn clothes. As I've mentioned, it's the manufacture of new clothing that has the biggest impact in the fashion industry, not shipping. Shipping our clothes all the way around the world to retail stores captures just 3 percent of fashion's carbon impact.[4] Ground-shipping routes for online shopping are also surprisingly efficient, especially when compared to driving in a personal vehicle to shop.[5]

It's packaging that gives online shopping and renting a hefty environmental impact.[6] Fossil fuels, paper, plastic, and chemicals are used to create packaging, much of which isn't biodegradable and ends up in landfills or out in the environment as plastic waste or microplastic pollution. This is a concern, not just with rental services but with virtually everything we buy, and it should be swiftly addressed. Rent the Runway ships in reusable garment bags and recycles their plastic dry-cleaning bags. Eliminating plastic and expanding the use of reusable and biodegradable packaging for all rental and resale companies would make these services all the more green.

The Transformative Power of Renting for Work

Q&A with Manhattan Newspaper Editor Emily K. *

ELIZABETH: We are all familiar with the concept of renting a dress or a tux for a formal event. But more women are renting clothes for their everyday lives. What inspired you to give it a try?

EMILY: It came about because I started a new job, and I'm still trying to figure out how to dress for work. Renting gives me a lot of flexibility and allows me to try different styles and looks. I can figure out how I want to present myself in a low-risk way. I also just get really excited to get a new dress in the mail! It's just fun.

ELIZABETH: I can see where some people might be wary of renting everyday clothes. Have you run into trouble with smells, stains, or items not showing up on time?

EMILY: I use the Rent the Runway. I was skeptical, too, but I haven't had any problems. One item was damaged, but the company was quick to send me a replacement. I've been amazed at the logistics, because all I do is drop off my bag using prepaid postage, and I'll get new items back in a few days.

ELIZABETH: Has renting changed your style?

EMILY: It's helped me refine how I get dressed. And it's helped me become a little more discerning. Because renting is just a flat fee, and you can get whatever you want, you're able to focus on the quality of the garment, how it looks, how it's made, how it feels, the cut. I'm able to just focus on the clothes themselves instead of the price, so I've been able to raise the bar a little bit on what I actually wear.

ELIZABETH: How do you justify the cost?

EMILY: I personally feel like buying clothes can be a pretty bad investment these days. They lose their value as soon as they leave the store. A lot of them wear out easily. Leasing the clothes rather than buying them just feels like a much better use of my money. What's more, could I have this dynamic and this high quality of a wardrobe for the same amount of money if I bought all of it? No.

ELIZABETH: Renting is also more sustainable. Was that part of the appeal?

EMILY: In theory, if we all have a smaller pool of clothes that we're borrowing from, then we're producing less stuff. Renting is like a big collective of people that have bought all of these clothes together, and hopefully we're producing fewer products to fill that pool. It really gives you fast fashion without the destruction of the planet in some ways. You can have as much clothing as you want, as many options as you want, and anytime you want, for a reasonable price.

ELIZABETH: You work in Manhattan, one of the most fashionable places in the world. Who else could renting work well for?

EMILY: People always have something they need to get dressed for, an event or a meeting, for example. I think it works for anyone who really enjoys feeling and looking their best.

*Interviewee is going by a pseudonym.

Yes, You *Can* Afford a Conscious Closet!

Fashion often feels tauntingly out of reach. A lot of it is! Celebrities are waltzing around in 800-dollar sneakers and gowns that cost more than our annual salaries. Instagram influencers are wearing something new every single day, piling on the pressure to keep up with style and spend beyond our means. There are many people who can't afford the basics, much less a rotating closet of the latest fashions. When it comes to fashion and money, there's *a lot* to talk about.

The conscious-closet approach asks you to look beyond the luxury lusting, logo-obsession, and the one-upmanship that often happens in fashion and focus on spending money mindfully and carefully on your wardrobe. I will never ask you to buy clothes you can't afford. Instead, I'll show you how to afford clothes that are perfect for you, your income, and your life, while dispelling the notion that all conscious fashion is expensive. Whether you're a Minimalist or Traditionalist looking to invest in classic wardrobe staples or a Style Seeker trying to keep up with fashion on a budget, I will show you how to straighten out your fashion finances, spend wisely, and invest far better in your clothes.

THE DISPOSABLE APPROACH TO SPENDING

Mass-market clothing is more affordable than it ever has been, and yet low-cost fashion can be a financially wasteful habit that adds up over time. I'll use myself as an example: Over the course of a decade, I amassed a hodgepodge of deals and steals that I estimate cost me somewhere in the ballpark of 6,000 dollars. It turns out I wasn't the bargain hunter I imagined myself to be.

But I wasn't an extreme case. I was the norm. Americans buy sixty-six garments and seven and a half pairs of shoes per year and spend just shy of 1,000 dollars per capita on what we wear.[1] That works out to a budget of 19 dollars per item, not exactly the kind of cash that equates to high-quality investments. If you spent this way for ten years, you would lay out 9,000 dollars and amass more than seven hundred items of clothes, clothes that we can safely assume have no resale value. Your wardrobe would be a total wash. I call this high-volume, low-quality method of spending on clothes the disposable approach.

THE CONSCIOUS APPROACH TO SPENDING

The conscious approach to spending is, like everything else in this book, about greater awareness: awareness of what you buy, what you paid, and how it worked out in the long run. Learning conscious spending habits can help you manage your money in all aspects of your life. It helped me to build the wardrobe I always wanted, and I actually *saved money* along the way. Here's how to start putting the conscious-closet strategy of spending into practice in your life.

- **Calculate the damage.** To know how much you can afford to spend on clothes, look first at what you already spend. Most of us have no idea what we spend on clothes. You might say, *I can't* *afford 40 dollars on a pair of jeans*—only to find out you spent 40 dollars *last month* on tops you haven't worn. To calculate your spending, look through your bank statements or your inbox for online shopping receipts. Or, you can use my method from Chapter 8: count your hangers or take the total number of pieces from your Impact Inventory and multiply that number by an approximate average price paid. Shocking, right?

- **Create a loose budget.** Financial analysts suggest spending no more than 5 or 10 percent of income on clothes, and then adjust based on your expenses and debt. It's a useful benchmark, especially when it comes to knowing what you can afford *per piece.* If you make 25,000 dollars a year and you have no debt, your clothing budget at 5 percent of your income would be 1,250 dollars for the year, 312.50 dollars for the season, or about a hundred bucks per month. A budget will help you to see that, no, you shouldn't splurge on a 2,000-dollar designer handbag, but you're also not relegated to the discount bin either. If you don't have much of a budget to work with, I have tips for you on shopping cheap toward the end of this chapter.

- **Set a goal.** Is your goal to invest in higher-quality clothes, to save up for something you've had your eye on, or to stop wasting money on clothes you don't wear? Set achievable goals and work toward them. It took me the better part of a decade to build the wardrobe I wanted. At first, I stopped buying 10-dollar disposable flats that wore out in a month and bought 40-dollar shoes that would last the season. I also bought less—instead of four 5-dollar tank tops, I'd buy two that were a little bit more expensive and looked a little better made, and scaled up over time. Take your time, carefully consider your spending strategy, and you'll make more lasting choices that are better for your bottom line.

- **Track your spending.** *Always* track what you spend on clothes. Personal finance apps are an easy way to keep track, or you can just keep a note in your smart phone with a list of purchases. At the end of each season, look back at what you've purchased and evaluate what you're wearing and what you're not. Which purchases were you really happy with? Which ones disappointed? Why? Continue to learn, tweak your spending strategy, and spend smarter. For example, if you're spending a lot on clothes you wear a few times, it might be time to consider renting your wardrobe, or shopping and selling on resale websites.

- **Pad out your budget.** A well-built wardrobe can layer you with confidence, open doors, and add a sheen of delight to your everyday existence. What I'm getting at is that clothes matter, and sometimes we have to get creative to find the money to spend on them. If your budget is feeling tight, refer to Chapter 5 and sell some pieces to pad out your budget. If you're overspending on areas like eating out, bars, and to-go coffees, those are obvious places to cut back. Making your own coffee instead of buying a latte in the morning can save about 25 dollars during a workweek, giving you an extra 100 dollars a month to spend on what you wear. The other way to pad out your budget is to save. Create a separate account for your clothes if you need to, drop as little as 10 or 20 dollars a week into it, and you'll have 120 to 240 dollars to spend after a single season of savings. There are also lots of tips on how to shop very inexpensively later in this chapter.

MY DISPOSABLE APPROACH FINANCES (2011)

Average Price per Piece: $19

Total Estimated Cost of Wardrobe: about $6,726 (purchased over a decade)

Total Estimated Resale Value of Wardrobe: about $100

Total Financial Loss on Wardrobe: $6,626

MY CONSCIOUS APPROACH FINANCES (2019)

Average Price per Piece: $40 per item (some cost far more, some cost far less)

Total Estimated Cost of Wardrobe: about $5,266 (purchased over eight years)

Total Estimated Resale Value of Wardrobe: about $3,417

Total Financial Loss on Wardrobe: $1,849

HOW TO INVEST WELL IN YOUR WARDROBE

Sometimes, we make less-than-stellar clothing choices not because we can't afford to spend more but because the idea of expensive clothes is terrifying. The fear is, *What if we're getting ripped off?* Or, worse, *What if we get it wrong?* It's time to undo that line of thinking. There are gorgeous, mood-altering pieces of clothing out there that are perfect for you. And sometimes they're going to cost you more money than you'd like. I don't relish buying expensive things. In fact, I hate it, but I can do it with the confidence that comes from knowing how to recognize a good buy. Here are my tips.

- **Know what you like.** Making a good buy is as simple and as difficult as knowing, *really knowing,* what you like to wear and what will fit well in your wardrobe. You've already laid important groundwork to make solid investments by reading "The Art of Less," particularly Chapter 11 on wardrobe building. You've thought about your personal style, your colors, shapes, and cuts.

You've learned to shop for quality. Now you can use these skills to spend well by choosing clothes you'll love for seasons to come. If you're considering buying pricey ethical or sustainable brands, use the same amount of scrutiny. Skip the ethical pity purchase, a phrase coined by conscious-fashion journalist Alden Wicker. You're not doing a conscious brand any favors if you buy their piece and then push it to the back of your closet.

- **Invest in what you're already wearing.** A safe place to start investing is in those signature pieces you find yourself buying again and again. My friend Gabby, who I mentioned in the Introduction, made her first investment in a classic black jumpsuit, one of her personal wardrobe staples. My first solid investment was leather cowboy boots with a replaceable sole. I've spent hundreds of dollars over the years on disposable boots. I sucked it up and bought a pair for 115 dollars, and they're still going strong after four years.

- **Check the resale value.** You should always protect your investments by buying brands that you can sell if you need to. Use the tips I taught you in Chapter 5 to look up the resale value of brands. (A refresher: Use resale websites like thredUP or the RealReal to check the pricing of similar items.) I recently sold a pair of Maison Margiela boots (bought to begin with on a resale site) that weren't quite my style to fund a new pair of sunglasses. I broke even on the transaction. My wardrobe is worth almost two-thirds of its retail value, meaning I could sell it right now and recoup a significant amount of the money I spent on it. Compare that to my fast-fashion wardrobe, which had a resale value of around 6 percent of what I paid for it.

How to Recognize a Good Buy: The Cheat Sheet

To summarize, when you find a beautiful but pricey investment piece that you're on the verge of buying, run it through this checklist to make sure you're spending smart. Expensive clothes should also *always* be:

- **Perfect.** If you've got any doubts, whether they're about color, style, or fit, skip it. Spend your money on clothes you know you can't live without.

- **Good quality.** Does the piece have great fabric, construction, fit, and details? That money you're spending should be going toward something tangible, including good materials and expert craftsmanship.

- **Made with creative, unique, or timeless design.** Are you paying to support someone's unique design vision? Alternately, is this piece so timeless that you'll wear it forever? If it's trendy, why not rent it or buy it on a resale site?

- **Ethically and sustainably made.** Not all high-quality pieces are ethically and sustainably made, but they should be. I can tell you that when you find that rare combination of superb quality, ethics, *and* design, it is so much easier to part with your money.

THE MAGIC OF COST PER WEAR

The absolutely cheapest clothes in your closet aren't your fast-fashion scores or your runway originals that you nabbed on clearance. They are the clothes you wear the most, and I have the math to prove it. Cost per wear is a formula that shows the price of clothing as a function of how much we wear it. CPW works like this:

$$\text{CPW} = \text{Total cost of the item} \div \text{Number of wears}$$

CPW is based on the simple yet profound idea that it costs a certain amount of money to get dressed every day. And it's *that* cost—rather than the price tag on our clothes—that we should pay attention to. Every time you wear a piece of clothing *again,* it, in theory, saves you from spending money on other clothes. A quick example: If you wear a 20-dollar shirt once, it costs you 20 dollars. But if you wear it again, the cost drops to 10 dollars, and so on. Calculating CPW as you're shopping has many benefits. Here are three.

- **CPW exposes fast fashion for being the bad deal it so often is.** A trendy 40-dollar dress bought for a party and worn once is a very bad buy indeed, with a 40-dollar CPW. If you kept that up and spent 40 dollars a day to get dressed over the course of the year, it would cost you *many* thousands of dollars. But CPW isn't biased toward cheap clothes. If you shop cheap and wear your low-cost clothes *a lot,* you will have a nonexistent CPW!

- **CPW protects against expensive and bad buys of all stripes.** If you have expensive tastes (as I do) or are drawn to eccentric clothes that you'll never wear (as I am), CPW will also save you from buying that 500-dollar designer dress or that sequin tube top that goes with nothing in your wardrobe, even if it is 50 percent off.

- **CPW encourages you to wear your clothes.** If you're laying out a squirm-inducing sum of money on something you're going to get a lot of use out of, CPW is your best friend. A pair of high-quality jeans that costs 100 dollars and lasts three hundred wears has a CPW of 33 cents! If you had a daily CPW of 30 cents throughout the year, you'd be spending a fraction as much as our example fast-fashion shopper. CPW isn't really about the money; it's about the wearing. It can work magic for core pieces and any wardrobe staple. For example, I bought a gorgeous Alexander Wang leather jacket at a consignment shop for 300 dollars (ouch!), but I've worn it about two hundred times over the course of four years, giving me a CPW of 1.50 dollars, and I could *still* sell it right now for at least 150 dollars.

SPENDING STRATEGIES FOR TRADITIONALISTS AND MINIMALISTS

Spending wisely on clothes looks different depending on your Fashion Personality Type. Most of the strategies I've mentioned so far in this chapter work well for Traditionalists and Minimalists, such as learning to make investments and using cost per wear to evaluate good buys. For Traditionalists and Minimalists, you're buying much of your wardrobe for keeps. Because you're buying fewer pieces and getting more wear out of your clothes than a Style Seeker, you have a bigger budget *per item*. Here are a few other spending strategies for your Fashion Personality Type.

- **Invest the most in your core pieces.** All the Fashion Personality Types have core pieces at the foundation of their closet, and it pays to buy these pieces once and buy them right, because you're going to wear them a lot. The beauty of investing in quality basics like jeans, a good winter coat, a classic button-down, or a few versatile dresses is that once you've bought them, you won't need to replace them for quite a while, perhaps even years.

- **The high-low trick.** Not everything in your closet will be a pricey investment. Another strategy is the high-low trick: Invest in a couple of great pieces each season and be super-cheap about everything else. By using the tips in the cheap-shopping section—see "Secrets for Dirt-Cheap Conscious Shopping" later in this chapter—you can avoid buying bad quality while shopping frugally.

- **The finish-line effect.** As you build out your wardrobe, more and more of your pieces will carry over from season to season. If you can, make your most significant investments in your wardrobe in the first few years. Once your main wardrobe is built out, your spending will plateau and then plummet. That's the money-saving power of the finish-line effect. If you're a Traditionalist, you can use your savings to, yes, save money, or use it to buy better accent, seasonal, and trendy pieces. My wardrobe is fully built out, so I am currently in a statement-jewelry-and-handbags phase. If you're a Minimalist, your overall spending on clothes could be *very* low once you complete your wardrobe. You can build a small, perfect wardrobe and spend next to nothing later.

SPENDING STRATEGIES FOR THE STYLE SEEKER

If you're a Style Seeker, the trick is to keep up with fashion without going broke. You should approach buying fashion as a service rather than a depreciating product you own. You'll save so much money over time. Thanks to the resale and rental market, which I've discussed at length earlier in Part Three, sharing and accessing fashion is much easier than ever before. Make sure you calculate what you're spending on fashion over the course of the year, and think about what it would cost you to keep that level of spending up for a decade. It's usually good motivation to switch to renting or resale. Still, not everything in a Style Seeker's closet is fashion and trends. You should have those core pieces at the foundation of your wardrobe that help you get dressed (unless you're renting everything). One idea is to spend on your basics and your fashion in totally separate ways. For basics and core pieces, buy those items for keeps. Look for better quality, and buy the best you can afford. For trendy or statement items you *know* you're going to wear only a handful of times, consider renting or buying them on resale sites and flipping them at the end of the season.

Here's an easy way to remember this strategy: Basics you buy. Fashion you DOI (don't own it).

SECRETS FOR DIRT-CHEAP CONSCIOUS SHOPPING

There are myriad ways to shop with your values when you're on a budget or simply love a good deal. Like many people, I have a split personality when it comes to shopping. I have my thrift store treasures next to my luxury designer pieces right next to my reasonably priced conscious brands. What matters when you're shopping is that you're getting a good *value,* meaning you feel like the product you're buying is worth your money. It is possible to be conscious, financially savvy, *and cheap* as you build your new wardrobe. Here's how to do it:

- **Thrift!** See Chapter 15 for tips. You can find whatever you're looking for—including trendy clothes, fast fashion, and brand-name and sometimes designer pieces—in a thrift store for practically nothing. I have a thrifted leather jacket that cost me a quarter!

- **Shop resale sites.** I've covered the glories of resale shopping extensively. You can find brand-name, high-end, and brand-new clothes for low, low prices on resale sites. You can also find conscious-fashion brands, which you'll learn all about in Chapter 20, on resale sites for less.

- **Shop sales.** No one said you have to pay full price! Even conscious brands have end-of-season sales and clearance sales, too. If there's a brand you want to own that's out of reach, get on their email list, like or favorite the item if it's online, wait for the price to drop, and pounce on discounts!

- **Use the high-low trick.** I've already mentioned the high-low trick once, but I like it so much I want to bring it up again. Don't feel pressure to invest in everything in your wardrobe. Choose a few items per season or year to save up for, and be cheap about everything else.

- **Start with the basics.** If you want to support brands that feel out of reach, start by scaling up your basics, like tank tops, underwear, or workout gear. This is a great way to support more conscious companies as well. PACT Organic, Mighty Good Undies, Maggie's Organics, and Etiko are just a few sustainable-fashion companies selling essentials under 20 dollars.

- **Borrow and swap.** Nothing is cheaper than free. Attend clothing swaps in your community or organize one with your most stylish friends. Look on social media for swap pages and groups and find deals there. There are tips in Chapter 6 on how to organize your own swap.

- **Refashion and DIY.** Why not reimagine what you already own? Go deep into your closet, dust off items you've forgotten about, and refashion, restyle, and remake them into something more personal. You can find inspiration for your DIY projects in Part Five: "Make It Last."

- **Shop budget brands with better ethics.** When shopping cheap fashion chains, make the effort to switch to a Better Big Brand. Not all discount or fast-fashion brands are created equal. Read Chapter 20 for tips on how to find brands that are more ethical and green.

PART FOUR

The Sustainable Fashion Handbook

I want to look good,
feel good, and do good—
that to me is a luxury.

–EMMA WATSON

Sustainable Fabric Lunatic

I'm a little bit of a fabric lunatic.

—JOHN MALKOVICH

I'm not sure exactly when I crossed over from normal human to fabric lunatic, but the transformation is complete. All textiles and their making fascinate me, from the ancient arts of silk spinning and leather tanning to the cold, calculated efficiency of a polyester mill. Everyone should be at least a little bit of a freak for fabric. Clothing *is* fabric. Fabric determines everything about what we wear, from how it feels next to our skin to how it washes, wears, and ages over time.

Yet the main reason I've dedicated an entire chapter to the materials we wear is this: The majority of fashion's environmental impact on the planet happens while manufacturing textiles, in the phase where fabric and materials are grown or made, then spun, dyed, and finished into something we recognize as clothing. In fact, this seemingly simple process of making the materials we wear requires many times more water and energy than shipping, packaging, or retailing our clothes.[1] Buying sustainable materials and educating ourselves about what defines an eco-friendly textile are two powerful ways we can help reduce fashion's footprint. It's a bonus that you'll learn how to add beautiful and eco-friendly new materials to your conscious closet along the way.

I'm often asked, is there a perfectly green fabric? I think it's the wrong question. Cotton consumes close to 19 million tons of chemicals each year, while synthetic materials gobble up 342 million barrels of oil.[2] The leather industry discharges the same quantity of emissions as 30 million cars driven over the course of one year.[3] We need to improve the sustainability of *all* the materials we wear. That's why, in Part Four, I give you both the good and the bad sides of the materials we wear—the beauty and the beast—so you can better enjoy and understand your clothes and help support brands in their mission to make them more sustainably.

I've featured full profiles for the top seven fibers and materials in use today, the ones in the lion's share of what we wear. In fact, just two—cotton and polyester—make up an astonishing 75 percent of the global fiber market.[4] I've also mentioned a few important others.

POLYESTER: ENVIRONMENTAL FRIEND OR FOE?

Polyester was once associated with leisure suits and flammable clothes from the disco era. Long maligned for being tacky and clammy, polyester has shed its old reputation and slipped into virtually everything we wear, from jeans and T-shirts to yoga pants and outdoor gear. Polyester is by far the world's most dominant fiber, accounting for more than half of all global fiber output and more than 80 percent of all synthetics.[5] Without polyester, there could be no fast fashion—it is the cheap, easy-to-produce material that an industry built on low price and speed depends on.

Polyester is plastic. It is made by refining crude oil or natural gas, breaking it into chemicals, and creating a polymer that is extruded and spun into fibers. That polymer is polyethylene terephthalate, also known as PET, the same ingredient that's in a plastic bottle. While natural materials like cotton, wool, and silk tend to support farmers and jobs in countries all around the world, the synthetics industry is high-tech and highly concentrated. More than 75 percent of the world's polyester fabric is made in just one country: China.[6]

Polyester's Impact
Nonrenewable · Chemicals · Microplastics

Polyester is made from fossil fuels, a nonrenewable and finite resource. Half of the fossil fuel used in the plastic-making process is used as the raw material that becomes plastic itself, and the other half is energy used to fuel the polymerization process.[7] Polyester's inextricable links to the fossil fuel industry (8 percent of every barrel of oil becomes plastic) and climate change can't be ignored.[8] Increasing demand for PET and plastic products is driving investments in petrochemical refineries in the United States, for example.[9] Compared to cotton, another widely used fiber, polyester requires more energy to make. Polyester also has hazardous building blocks. The catalyst to produce polyester is antimony trioxide, a heavy metal that's a known carcinogen.[10] As I'll explain in the next chapter, the use of hazardous substances to manufacture clothes is all too common. These substances, if handled incorrectly, can negatively impact textile and garment workers and the environment, but they also have the potential to impact consumer health as well. Antimony-free polyester is available on the market, and we need to demand more of it.

Last, but certainly not least, polyester and other plastic-based synthetics do not readily biodegrade. All of the plastic clothing being made in the world is manufactured without much of a plan for how to collect or recycle it, even though we know that plastic persists and accumulates in the environment. There is only a sliver of recycled polyester content being used in fashion, and it's made out of recycled PET bottles, not plastic clothing. What's more, our clothing is shedding tiny microfibers at an alarming rate. A study commissioned by Patagonia found that, on average, synthetic fleece jackets can shed up to 250,000 fibers per wash.[11] A similar study showed that acrylic garments shed as many as 700,000 fibers in a single spin cycle.[12] The final destination for these fibers is the ocean.

According to the International Union for Conservation of Nature, there are 1.5 million tons of small pieces of what are known as microplastics entering the ocean each year, and as much as 34.8 percent of that pollution is coming from synthetic textiles.[13] Newer studies show that microfiber pollution is also coming from cotton, linen, and viscose rayon fibers as well, challenging what we know about how textiles biodegrade in marine environments.[14] These little fibers from our clothes have been found everywhere from beaches to lakes, and in everything from beer and table salt to seafood and drinking water.[15]

Microfibers travel from our garments to the ocean in a number of ways, including friction from wearing, but scientists believe their primary means of transportation is through our laundry machines. They slip through the filters in our sewage treatment plants and escape into the sea. Scientists are racing to understand the impacts of these tiny particles that are circulating all around us.

How plastic pollution impacts human health and marine life is inconclusive at the time of this writing, but the evidence is troubling at best. Plastic fibers can absorb persistent organic pollutants from the surrounding environment.[16] From there, there's evidence that these toxins can accumulate in the tissues of fish and could move up the food chain to our plates.[17] While the extent of the danger is unknown, microplastic pollution is an urgent problem that we cannot ignore.

How to Buy Polyester Consciously

Even though polyester is typically cheap, it's not a disposable product, so don't treat it as such. Take care of your polyester clothes, buy as needed, and always donate or recycle when possible. Most of us are familiar with the little labels that tell us where and how our food is grown: organic, grass-fed, non-GMO, and free-range are all familiar sightings in our grocery stores. The same type of labeling exists for clothing, including animal welfare standards, organic standards, and safe-chemistry standards, all of which I'll touch on in this chapter. We need to pressure brands to certify more of our fashion! To buy safer, nontoxic polyester, look for third-party certification labels that test for hazardous substances, such as bluesign, Cradle to Cradle (C2C) Certified, and Oeko-Tex. Keep an eye out for antimony-free polyester, as well. You can also shop for recycled polyester (rPET) garments and shoes, made out of plastic bottles, which saves around 60 percent in energy consumption and up to 45 percent of CO_2 emissions, while reducing the need for virgin polyester.[18] Patagonia, Rothy's, Everlane, Adidas, and Timberland are just a few of the many brands carrying recycled polyester. As for microplastics, here are a few ways to lessen your impact:

- Support organizations fighting plastic pollution. A few are 5 Gyres, Greenpeace, Oceanic Society, and the Plastic Pollution Coalition.

- Purchase a Cora Ball or a Guppyfriend laundry bag, which can be used in the washing machine to capture microfibers.

- Hand wash and air-dry more of your clothes. It's better for them anyway. The agitation from the washing machine is thought to cause the most microfiber shedding.

- Pick up a copy of Lucy Siegle's book *Turning the Tide on Plastic,* a tremendous resource full of tips for curbing your plastic habit and its impacts.

Consumer changes won't go far enough to solve this problem. Because microfibers are coming from so many sources (car tires, microbeads, even shoe soles) and are ingested without our knowing, we need widespread scientific, industry, and government solutions. Patagonia, for example, is investigating how to change fabric finishing to reduce microfiber shedding. Other big-picture ideas include retrofitting washers or even water treatment facilities with better filters. Demand that brands and government act now to study the impacts of microplastics and to curb harmful plastic pollution.

SPANDEX, NYLON, AND OTHER SYNTHETICS TO CONSIDER

There are many other synthetic fibers in use today, from the spandex in our skinny jeans to the nylon in our windbreakers, each with its own benefits and environmental challenges. A known carcinogen is used and air pollutants caused while making our stretchy spandex, for example.[19] Spandex is also challenging to recycle and downcycle, as it clogs up shredding machines. Polyurethane (also called PU) used in coatings, shoe outsoles, and faux leather is made using some toxic compounds, and can release dioxins and other toxins when incinerated.[20] Nitrous oxide, the gas produced during nylon production, is three hundred times more potent than CO_2.[21] Acrylic, a cheap, often poorly performing alternative to wool, is made from acrylonitrile, a chemical listed as a "probable human carcinogen" by the EPA.[22] What's more, all synthetics require quite a bit of energy to make.

Alternatives

Most materials we wear *can* be manufactured *far* more safely and sustainably. Certain hazardous chemicals used by the textile industry can be handled with care or eliminated so that consumers and workers are safe and protected. Look for safe-chemistry labels, including bluesign, Cradle to Cradle Certified, and Oeko-Tex, as you shop. Adidas, PrAna, and Patagonia are just a few of the brands using bluesign-approved safe chemistry in their synthetic products, for example. You can also shop for recycled nylon, which uses far less energy than virgin nylon and is becoming increasingly common. Repreve and Econyl are two textile companies manufacturing recycled nylon, and Patagonia and Stella McCartney are two brands using it. There are also products testing recycled spandex and polyurethane, alongside exciting breakthroughs in what's known as "biosynthetics," synthetic fibers made from 100 percent renewable and biodegradable sources like sugar or yeast instead of fossil fuels. Adidas and Stella McCartney have used bio-based plastic alternatives, and there's a flurry of innovation happening, so the options will multiply from here. One material to avoid at the time of this writing is polyvinyl chloride, or PVC, which is used to make vinyl and some faux leather; it often includes a type of phthalate to soften the plastic that's linked to endocrine disruption.[23] Many brands have already banned the use of PVC textiles.

COTTON: THE FABRIC OF OUR LIVES?

Cotton is one of the most versatile and universally loved fibers. It is comfortable, breathable, biodegradable, and affordable. I own more cotton garments than anything else. While no longer the world's leading fabric, cotton makes up a massive 24.5 percent of total global fiber production.[24] It's hard to overstate the importance of cotton to the economy, culture, and human history. Cotton is a significant industry wherever it grows, including across Africa, the Middle East, South America, the southern and western United States, China, Australia, Pakistan, India, and beyond. In China alone, there are an estimated 49.7 million cotton farms, mostly small household farms.[25] In India, there are an estimated 6.9 million cotton farmers.[26] China, India, and the United States together grow well over half the world's cotton.[27] Considering the vast number of people and places that depend on the cotton industry, making cotton more sustainable and ethical will have far-reaching benefits.

Cotton's Impact
Pesticides · Water · Child Labor

Cotton can be difficult to grow, succumbing to flooding, drought, and weed and insect infestations. Heavy chemical use has been the response on many farms and in many countries. Cotton uses an estimated 6 percent of all pesticides, more than any other major crop.[28] The production of cotton demands an estimated 220,000 tons of pesticides and 8.8 million tons of fertilizer each year.[29] These are staggering sums. Many pesticides are highly toxic to human health and the environment and can poison workers, cause long-term illness, and escape into the air, water, and soil, negatively affecting the many millions of people who live in cotton-growing regions. According to the United Nations, poisonings from industrial and agricultural chemicals are among the top five leading causes of death worldwide.[30]

Compared to other fibers, cotton requires a lot of water to produce. As much as 2,168 gallons of water is required to grow the cotton in a single T-shirt.[31] That's according to Textile Exchange, a nonprofit organization that researches and advocates for sustainable fiber usage. While water is plentiful in some cotton-growing areas, almost 60 percent of all cotton is grown in regions affected by water scarcity and where demand for water often outstrips the supply.[32] And while cotton could be a major source of poverty alleviation in rural and poor areas, in many places it is exploitative instead. Labor rights activists have worked for decades to eliminate the use of state-sponsored forced labor and child labor in Uzbekistan, a leading cotton exporter. Many child laborers in India (of which UNICEF estimates there are 10.1 million) work in the cotton industry, either picking cotton or cotton-seeds or even applying harmful pesticides.[33]

How to Buy Cotton Consciously

Cotton is affordable and plentiful, but we shouldn't take cotton clothing for granted. We should care for cotton products. To choose more sustainable cotton, you have many options. You can look for organic cotton, grown without harmful chemicals or pesticides or genetically modified seeds. The two leading organic certifications for clothing are the Global Organic Textile Standard (GOTS) and the Organic Content Standard (OCS). Look for these labels as you shop. According to an assessment by Textile Exchange, organic cotton uses up to 91 percent less irrigated water than conventional cotton.[34] Cradle to Cradle Certified is another label to look for. The clothing retailer C&A made the first pair of gold-level Cradle to Cradle Certified jeans in 2018. You can also purchase cotton from one of the thirty-plus brands that are members of Cotton Made in Africa, which supports small growers and environmentally friendly growing practices in sub-Saharan Africa. A list of members can be found on the CmiA website. Keep an eye out for fair-trade-certified cotton products as well, which are made without the use of hazardous pesticides and provide a stable income to small farmers. Fair-trade products are certified by a number of international organizations, including Fair Trade USA and Fairtrade International. You can look for these labels when you're shopping. Athleta, Madewell, Nudie Jeans, People Tree, and PrAna are just a few brands carrying some fair-trade clothing. Another sustainable option is recycled cotton, which uses much less water to make. Evrnu is one startup pioneering chemical-to-chemical cotton-recycling technology. And one last tip: You can shop with one of the more than one hundred clothing brands that are members of the Better Cotton Initiative, a nonprofit organization transitioning cotton farming in twenty-one countries toward more sustainable practices. Gap, ASOS, H&M, and Levi's are just a few BCI members. BCI cotton isn't always marked on labels, but you can check the website for a full list of member brands.

VISCOSE RAYON: THE FOREST CLEAR-CUTTER IN YOUR CLOSET?

Viscose rayon is the most overlooked and least understood of the common fibers we wear. And yet, I'm sure you have at least a handful of garments in your closet made of this material. We often miss viscose rayon because it disguises itself under a multitude of other names, from bamboo and modal to Tencel. What these materials (sometimes called "semisynthetics" or "regenerated cellulosic fibers") all have in common is that they're crafted by chemically dissolving wood from eucalyptus, beech, or bamboo trees, and the chemical pulp is re-formed into a fiber. These materials share a soft and slinky hand feel and are a cheaper cousin to silk or cotton. Viscose rayon is a very concentrated industry, with 80 percent of the market controlled by ten industrial textile giants.[35] Austria's Lenzing and India's Aditya Birla Group are the two largest viscose rayon producers in the world. Many of the dissolving pulp mills that supply the wood pulp for fiber are concentrated in Brazil, Indonesia, and Canada, while the vast majority of mills producing the fibers and finished textiles are in China.[36]

Here is a breakdown of the different types of viscose rayon:

- **Viscose or rayon.** Viscose and rayon are two words describing the same material. Typically, you'll see "rayon" used to label clothes sold in the United States, while "viscose" is the more common term on labels in Europe. In either case, conventional viscose rayon is often made using more hazardous chemicals compared to some of the following varieties in this list, and it makes up 70 percent of the viscose rayon fibers market.[37]

- **Modal.** Made via a modified and higher-energy process using beech trees,[38] modal is a more durable, more machine washable type of viscose rayon. Lenzing controls a majority of modal production.

- **Bamboo.** Bamboo can be made into a fabric similar to linen, but it's most often used to create a type of viscose rayon. It can be made using either the original, chemically intensive viscose rayon process (and mislabeled as eco-friendly) or in an environmentally friendly process.

- **Lyocell.** A more modern and sustainable viscose rayon, lyocell uses sustainably managed eucalyptus forests for its wood pulp and recycles the chemicals it uses in a closed-loop system. It also has improved performance features. This material is often sold under its brand name, Lenzing Tencel. There are a few other less-common viscose rayon fibers you might look up on your own, Cupro, Bemberg, and acetate among them.

Viscose Rayon's Impact
Chemicals • Global Warming • Deforestation

It's time to start paying attention to viscose rayon and its environmental impact, as production of these tree fibers has doubled in the past decade and is projected to double again in the next ten years—and the process of making the most common varieties is the furthest thing from natural or green.[39] Making viscose rayon requires a lot of energy and the material has a higher global-warming impact than the manufacture of polyester and cotton.[40] It is a very inefficient process, as well. According to Canopy, a forest preservation group, 70 percent of the tree becomes waste in the manufacturing process. High volumes of harsh and hazardous chemicals are used, including large amounts of bleach and carbon disulfide, a neurologically toxic chemical that has a long history of causing insanity in exposed workers.[41] Without proper regulations, pulp mills can contaminate water as well.[42]

Viscose rayon is also driving deforestation. As demand for printed materials goes down, pulp mills are banking on trees going into more and more of our fashion. According to research conducted by Canopy, more than 150 million trees are logged annually and turned into viscose rayon fabrics; if placed end to end, those trees would circle the earth seven times.[43] Most alarmingly, many trees logged for fabrics are coming from fragile, valuable ecosystems. As much as 45 percent of all viscose rayon is being sourced from ancient and endangered forests, including those in Indonesia, Canada's boreal forest, and the Amazon.[44] Forests are a major source of biodiversity and carbon sequestration, making old-growth deforestation a major climate-change threat. Beware of greenwashing of viscose rayon products, as they're often marketed as "natural" or "eco-friendly" or as "tree fiber" or "eucalyptus" to mislead consumers.

How to Buy Rayon Consciously

Thanks to pressure from advocacy groups like Canopy, the viscose rayon industry is working to clean up its act. When shopping, look for lyocell or brand-name lyocell, known as Lenzing Tencel, as it's the most sustainable type of viscose rayon, sourced from fast-growing eucalyptus trees (instead of endangered forests), and using careful chemical management that recycles substances rather than letting them out into the environment.[45] You can also look for bluesign and Oeko-Tex safe-chemistry certifications on viscose rayon, bamboo, modal, or lyocell. There are efforts underway to make conventional viscose-rayon less environmentally damaging. Lenzing now makes a more sustainable viscose rayon, called EcoVero, as does Birla, and you can look for these brand names on your fabric label. Or shop with the dozens of brands partnering with Canopy, which is working to protect forests from the viscose rayon supply chain. You might also shop with brands that are members of the Forest Stewardship Council, a sustainable forest management group. There is also growing investment in viscose-rayon sources from recycled material and those that require no trees. For example, Lenzing's Refibra is a type of lyocell made from recycled cotton scraps, as is Asahi Kasei's Bemberg.

LEATHER: CAN THIS ANCIENT MATERIAL GO GREEN?

Long before humans figured out how to weave cloth, we wore animal skins. Our preoccupation with leather isn't surprising, given its incredible durability, versatility, and beauty. It's a rare material that can improve with age and wear. I adore leather and collect secondhand leather jackets, pants, and vests.

The leather industry is a vast and valuable titan that touches many continents and lives. In 2016, the global leather goods market was valued at 93.2 billion dollars, with almost 5 billion square feet of leather produced each year.[46] Footwear is the biggest part of the leather industry, with China producing more than 4.4 billion pairs of leather shoes annually.[47] The largest hide producers are Brazil, the United States, and China. China also produces the largest amount of finished leather goods, followed by Italy, India, and Brazil. Cowhides are by far the most commonly used leather, but goat, pig, lamb, and more exotic skins like snake and crocodile are also used as leather.

Leather's Challenges
Chemicals · Carbon Impact · Animal Welfare

The leather industry has a way to go toward being ethical and green. Cow leather, the most common variety, is considered a waste by-product of the beef industry.[48] And yet we shouldn't ignore the cattle industry's environmental impact when evaluating leather. The planet's cattle herds and the fertilizer- and pesticide-intensive way they're raised and fed are major drivers of deforestation, land degradation, climate change, and water pollution.[49] Cows are also a major emitter of methane, a powerful greenhouse gas.

While our ancient ancestors tanned leather one hide at a time with natural ingredients like oil and smoke, today's leather is massproduced and preserved using a multitude of harsh and, in some cases, hazardous chemicals. Leather tanning relies on three hundred to four hundred different chemicals, and as much as three pounds of chemicals are used to produce one pound of leather.[50] The most common tanning agent in use today is trivalent chromium, or chromium(III), which is not toxic to human health. The carcinogenic type of chromium, called hexavalent chromium or chromium(VI), has been phased out at most tanneries. But, without proper chemical management, chrome(III) can oxidize into the more toxic type of chrome.[51] Leather also produces a high volume of solid waste, including skin, fat, hair, and polluted water, which has to be carefully managed.[52]

A large segment of the modern leather industry is highly regulated, but there are some major exceptions. In some Bangladeshi tanneries, for example, leather workers lack protective gear (and many stand directly in vats of chemicals), and toxic wastewater is dumped untreated into local rivers. The leather-tanning district of Hazaribagh, Bangladesh, has been named one of the most toxic places in the world, although efforts are underway to clean it up. Animal welfare on cattle ranches, small farms, feedlots, and slaughterhouses varies greatly from area to area. The extent of animal cruelty in the cattle industry—and by association the leather industry—is difficult to quantify and thought to be widespread, and calls for a more transparent and ethical beef and leather industry grow by the day.

How to Buy Leather Consciously

Leather is one of the most durable and long-lasting materials we wear. Purchase leather pieces for keeps. Repair and condition leather products to make them last for years. To shop more sustainably, choose leather from one of the seventy-plus brands that are members of the Leather Working Group, which certifies and audits leather tanneries, covers almost 20 percent of the world's leather output, and ranks tanners from bronze to gold based on strict environmental standards, such as safe chemistry and proper energy and wastewater management. Aldo, Zara, Clarks, and Timberland are just a few LWG members. The rest can be found on the LWG website. You can also, once again, look for safe-chemistry certifications like bluesign and the Oeko-Tex Leather Standard as you shop. As of this writing, Textile Exchange is developing a global Responsible Leather Standard that will help brands certify their leather products as safe, sustainable, and humane. Brands are starting to work with ranchers and farmers to provide transparency and show consumers when leather is sourced from humanely raised animals. Shop around for brands that are transparent and can tell you where their leather is sourced and tanned and can confirm that it's made under eco-friendly and ethical conditions (footwear company Nisolo and Amsterdam-based O My Bag are examples). If it's not clear where your brand stands, ask them (more on how in Chapter 20). Keep an eye out for products made from upcycled leather, meaning leather garments that are deconstructed and sewn into new products, and recycled leather. Recyc Leather and Nike Flyleather are two initiatives using recycled leather scraps. If you are avoiding animal fibers, there are a fast-growing number of leather alternatives that are animal-free and don't have the high environmental impact of a plastic-based faux leather. Modern Meadow's Zoa is made from yeast, Apple Peel Skin is made from organic apples, and Vegea uses grape skins, in just three examples.

You can also follow Joshua Katcher (author and designer of vegan menswear brand Brave GentleMan) on social media, at either @Brave_GentleMan or @DiscerningBrute, as he is an authority on innovation in the vegan textiles space.

WOOL: CAN THIS DURABLE FIBER MAKE A GREEN COMEBACK?

We've covered the fiber giants. Now it's on to the more exclusive fibers in our wardrobes. Wool is gorgeous and durable. It has the magical capacity to resist odors, wrinkles, and stains. What's more, wool items can be mended and tended and can last for many years. Higher-quality wool has also shed its itchy and high-maintenance reputation, and many modern wool varieties are so soft, machine-washable, and lightweight that they're being used in T-shirts, workout gear, and sneakers. One of my softest garments is neither my cashmere sweater nor one of my cotton tops: It is a fine-knit merino wool cardigan.

As of 2015, more than 1 billion sheep are raised around the world, producing 2.5 million pounds of raw wool.[53] Wool is raised in about a hundred countries on half a million farms, with Australia, China, and New Zealand together producing almost half the world's wool products.[54] And yet wool makes up less than 1 percent of global fiber output. Wool, it should be noted, can also refer to other more rarified animal hairs, like cashmere, llama, vicuna, camel hair, angora rabbit, yak hair, mohair, and alpaca. Peru is home to the world's largest alpaca and vicuna herds. However, sheep's wool makes up 95 percent of the wool market, according to Textile Exchange.

Wool's Impacts
Desertification · Chemicals · Global Warming

Wool can have a sizable impact on the environment, or it can be ultra-sustainable. It all depends on where and how the animals are grazed and raised and how their wool is processed. Cashmere, which comes from the downy-soft undercoat of cashmere goats, is a key example of how wool can harm the environment. Huge spikes in demand for cashmere have led to a large increase in goat herds, which is causing land degradation and desertification in the Mongolia region of China, where a third of all cashmere is produced.[55]

On many standard sheep farms, overgrazing can also lead to soil erosion and desertification.[56] Fertilizers and pesticides are often used on pastures and the sheep themselves, driving up wool's chemical impacts. Scouring and cleaning raw wool requires harsh alkaline and bleaching agents and creates high quantities of wastewater.[57] Wool, like leather, also has a much-higher-than-average global-warming footprint for a fiber, due largely to methane released by sheep. Mulesing is another area of concern. The process involves cutting flesh from the tail area of the animal to prevent an infection caused by flies and is considered by many to be inhumane.

How to Buy Wool Consciously

While pricier than cotton and synthetics, wool lasts longer than most other fibers, and quality wool pieces more than pay for themselves over time. Buy timeless wool pieces, and mend them to make them last (more on this in Chapter 24). To choose more sustainable wool, you can shop for organic wool certified by GOTS or OSC. Or look for safe-chemistry certifications like bluesign, Cradle to Cradle Certified, or Oeko-Tex on wool products. Stella McCartney became the first brand to make a Cradle to Cradle Certified wool yarn, in 2018. Or shop from brands that are certified by the Responsible Wool Standard, run by Textile Exchange, which ensures that animal welfare and sustainable land management standards have been met. H&M, REI, and Marks & Spencer are a few brands that have made RWS commitments. Another organization to know about is Fibershed, a nonprofit fostering the resurgence of small-scale farmers and regenerative farming practices around the world. The North Face makes a Climate Beneficial wool beanie that is carbon positive, meaning raised on a wool farm that absorbs more carbon than it releases, and sourced from a Fibershed member. When shopping for cashmere, shop with brands that are transparent and can reveal where they source their fiber and the steps they've taken to source it sustainably. Naadam cashmere is an example. You might also look for recycled wool products, one of the oldest recyclable materials, and ask brands to carry more recycled wool and cashmere. PrAna and REI are two examples of brands carrying a selection of recycled wool.

DOWN AND FUR: ADDITIONAL ANIMAL MATERIALS TO CONSIDER

Any animal-based fiber comes with tremendous ethical responsibility. Down is a layer of fine feathers sourced from geese and ducks and commonly used to insulate jackets. Forced feeding and live plucking are common on factory farms that raise animals for down. If you buy down, shop with brands certified by Textile Exchange's Responsible Down Standard, which verifies high animal welfare standards. Alternatives to down include wool and polyester stuffing. As for fur, there are a number of more sustainable and humane alternatives. Skip the acrylic faux fur, which has a high environmental impact and can't be recycled. Ecopel makes faux fur from recycled PET, for example; Reformation sells faux fur from dead stock or leftover materials, a better choice. There are also innovations in lab-grown fur that use a percentage of renewable materials. In addition, shopping vintage and secondhand can be a way to sidestep any ethical and sustainability concerns you might have about real fur.

LINEN AND HEMP: CRISP, WRINKLY, AND NATURALLY SUSTAINABLE?

Linen is a textured and ancient fiber made from the flax plant. While linen comprises less than 1 percent of all fiber in production, similar bast-plant fibers like hemp, jute, and ramie, along with linen, capture more than 5.5 percent of the global market.[58] Many people in the sustainable-fashion community are investing in bast fibers, so you can expect to see more of them as you're out shopping.

Western Europe grows 85 percent of the world's flax that goes into linen, while China manufactures and finishes most linen textiles.[59] In the United States, hemp fibers are on the cusp of a comeback. In 2018, the Hemp Farming Act was passed, legalizing the growing of hemp (it was classified as a controlled substance for decades, despite containing only trace amounts of THC).[60] Hemp is a fast-growing plant that needs few chemical inputs to grow. My absolute favorite T-shirt is a 100 percent hemp tee by Emerson Fry. It's soft, resilient, and breathable.

Linen's Impacts / How to Buy Consciously

Compared to other fibers, bast fibers use less energy and few chemical inputs like pesticides and fertilizers to cultivate.[61] These materials can be cultivated quite sustainably. Look for linen products and their kin when you shop. (And buy a small travel steamer if the wrinkling bothers you. Or just embrace it.) You can also shop for recycled or organic linen, hemp, jute, ramie, or flax, certified by GOTS or OCS. CRAiLAR flax fiber, produced in the United States, is grown sustainably. Start looking for more hemp. North Carolina's TS Designs, which manufactures sustainable T-shirts for the wholesale market, is one company planning to grow and sew industrial hemp, right in the United States.

SILK: A LUSTROUS MATERIAL OR ENERGY HOG?

Silk is stunning, with a luster and drape that has captivated humans throughout its eight-thousand-year history. Although it comprises a small corner of the global fiber market, at just 0.2 percent, there are still some three hundred thousand households around the world involved in the production of raw silk.[62] Currently, China is the world leader in silk production, followed by India, Uzbekistan, Brazil, Iran, and Thailand.[63] Silk is produced by the saliva of silkworms that feed on the leaves of mulberry trees. A single silkworm can spin almost three thousand feet of usable silk thread while making one single cocoon.[64] To extract the silk, a silkworm's cocoon is boiled and the filaments unraveled.

Silk's Impacts / How to Buy Consciously
Global Warming · Energy · Chemicals

Silk is made from renewable resources and its production creates very little waste. However, fertilizers and insecticides are often used to grow the mulberry trees, and more energy is used to make silk than for most other textiles.[65] The silkworms are kept at a controlled temperature and the cocoons are dried using steam and hot air, requiring large amounts of energy. Some silk is dyed using heavy metals like chromium(VI) and made weightier by applying what's known as metallic salts. These chemicals can be toxic to humans and the environment.[66] Silk is pricier than most of the other materials I've mentioned, but it's extremely durable, long lasting, and gorgeous. Care for your silk pieces and they will more than pay for themselves over time. To buy better silk, you can choose organic silk (GOTS or OCS) and look for safe-chemical certification labels like bluesign, Cradle to Cradle Certified, or Oeko-Tex as you shop. Everlane and Eileen Fisher are two brands selling bluesign-certified silk. Peace silk is made without killing the silkworms, while Bolt Threads manufactures a lab-grown silk alternative made out of yeast and sugar. Stella McCartney has used it in her collections.

Sustainable Fiber Cheat Sheet

Now that you've read the fine print about textiles and their environmental pros and cons, here are some easy tips and shortcuts for shopping for sustainable materials, in no particular order.

- **Recycled.** Whether it's recycled polyester, nylon, cotton, cashmere, or wool, most recycled content requires less energy and fewer resources to make and cuts down on waste. Look for the Recycled Claim Standard certification on labels as well.

- **Safe and Nontoxic.** Choose clothing certified for safe and sustainable chemical management when you shop. Your best options are bluesign, Cradle to Cradle Certified, and Oeko-Tex. Organic certifications also verify safe-chemistry usage.

- **Organic.** Organic certifications cover natural fibers—linen, cotton, wool, and silk—and ensure these materials are grown without harmful chemicals or pesticides or genetically modified seeds. GOTS is the most rigorous organic standard, as it covers not just the cultivation of the raw material but the processing of the textiles as well.

- **Fair trade.** Fair-trade products support small-scale producers in developing regions through poverty reduction and sustainable development. Fair-trade products are certified by a number of international organizations, including Fair Trade USA and

Fairtrade International. Check the Fairtrade International website or Good on You for a comprehensive list of participating brands.

- **B Corporations.** One other easy way to shop for more sustainable materials is to shop with B Corporations, for-profit companies that are monitored by a third-party group to meet high ethical and sustainability standards. Some B Corps label their products with the signature "Certified B Corporation" label. A quick Google search will turn up more. A few well-known clothing companies that are B Corps include Patagonia, Reformation, Eileen Fisher, Dansko, MUD Jeans, Allbirds, Nisolo, and Outland Denim.

THE NEXT GENERATION OF FIBERS

Throughout this chapter, I've mentioned next-generation textiles that are reshaping the fashion industry. We don't have to imagine synthetics made without oil, leather made without animals, and textiles made out of fruit skins, mushrooms, and—crucially—old clothes. They are already here. Most traditional textiles will stay in production for the foreseeable future, but we need these breakthroughs to meet the growing demand for fashion, sustainably. Here are a few other sustainable fibers that I haven't yet mentioned that might soon vie for space in your closet: Piñatex creates leather alternatives from pineapple leaves (Hugo Boss is a client). Bolt Threads' Mylo is a faux leather made from mushrooms. Orange Fiber, an Italian startup, is creating fiber from citrus waste (Salvatore Ferragamo has used it). Worn Again is using blended polyester-cotton textiles and plastic bottles as the feedstock for new clothes, and Modern Meadow is crafting a lab-grown leather alternative from yeasts. VitroLabs is working on lab-grown leather and fur, free of animals, while 10XBeta is creating shoes out of—get this—recycled carbon dioxide. Keep your eye out for these and other exciting new materials as you shop.

Almost any fiber or material we wear can be cultivated and manufactured in a more sustainable way. A material's better version of itself is known as a "preferred textile," shorthand for fiber-production methods that are on the road toward being more sustainable when compared to conventional production methods. For example, recycled polyester is a preferred version of polyester; organic cotton or Better Cotton Initiative cotton are preferred versions of cotton; leather certified and audited by the Leather Working Group is a preferred version of leather. The idea of preferred materials helps to move us away from black-and-white thinking about sustainability toward the achievable and significant goal of reducing the environmental impact of every aspect of what we wear.

Kick Nasty Chemicals Out of Your Closet

Thousands of different chemicals are used to create our clothing. They are used to bleach, scour, soften, brighten, and repel water and stains. Many more are used to add color or, in the case of synthetics, to make the fibers themselves. Chemicals are indispensable to the textile industry, but there's growing alarm about the potentially hazardous ones that lurk in what we wear. This chapter aims to help you protect yourself from hazardous chemicals and push the clothing industry to banish nasty substances from fashion.

Forty-six million tons of chemicals are used to process textiles each year.[1] While most don't pose a threat, others are known hazards to human health and the environment and are in use anyway. According to a 2014 study commissioned by the Swedish government, 10 percent of the twenty-four hundred textile-related chemicals in use today are known to be a "potential risk" to human health, including many that cause skin irritation, allergic reaction, and asthma.[2] A bigger threat is that some textile chemicals are linked to cancer, endocrine disruption, and reproductive and developmental problems. Here are just a few examples: Formaldehyde, used in anti-wrinkle finishes, is known to cause nasal cancer in rats.[3] Certain types of phthalates used in faux leather and vinyl cause reproductive development delays in animal testing.[4]

What's the threat for humans? Small traces of hazardous

chemicals can remain on clothing we buy, and some of them can be absorbed into our skin or inhaled. While the chemical residue on any one shirt is low, repeated exposure to hazardous substances accumulates over time, which concerns experts. "Maybe the exposure coming from your shirt is completely harmless, but when it starts to become a cumulative thing, that's a different story," warns Jay Bolus, president of McDonough Braungart Design Chemistry, and main author of the Cradle to Cradle Certified product certification program. For example, formaldehyde is not only used in fashion; it's a common wood preservative found in furniture and is sometimes used to manufacture mattresses, meaning we could be exposed to this chemical not only through our shirts but also while we sit at our desks and sleep.

It's very difficult to draw a straight line between, say, the shirt you're wearing or the bed you sleep on and a long-term illness like cancer. But that's a problem in itself. There are hazardous chemicals used in most consumer products. What's more, there are too many variations in what we wear, what chemicals we're exposed to, and the length of that exposure. "People should *at least* be aware that these problematic substances are being used," says Bolus.[5] You can read my Q&A with Bolus at the end of this chapter to learn more about the difference between hazard and risk.

What we don't know about the safety of chemicals on the market is almost as troubling as what we do know. Prior to the EPA's 1976 Toxic Substances Control Act, sixty thousand chemicals were let onto the market without any government testing for safety.[6] And they remain there, untested. While scientists are trying to study the connection between chemicals, clothes, and illness, there are too many unknowns to assure consumers that a safe level of exposure to harmful chemicals exists.

What's more, fashion's addiction to harmful substances is polluting the waterways of textile-making countries, poisoning marine life, and even contaminating the food chain.[7] Whether we're concerned about workers, the environment, or our own health, there's a growing consensus that the use of known hazardous chemicals is unsafe and unethical. "The textile industry is under increasing scrutiny," says Bolus. "People are becoming more aware of the toxic stuff that's either going into their clothes or going out into the wastewater and the rivers."[8]

Until recently, the approach to hazardous chemicals (in the United States especially) was to put the burden of proof of risk on consumers: an innocent-until-proven-guilty approach to chemicals that puts our health and environment on the line. "We're now saying you've got to prove to me that this is safe versus me prove to you that it's harmful," says Bolus.[9] A growing number of governments and brands are working to eliminate hazardous chemicals whenever possible, and test and regulate the rest of them. This safety-first and precautionary-based approach to chemical usage is becoming the norm. It certainly makes the most sense to me. We don't need to fear all or even most chemicals—they're essential to modern life—but we need to change the standards surrounding their use.

Who's doing something about the chemical threat in clothes? Since 2006, the European Union's REACH (Registration, Evaluation, Authorisation and Restriction of Chemicals) has set the world's most stringent standards for chemical usage in textiles, banning dozens of carcinogenic, mutagenic, and reproductively toxic substances, including formaldehyde. In the United States, the long-overdue reform of the Toxic Substances Control Act in 2016 marked a huge step forward, giving the Environmental Protection Agency the power to review *all* chemicals in use and requiring new chemicals to be evaluated for risk before hitting the market. Environmental nongovernmental organization (NGO) Greenpeace has investigated hazardous chemicals in clothing supply chains and is a leading instigator of industry reform, thanks to its landmark Detox campaign. In response, many brands have developed manufacturing restricted substances lists, or have joined the ZDHC Roadmap to Zero, a group of brands and suppliers working to synthesize industry standards around hazardous substances in the fashion supply chain, all with huge benefits to shoppers and the environment. As I've mentioned, there are also a number of third-party certifications such as Cradle to Cradle that have formed to help give consumers and manufacturers peace of mind that what we're wearing is safe.

Hazardous Chemicals to Watch Out For

Unfortunately, I can't list all the harmful chemicals used by the textile industry here. For a more comprehensive list, look up Greenpeace Detox's hazardous chemicals list or the ZDHC Roadmap to Zero Restricted Substances List.[10] But here are a few hazardous chemicals to know about, followed by tips on how to avoid them.

- **Formaldehyde.** Anti-wrinkle or permanent-press properties in clothes can be derived from a chemical treatment that releases formaldehyde, a known carcinogen.[11]

- **Triclosan/triclocarban.** Used often in antimicrobial finishes, these chemicals are designed to kill bacteria that cause odor in workout clothing. Those that include silver and triclosan/triclocarban have been linked to antibiotic resistance and endocrine disruption.[12]

- **Phthalates.** Phthalates are chemicals most commonly used to soften plastic and are often used in PVC as faux leather and synthetic rubber, in plastic coatings on clothes, and in some dyes. Of particular concern is a phthalate called DEHP, which is toxic to reproduction.[13]

- **Flame retardants.** Several flame retardants are toxic. Short-chain chlorinated paraffins (SCCPs), used as flame retardants and finishing agents for leather and textiles and in plastic

coatings, are toxic to marine life and linked to cancer,[14] and brominated and chlorinated flame retardants (BFRs, CFRs) are persistent in the environment and linked to reproductive toxicity.[15]

- **Perfluorinated chemicals (PFCs).** Perfluorinated chemicals
(PFCs) are often used for their water-repellent and stain-
proofing properties, and they persist in the environment. Some
can affect the liver or act as endocrine disruptors, altering levels
of growth and reproductive hormones.[16]

HOW TO REDUCE EXPOSURE TO TOXIC CHEMICALS IN CLOTHING

Here are some simple steps you can take to reduce your exposure to
harmful chemicals in clothing:

- **Question unnecessary performance features.** There are innovations in nontoxic versions of performance features, but you might
consider avoiding clothing with anti-wrinkle, stain-resistant,
water-resistant, and antimicrobial coatings until standards are
more uniform. Or, if you're buying a performance garment, get
in touch with the brand and ask if the finish on the garment is
nontoxic.

- **Wash before wearing.** Chemical bonds do tend to break down
over time and with repeated washings, which means washing
your clothes can cut down on some exposure.[17] Just keep in mind
that your laundry detergent can be another source of hazardous
chemical exposure. More on this in Chapter 22.

- **Shop brands with chemical-reduction strategies.** Many brands
are on the path to better, safer chemical usage. You can Google your
brand's restricted MRSL (manufacturing restricted substances

list), which shows which chemicals are banned in their supply chain. Or shop with one of the eighty major brands that have committed to Greenpeace's Detox campaign or that have signed on to the ZDHC Roadmap to Zero program. If it's not clear where your brand stands on chemicals, contact them and ask!

- **Buy certified nontoxic.** Shop for clothes with third-party certifications that regulate chemical usage, including bluesign, Cradle to Cradle Certified, Oeko-Tex Standard 100, and the Global Organic Textile Standard (GOTS). You can Google any of these standards for lists of participating brands.

- **Contact your legislators.** As citizens, we need to demand thorough testing and regulation of hazardous substances. It shouldn't be a choice—toxic versus nontoxic—when we shop. Let your elected leaders know that you want harmful chemicals out of all consumer clothing products!

How Certifications Can Protect Us from Toxic Clothes

Q&A with Jay Bolus of McDonough Braungart Design Chemistry, Creator of the Cradle to Cradle Design Framework

ELIZABETH: There are thousands of chemicals used in the manufacture of clothing. Many are a serious danger to our health and the environment, and most consumers aren't even aware of the problem. Can this be true?

JAY: Unfortunately, a lot of that is true. We are part of a massive global human experiment when it comes to chemicals in ourselves and in the environment. The majority of [chemicals used in clothes] don't have complete human and/or environmental health profiles associated with them. And there are new chemicals being developed every day, and some are used without knowledge of what their impacts are.

ELIZABETH: We wear clothes on our skin day in and day out. Why is the threat of chemicals to human health being overlooked?

JAY: Some chemicals have been used for such a long time that they are deemed acceptable, and therefore nobody's really challenged that. Another part of the issue is that some of the chemicals end up in the finished garment in low concentrations, so people think there's no concern.

ELIZABETH: Hazardous substances are also being released into the water and the air from textile mills. Is that a threat to us as consumers?

JAY: Yes. Because there are two ways you're going to be exposed to these nasty chemicals. They can be in the shirt you're wearing on your back, or they can be in the food you're eating on a daily basis. We're discharging these chemicals into our waterways in textile-making countries, and they bioaccumulate and ultimately find their way into fish and people as a result.

ELIZABETH: Can you give me an example of a known hazardous chemical used in clothes?

JAY: Yes. Anti-wrinkle treatment made from formaldehyde has been tested pretty extensively, and we know it's a problem. But there's no watchdog or regulatory body that's overseeing all of this and saying, "No, you can't use this." It's used all the time even though we know formaldehyde causes cancer.

ELIZABETH: There's an important difference between saying formaldehyde causes cancer and saying that wearing clothes made using formaldehyde will definitely give a person cancer. Can you explain?

JAY: There is a difference between hazard and risk. When I say formaldehyde causes cancer, that's a hazard. That's an intrinsic property of formaldehyde. But then the question is, What is the risk to human beings if I were to use formaldehyde as an anti-wrinkle treatment on a cotton shirt? Am I then going to get cancer by wearing the shirt? Can that translate into risk if it's used in certain ways on a garment? How that risk is analyzed depends on who you talk to. There's a whole science around risk assessment that the big chemical companies do, and it's really about dose and duration.

ELIZABETH: Do you think measuring the risk of a chemical on a single garment goes far enough to protect consumers?

JAY: No. The big weakness in the way risk assessment is being done is that it doesn't take into account multiple contributions from multiple sources, right? So you might say that, okay, if formaldehyde stays below a certain airborne level in my breathing space, I'm fine. But what if it's also emitted from my desk and then I've got it coming from someplace else? And then all three of those sources of emissions together could put a person over the threshold where it's going to cause a problem. So risk assessment is a hotly debated topic in the scientific and sustainability communities.

ELIZABETH: Will it ever be possible to directly link these chemicals to real-world health effects caused by wearing toxic clothes?

JAY: It would be really hard to create a study like that, that would give you some meaningful results. There are so many factors that come into play and so many variations in the population. For example, there are certain classes of compounds, like these anti-wrinkle agents and flame retardants, that definitely have hazardous substances in them. They are linked to specific risks. But then the question is, Well, how long do I have to wear this in order for that to truly be a risk? Eight hours? Ten years? It would be hard to measure.

ELIZABETH: How does Cradle to Cradle think about risk from toxic substances in clothes?

JAY: If there is a relevant route of exposure to a hazardous substance, we're going to assume there's a risk, regardless of the level of exposure. For consumers, our silver-level label or higher label assures you that there are no carcinogens, mutagens, or reproductively toxic substances being used in your product.

ELIZABETH: And there's also Oeko-Tex and bluesign offering certifications for nontoxic clothing, too. What other certifications help?

JAY: If you can go with GOTS or some other organically certified natural fiber, you'll know that the chemical use in your clothing is pretty limited.

ELIZABETH: It's easy to slip into thinking that all chemicals or chemistry is bad and the goal should be to make everything natural. How do we not go there?

JAY: We are not anti-technology. In our world there are two cycles at play. There's the biological cycle, which are your natural materials, and then there's the technical cycle, which are synthetic materials. Both are equally important and both can be designed with safe, healthy materials.

Conscious Superstars and Better Big Brands

Every time we buy new clothing, it's a small vote for the world we want to see. Or so the saying goes. But that's selling our clothes a bit short. Fashion creates massive opportunity, as clothing brands and retailers are some of the most powerful entities in the world today. A conscious clothing company can help to revive artisanship, reduce poverty, empower women, and push sustainable practices forward, all while leaving style lovers doing good while looking good.

Conscious Superstars are those brands that set the highest standards for fashion. They are pioneers of new ethical and sustainable business models. They tend to choose more sustainable materials, they're more transparent, and they are working to pay the people in their supply chain fair wages. No brand is perfect, but conscious brands hold themselves accountable and respond to citizen pressure to always be doing better. At the end of this chapter, you'll hear from sustainability experts at Reformation and Eileen Fisher, two Conscious Superstars. There are *many* others. If you can wear it, you can shop for a beautiful, ethical, and sustainable version of it. Not surprisingly, Conscious Superstars—my term for brands that have sustainability and ethical production as part of their company DNA—are growing faster than their stuck-in-the-old-ways competitors.

HOW TO SEEK OUT CONSCIOUS SUPERSTARS

There are many thousands of Conscious Superstars out in the world today. These companies tend to be newer, smaller, and online, compared to the brick-and-mortar retail giants they're up against. Instead of endorsing any one specific brand (I can't possibly list them all here anyway), I want to give you the tools to find companies that represent *your* style and values. Here are my tips for seeking them out.

- **There's an app for that.** There are several apps and websites that curate and recommend conscious brands. The Good on You app ranks the ethics and sustainability of fashion brands from "Avoid" up to "Great," offers more ethical alternatives, and allows you to search by category, seeing results for swimwear, dresses, kids' clothes, and more. Similarly, Done Good is a brilliant browser extension and website that will light up your Google searches with approved sustainable and ethical brands. You can also directly search the Done Good website directory. There's also Rank a Brand, which provides an A-through-E pass-to-fail grade for brands. It's a good idea to look at brand rankings and ratings across a few different sites and sources, to get a complete picture of a brand's performance.

  For a more granular perspective, look up brand rankings within these two annual reports: *Ethical Fashion Report,* released by Australian charity Baptist World Aid, measures labor rights and sustainability efforts, while the Fashion Revolution *Fashion Transparency Index* scores more than one hundred top global brands on their labor and environmental reporting and transparency. Both are available online for free. At the time of this writing, People Tree, Etiko, Veja, Loomstate, Nudie Jeans, Kowtow, and Amour Vert are just a *very few* of the independent conscious brands that rise to the top across these apps and websites. There are also so many more to choose from and discover. I will keep an updated list of Better Big Brands and Conscious Superstars on my website.

- **Just Google it.** There are an abundance of ethical and sustainable fashion brand directories online. You can start with the shopping directories on my website, but there are *many* others. Typing "ethical and sustainable brands" will get you started, or you can get specific and search for upcycled leather, sustainable denim, organic cotton underwear, and so on. A search for "upcycled streetwear" might turn up the brand Public School, for example.

- **Browse social media.** Conscious brands are major style leaders on social media. This is where you can find out about exciting startups and independent, socially conscious designers, such as Proclaim, Study New York, and Grammar, three American-made lines making intimates and women's fashion. Hop onto Instagram and search hashtags like #ethicalbrands, #fairtrade, #conscious fashion, #sustainablestyle, #sustainablebrands, and #inclusivefashion. Once you follow a few, your feed will start to fill with recommendations of similar users and brands to follow.

- **Follow conscious-fashion influencers and bloggers.** There are stylish influencers and bloggers on social media whose job it is to seek out and raise the profile of conscious fashion. You can Google lists of "ethical fashion influencers" and follow them on social media. Good on You runs roundups of them as well. Keep track of high-profile conscious-fashion icons online as well: Emma Watson, Rosario Dawson, Olivia Wilde, and Amber Valletta are a few of the stars advocating for fair and sustainable fashion. Watson, a tireless advocate for conscious fashion, introduced almost half a million followers to conscious clothing on her Press Tour

Instagram account. And actress Rosario Dawson cofounded the artisan-made Studio 189 fashion line, which won the Council of Fashion Designers of America's sustainability prize in 2018.

- **Keep learning.** In time, as conscious fashion grows, these tips will change and expand, and I'll offer additional help on my website, TheConsciousClosetBook.com.

WHICH BIG BRANDS ARE ETHICAL AND GREEN?

Thank goodness for Conscious Superstars, but what about the giant fashion companies that make most of the world's clothing? What are *they* doing to be ethical and green? Big brands and fashion conglomerates work with hundreds and sometimes thousands of suppliers around the world and churn out *hundreds of millions* or even upward of a *billion* items per company per year. Sweeping ethical and sustainable changes are more challenging for big brands. But, by nature of their size and influence, any change a big brand makes can have immense positive impact, whether it's by using more sustainable materials, paying higher wages, or making boardrooms, advertising, and runway shows diverse and inclusive. Here's how to do your own research into big brands and seek out those making efforts to be sustainable and ethical:

- **Yes, there's an app for that, too.** Once again, Good on You is a great resource, as are the *Ethical Fashion Report* and the Fashion Revolution *Fashion Transparency Index,* which all rank and score major brands. While most of the top ratings go to smaller companies, a few big brands like Reebok, Patagonia, Adidas, C&A, G-Star, and Marks & Spencer all currently have "Good" ratings on Good on You. Adidas, Reebok, Puma, and H&M rank higher than their competitors on the Transparency Index and Adidas, Inditex, Lululemon, Hanes, and Patagonia are A-ranking brands according to the 2018 *Ethical*

Fashion Report. Again, these are not endorsements. It's important to do your own research or look for concrete standards, such as third-party certifications (like the ones I mentioned in the last chapter), and look up rankings for a wide range of brands. Also, make sure whatever information you're looking at has been updated recently, as this space and the standards are changing fast!

- **Hop onto the home page.** You can tell a lot about a brand or retailer by doing your own Internet research. Information about sustainability and social issues is typically grouped together on one or two sections of a brand's home page. Look for a link or section that says "Sustainability," "Corporate Responsibility," or something of that nature. The more in-depth information, fine print, data, and photos and videos of the supply chain you find, the better. It's a red flag if you find yourself having to dig to find basic information. Look around the website of multiple clothing companies to see the differences in what each brands reveals. Eileen Fisher, Patagonia, G-Star, and Reformation have an easy-to-find link for their social and sustainability efforts, for example. Even better is when brands go the extra mile and outline clearly defined, measurable labor and environmental commitments. These might include:

  - **Sustainability benchmarks.** Look for measurable goals for sustainable water, energy, chemicals, carbon, and waste usage, target dates for meeting these goals, and regular progress reports.

  - **A full list of all factories and suppliers.** Ethical brands are transparent brands. Look for a full list of factories and any suppliers going back to raw material suppliers (meaning cotton farms, leather tanneries, etc.). Look for detailed information on life inside factories, including wages paid. According to Fashion Revolution, as of November 2018, 172 brands across 68 companies are disclosing at least some of the facilities making their clothes.[1]

- **Defined goals to meet a living wage.** There are very few brands in the world paying a living wage to garment workers, but try to shop with those that set targets to work toward a living wage. I'll talk more about the fight for a living wage in Part Six: "Fashion Revolution."

- **Ask a brand.** If you can't tell if a brand has social or environmental commitments, ask them! The easiest way to connect with companies is in the comments or direct messages on social media or through a customer service email address. Here are some of the things you might ask a brand: "Hi, I love your clothes, but I'm wondering if you can tell me more about how they're made. Are they sustainable?" or "Hi, I am a huge fan of your bags, but I'm worried about dangerous working conditions. Can you tell me more about your factories?" Reach out multiple times if necessary. A responsible brand will make it easy to get in touch with them and will respond to your queries.

- **Google environmental and social justice progress.** Take your investigation further by doing an Internet search on your company's labor rights and environmental problems and progress. Search for recent news of labor strikes, calls for minimum-wage increases, or efforts to be inclusive of women of color in the company's hiring and advertising. Next, check the websites of nonprofits and labor rights organizations fighting for a fair fashion industry to see if a brand is the target of a human rights campaign. Clean Clothes Campaign, Fashion Revolution, International Labor Rights Forum, United Students Against Sweatshops, the Garment Workers Center, and Labour Behind the Label are all working to protect garment workers, while Greenpeace, World Wildlife Fund, and the Natural Resources Defense Council are leading environmental campaigns connected to fashion.

WHAT TO DO IF A BRAND YOU LOVE IS UNETHICAL

It is always disappointing and even horrifying to discover that the brand you love has been accused of polluting the environment or using sweatshops, or that there's zero information available on their human rights and environmental initiatives. Here's what you can do about it:

1. **Voice your concerns.** It's so important to hold all clothing companies accountable by voicing our concerns. Reach out to brands via email, social media, or phone using the tips I just mentioned in the "Ask a brand" section. Or, take your concerns to a store manager in person. Keep the pressure on companies to move forward on diversity, workers' rights, and the environment!

2. **Channel your energy into fashion activism.** It's just as important to join an organization and collectively fight for widespread change in the fashion industry. Much more on this in Part Six: "Fashion Revolution."

3. **Avoid the worst actors.** Some brands are doing *a lot* more than others to be sustainable and ethical. Consider shifting your purchases from the brands ranked at the very bottom, based on the rankings of Good on You or one of the brand-ranking reports, toward better-ranking brands. Supporting brands that are making *some* changes and are on the road to being conscious sends a positive message to the rest of the industry to step up.

HOW TO AVOID GREENWASHING AND ETHICAL FAKES

As the sustainable and ethical market grows, so do imposters looking to ride the coattails of our conscious-fashion movement. False claims of "green," "eco-friendly," "organic," and "ethical" clothing are growing. Feminist slogan T-shirts made in sweatshop conditions or "natural" rayon clothes made from endangered forests are two examples of conscious fakery. Luckily, greenwashing and ethical fakes are easy to spot with just a little digging. You're already quite the expert in sustainable materials just by reading this section of the book. Before you buy, look for the following four signs that an ethical and sustainable brand is authentic. A conscious fashion brand will always:

- **Practice what they preach.** Conscious brands go beyond recycled packaging and solar panels on the head office to making their own products sustainably. Likewise, look for brands that don't just give money to good causes but that make their money by running their business sustainably, inclusively, and by paying fair, living wages.

- **Offer fine print.** Any brand marketing its products as green or ethical should back up its claims, either on the product label or on its website, with detailed information about how those claims are defined.

- **Engage with outside stakeholders.** Alignment with outside groups, including third-party certifications, nonprofits, labor unions, and multiparty stakeholder organizations are signs that a brand is operating more responsibly. Look for memberships to groups like the Leather Working Group, Canopy, the Sustainable Apparel Coalition, Ethical Fashion Initiative, the Bangladesh Accord on Fire and Building Safety, the Organic Cotton Accelerator, or Textile Exchange, to name a few.

- **Hold themselves accountable.** A conscious brand has nothing to hide and will answer any questions about their business practices and the story behind them in full, including admitting when they make a mistake and that they're a work in progress.

THE TRUE COST OF FASHION

Whether we're deal hunting or splurging on a designer item, we are rarely asked to pay the true cost of fashion. The pollution, carbon emissions, waste, and poverty our clothes create aren't tallied up and included in the prices we enjoy. It does cost a bit more to do things the right way, to operate safer, well-paying factories and farms and to use longer-lasting, sustainable materials and craft more durable products. Ethical and sustainable clothing doesn't have to be unaffordable, though.

Why are ethical and sustainable brands sometimes more expensive? Here are a few reasons: Many create higher-quality products, and material costs are higher, and some but not all manufacture in so-called high-wage countries like the United States and Italy, both for the quality and the fast turnaround. Those that source from overseas commit to paying higher wages, which has an impact on the retail price, although, as I'll further explain in Part Six, paying living wages adds as little as a dollar to the retail price of a garment.

The biggest factor that determines retail price is volume. As I explained in *Overdressed,* it's not unusual for a major clothing brand like Gap, Nike, Target, or Walmart to churn out tens of thousands, hundreds of thousands, or even millions of pieces of the same style.[2] Fast-forward a few years and Inditex, the company that owns Zara, is now making 1.4 billion garments per year.[3] These companies can spread out any development, advertising, and material costs over the colossal amount of product they make. Conscious fashion by contrast is made up largely of independent startups and smaller companies, some of which you've learned about in this chapter. We should want Conscious Superstars to continue to make great clothes in smaller batches. Our economy is stronger and our choices as consumers are better when we foster independent business. These companies also have a tiny fraction of the ecological footprint of big brands, just by the nature of their smaller size.

But it's time for more big brands to step up to the plate. Big companies are the ones with the huge economies of scale that could bring down the price of sustainable materials and fund the research and development of eco-friendly innovations, from textile recycling and nontoxic dyes to factories powered by clean energy. They can certainly afford to pay higher wages. Rather than ask small companies to drop their prices, big companies should do their part to make sustainable and ethical fashion more widespread.

Imagine what the world would look like if we all dedicated just a few extra minutes a week or a portion of our shopping dollars to seek out and support more ethical and sustainable brands. What if we spent just a little extra time holding big brands accountable, demanding they tell the whole story behind the clothes we wear, and asking them to craft more safe, sustainable, and ethical products? The world would change. We'd see a much brighter fashion future, and we're already seeing glimmers of it today.

Making Sustainability Stylish

Q&A with Kathleen Talbot, Vice President of Operations and Sustainability at Reformation

ELIZABETH: Tell us about Reformation. What kind of brand are you?

KATHLEEN: We're a sustainable fashion company based in Los Angeles. We want to push the boundaries of what sustainable fashion looks like. We make everything from basics and jeans to sustainable wedding dresses and event wear. It's our goal to meet the full needs of your closet and to make something beautiful and sustainable that you would want to buy anyway.

ELIZABETH: What prompted you guys to make sustainability part of the core mission of Reformation?

KATHLEEN: It's our leadership. We are lucky to have a founder, our CEO, Yael Aflalo, who had this vision from the beginning. She worked in conventional fashion and really saw the impacts of the industry firsthand. The impact of fashion is so massive. Reformation was founded on the premise of challenging the status quo and looking where waste occurs, where the climate change impacts occur within this industry, and designing out or around these issues.

ELIZABETH: Your company makes sustainability look easy. Is the actual process of designing clothes more sustainably challenging?

KATHLEEN: For us it *is* pretty easy. Our goal is no trade-offs. When we started the brand and we built our supply chain, we built all of our processes with clear sustainability parameters. Our designers pull from a library of materials that have been preapproved based on fiber impacts and clean chemistry. And then they can just go as wild as they want in terms of the actual design and construction. We make upwards of thirty new styles a week that are meeting 100 percent of our sustainability criteria, so you don't have to worry that sustainability will necessarily limit creativity.

ELIZABETH: What can bigger brands and even fast-fashion chains learn from what Reformation is doing?

KATHLEEN: There's a ton of what we are doing that's transferable to bigger brands. And we're already seeing it. The big players can come up with their own fiber standards and build a sustainable material library. And it can have a huge impact because of their volume. Even if they just become 10 or 20 percent better, it has a big impact in terms of environmental performance, but it also has ripple effects within the industry by making these fabrics or technologies more widely available. Every brand has their next steps and can keep pushing sustainability forward in their own way.

ELIZABETH: As anyone who's shopped with Reformation knows, your clothes are displayed beside the embedded resources for each piece, so you can see how many pounds of carbon or water your garment saves. How do you come up with these fascinating metrics?

KATHLEEN: We do life-cycle assessments of everything that we make, and what we've discovered is that up to two-thirds of the impact of our stuff depends on the materials used. Packaging and consumer care and all these other things are really important (and included in our calculations), but the materials are by far what dictates the sustainability of our stuff. So most of our clothes are made from biodegradable and rapidly renewable fibers. We try to keep them plant-based. We definitely layer into our material choice the potential for circularity, meaning the potential for it to be taken back and turned into second-generation materials.

ELIZABETH: What fabrics are meeting your standards?

KATHLEEN: We use a lot of cellulosic fabrics, so those are in the Lenzing Tencel, Lenzing modal, Lenzing viscose family and are made from sustainable, traceable wood pulp [these materials are explained in depth in Chapter 18]. Other materials we use include silk, flax, organic cotton, and hemp. We also use dead stock, meaning overstock materials.

ELIZABETH: Would you ever use a synthetic, like polyester, in your clothes?

KATHLEEN: We call synthetics fossil-fuel fabrics. We do not use synthetics unless it's recycled, it's dead stock, or it's really needed for performance needs, like a little spandex for stretch. We are even scaling back our use of recycled synthetics until the research on microplastic pollution is more robust. [For more information on the impact of microplastic pollution caused by fashion, see Chapter 18.]

ELIZABETH: A lot has changed in the years since I wrote *Overdressed* and in the years since Reformation started. How much increased awareness are you seeing on your end?

KATHLEEN: More and more brands are getting involved in the space. And it's been really interesting to see the level of consumer awareness increase. We can start the conversation basically three steps ahead of where we could five years ago. Five years ago, most people did not connect their consumer habits, particularly within fashion, to an impact on people or the planet. That's all changed.

ELIZABETH: What's the holy grail for sustainable fashion? Can we go beyond making it less bad to making it actually good for the planet?

KATHLEEN: It would involve designing something that is carbon neutral, water neutral, or even restorative. That's what we should all be pushing for, and those things can go hand in hand with bigger systemic changes around garment recovery and recycling.

ELIZABETH: Some people might say that the only way to make fashion sustainable is to dramatically cut our consumption of style. Can we still enjoy fashion and create a sustainable world?

KATHLEEN: We do need to think about overall consumption. But we 100 percent believe that a sustainable future doesn't need to sacrifice your sense of style, or using fashion as a form of self-expression.

Eileen Fisher's New Way to Sell Old Clothes

Q&A with Cynthia Power, Director of Eileen Fisher Renew

ELIZABETH: For those new to Eileen Fisher, tell us about the brand.

CYNTHIA: Eileen Fisher started her company in 1984. She was very inspired by Japanese design and the idea of classic, simple shapes. She was having trouble putting herself together, and so she had this idea to make a very small collection of five simple shapes in really high-quality natural fibers.

ELIZABETH: Eileen Fisher was doing capsule wardrobes long before the rest of us! The brand is also ahead of the curve on sustainability; you've been using nontoxic dyes and organic fabrics for years. Why does sustainability matter to Eileen Fisher?

CYNTHIA: Part of it comes from the fact that we use natural fibers, whether it's cotton plants or cashmere from goats. We want to make sure that we're respecting those resources and our connection to the earth. The dyeing process can also be a really chemically intensive process, so we want to make sure that we're not contributing to water pollution in other countries. We try to make the best decision we can make for each garment, for each process, and for each fiber that we're producing.

ELIZABETH: As environmentalists, we often think that natural is better. But making clothes with natural materials can do a lot of harm. How do we use them carefully?

CYNTHIA: Right. Take, for example, cashmere. There is desertification that is happening because of cashmere goats. [For more information on this issue, see Chapter 18.] As a brand, we have to think about the responsible place to source cashmere, so we've been offering recycled cashmere sweaters as well. All resources are getting more precious. I think in ten years, I hope to see more of the cashmere supply being recycled, and we should do the same for cotton and wool.

ELIZABETH: You're the director of Eileen Fisher Renew, the resale part of the brand. How does Renew work?

CYNTHIA: Eileen Fisher has a commitment to every piece of clothing we've ever made. So, with our Renew program, we take our clothes back at any of our retail stores in the United States and give a 5-dollar gift card in exchange for each piece of Eileen Fisher clothing. Then we'll figure out a responsible way to reuse, recycle, or remake it. I manage the take-back and resale program, so I oversee our recycling centers and our dedicated Renew stores.

ELIZABETH: Do clothes come back to you in really bad condition?

CYNTHIA: We have seen crazy cardigans just filled with moth holes. We've seen pieces with big wine stains on them. We see things in terrible condition and in pristine condition. Sometimes we get things back with the tags on that people never wore.

ELIZABETH: What do you do with the pieces you get back?

CYNTHIA: We get back two hundred thousand garments a year, and almost half of it is actually in perfect condition and can be cleaned and resold as is. The other half of what we get back has just very small damages, very small imperfections like a tiny pull in a sweater. We call those the not-quite-perfects, and we are experimenting with different ways to sell those pieces for much less. We are also experimenting with some remade collections. Another one of our employees, Lilah Horwitz, makes these collections called Broken Clothes where she'll take three shirts and cut them up and match them back together. They're beautiful.

ELIZABETH: Does reselling only work for brands that make really high-quality clothes? Can fast fashion or brands with lesser quality learn from what you're doing?

CYNTHIA: If they're damaged, that's where chemical and mechanical recycling could come in. My hope is that a fast-fashion brand could take back all of its clothes and use it as raw material for their future collections.

ELIZABETH: I keep hearing about chemical textile recycling, where fibers from old clothes are broken down and remade into fibers for new clothes, but it's not common yet. Are you seeing breakthroughs?

CYNTHIA: It's starting to happen. We've been doing some experimental collaboration with some of the mills that we work with. We successfully worked with one to create a fabric that's 90 percent virgin and 10 percent recycled silk. It's a good place to start. In my mind, in ten years, everything will have recycled content.

ELIZABETH: Shopping on the Eileen Fisher Renew site feels like a traditional retail experience, but also like something very different and very exciting. Can you explain to someone who hasn't tried it what makes it special?

CYNTHIA: The precertification piece of it is what's different. We've guaranteed the quality of the product you're buying. It's a hugely different feeling than going to a thrift store and just trying to find a treasure, but you're just buying it as is. I wish all of my favorite brands would do what we're doing. We have customers that love Renew so much they'll come into the store with a suitcase from Ohio or elsewhere and they fill it up. That's how excited they are about what we're doing. It's a much better experience.

ELIZABETH: What's the consumer's role in pushing a more circular, less wasteful fashion industry?

CYNTHIA: Consumers have a huge role to play. You have to care about what you're buying. There's this whole problem with apathy, especially with fast fashion. When you can buy something for 5 dollars, it feels like it doesn't really matter. We want the consumer to feel really proud when they buy something secondhand because they know the environmental impact is so much smaller. I do think that the brand's reselling its own product is a huge step toward changing that stigma around secondhand.

PART FIVE

Make It Last

**Care for your clothes,
like the good friends
they are!**

–JOAN CRAWFORD

Our Clothes Have *Got* to Last Longer!

Once you've built a more conscious closet, you'll no doubt want to make it last! Whether we paid a pittance or a small fortune or plan to wear a garment for one night or years to come, taking proper care of clothing is a must. You might come into this section with a bit of dread. No one likes laundry days or scrubbing stains, *do they?* You might be surprised. It is possible to love caring for clothes, as I hope to show you. Part Five is dedicated to easy, sustainable, and—yes—enjoyable clothing maintenance skills that will help you keep your clothes looking great for longer.

A 2014 study found that the millennial generation, raised on fast fashion, lacks mastery of basic clothing repairs and laundry skills when compared to their parents and grandparents.[1] Another study, of UK consumers, found that a third of consumers toss out a garment if a stain doesn't lift on the first try. A quarter admitted to not even bothering to lift a stain, if the item was cheap.[2] The fashion industry is peddling so-called easy-care clothes, while laundry detergent brands and appliance makers have automated the process of stain removal and cleaning, all with higher and higher environmental costs. We've adopted a disconnected, throwaway attitude that extends into the laundry room, and it has erased our knowledge of caring for clothes. I see wearable clothes in trashcans on my block on a regular basis. While sorting clothes, I see pieces tossed out with stains and small rips that, with proper know-how, can be tackled in minutes. We're doing laundry around the clock, calling into question the idea that washing machines are saving us time. We can do so much better.

How long should clothing last? We don't often find out. Most everyday casual clothing like jeans, T-shirts, socks, and basic knits can and should last at the bare minimum one hundred to three hundred wears, or *three years* of regular wear and washing.[3] Let's put that in perspective. We know from Chapter 16 that some consumers wear their clothes only three times, which amounts to 3 percent of a typical garment's useful life.[4] More durable items like suits, blazers, jackets, coats, and tailored dresses can last even longer, five years to a decade at the least, if cared for properly. Whether you plan to wear, sell, or donate your clothes, we should each do our part to make all clothing last several years or 100 wears. Let's get to it!

Part Five: "Make It Last" will show you how, focusing on three areas of clothing maintenance: laundry and stain removal, mending and patching, and working with a professional to repair your garments and shoes. These might seem like old-fashioned practices, and they are, but they are filled with renewed relevance and urgency in our resource-scarce world. Clothing maintenance is something I'm evangelical about, and not just because it's better for the environment: A well-cared-for closet looks as great as it feels.

Level Up Your Laundry

If **you are** looking to change one single set of habits that will slash your fashion footprint and keep your clothes looking better longer, look no further than your laundry room. Washing clothes has the second-highest environmental impact of any part of the life cycle of clothing, second to the manufacture of new textiles.[1] And we have complete control over our laundry routines.

Americans have very high-impact laundry habits. Just by doing our laundry, Americans consume as much electricity (66 billion kilowatts) per year as the entire state of Minnesota, and we emit more than 46 million tons of carbon dioxide equivalents.[2]

The most energy-intensive step of doing laundry by a long shot is heating the air in our dryers, followed by heating the water in our washers. We all need to wash less, wash on cold whenever possible, and consider giving up our dryers altogether. This might sound disagreeable, but I think I can change your mind. We stand to save time, money, and the condition of our clothes by deeply rethinking our laundry habits.

YOUR MACHINE IS RUINING YOUR CLOTHES

Let's put aside our mission to save the planet for a second. Machine washing and especially tumble drying are not good for our clothes. Machine washing gets them clean in a jiffy, yes, but at a cost. Every go-round in the machine shortens the life of a garment. Studies show that mechanical agitation, forced air, and heat from our washers and dryers combine to cause shrinkage, fading, and tears in our clothes.[3] The lint in the dryer is residue from fibers breaking down. One study showed that just twenty rounds of laundering and drying can make textiles twice as easy to tear.[4] And anyone using his or her machine more sparingly will tell you the same thing. Parsons professor of sustainability Timo Rissanen, whom you heard from in Chapter 9, doesn't tumble-dry any of his clothes. "I grew up in Finland where they [dryers] weren't a common thing. Line drying was and is most common," he says. As a result, his clothes last forever. "I still wear cotton T-shirts that are seventeen years old."[5] For the sake of your clothes, wash and dry them less!

NON-GROSS WAYS TO WASH LESS

The vast majority of Americans have their own washing machines, as well as separate and very-high-heat dryers. Eighty-five percent of the population has tumble dryers, an anomaly in other countries.[6] And while we claim our modern machines are ultraconvenient, we are still doing laundry all the time. Americans run a load of wash at least every other day, doing between three hundred and four hundred loads of laundry per year on average.[7] Assuming we spend an hour on laundry, that's more than two weeks a year spent sorting, loading, folding, and putting away clothes. Just by committing to skip a wash or two you could free up precious time, not to mention energy and resources. Cutting the number of loads you run by just 10 percent could save as much as five thousand gallons of water a year, not to mention shave dollars off your electric bill or the number of quarters you're using at the laundromat.[8]

Many of us live lives that our ancestors would describe as shockingly free of dirt, disease, and sweat (though parents with small children might disagree), and yet we're often washing clothes after one or two wears. We are overusing machines to freshen our clothes, rather than get them clean. And it's time to break the habit. Before you run a load, ask yourself, could this be worn again? Is it *truly* dirty and smelly? Wrinkled does not count as dirty. Lint or fuzz does not count as dirt either. Small stains should be spot-cleaned. And if your shirt doesn't have that laundry-fresh scent, chances are that's a good thing (more on the potentially hazardous fragrances and chemicals in our cleaning supplies shortly).

What garments can skip regular washing? Apologies for being graphic, but anything that sits next to your crotch, armpits, feet, or underboob (that's the scientific term, right?) and comes into close contact with sweat and skin is a good candidate for regular washing. This includes underwear, tight-fitting T-shirts, pajamas, socks, and your activewear. Anything that goes *over* your undergarments and doesn't cling to your body can be washed *far* less frequently. Really, your nose is the best guide. Good candidates for washing less: jeans, button-down shirts, trousers, coats and blazers, sweaters, and dresses that don't cling to the skin. I wash my sweaters and cardigans rarely, maybe once a year. Some of my tailored pieces are rarely or never washed. And there are of course premium-denim fans, including the CEO of Levi's, who are famous for never washing their jeans.[9]

Your ability to skip washes also depends on what fibers you own. Synthetics, especially polyester, tend to trap oil and odors, so you might consider switching to more natural materials like cotton, wool, and linen for your everyday clothing to reduce your need to wash clothes.[10] By building your wardrobe around mostly natural materials and by wearing proper undergarments that protect your outer layers, you can live a life of only doing small loads of underthings and work-out gear and washing everything else only as needed.

What about, you know, *germs?* The truth is, there are microorganisms and bacteria all around us, including on our bodies, on our clothes, and *even in our washing machines,* and the vast majority are harmless. There's no need to be concerned about getting sick just from wearing your clothes a bit longer. A 2015 study found that the bacteria in jeans worn for a year were present in the same concentrations as in those worn for a week, and none were harmful.[11] If you or someone in your home has a cold or other contagious illness, you can disinfect clothes by washing them in hot water, tumble drying them for half an hour, *or* ironing them. All work equally well.[12] Another eco-friendly way to kill germs is to wash your clothes on cold and then line dry them in the sun, as UV rays are as effective at killing germs as bleach.[13]

HOW TO FRESHEN YOUR CLOTHES BETWEEN WEARS

Here are some simple and convenient ways to keep clothes fresh between wears that don't require washing:

- **Air your garments out overnight.** Do *not* leave worn clothes in a heap on the floor, or moisture, creases, and odors will set into them. As soon as you take your clothes off, immediately smooth out the fabric and any wrinkles while they are still warm from wear. Hang your garment in a place where air can circulate through the fibers, like the back of your bedroom door versus crammed in your closet. This simple step will remove many odors, including food and body odor, naturally.

- **Spot clean.** If you've gotten just a spot of dirt or food on your otherwise clean garment, there's no need to put it in the laundry machine. Save machine laundering for all-over dirt and smells. Spot-clean the piece by dabbing the spot in water (or a little bit of dish soap and water), rubbing it very gently with a toothbrush or paper towel if necessary, and running just the spot under water to remove any soap. Use distilled water on silk to prevent a water ring from forming. Hang it up to dry. If it's a delicate piece or a stubborn stain, I'll describe how to clean these items later in the chapter. Spot cleaning is such a huge time-saver as it'll help you avoid running loads of laundry every day.

- **Spritz them.** If your clothes have extraclingy smells, try spritzing them lightly with a mixture of one part vodka to four parts water mixed together in a spray bottle. This is really useful for food odors, perfume, light body odor, and even cigarette smoke and can also help you avoid a trip to the dry cleaner.

- **Use a lint roller and fabric shaver.** Your clothes will look worn and dirty if they're covered in lint, pills, and hair. Keep a lint roller, fabric brush, or fabric shaver on hand. A small battery-operated fabric shaver costs about 15 dollars. A lint roller costs a few bucks. Remove lint and other particles before you step out in the morning to keep your clothes looking fresh and sharp.

- **Steam them.** You can use a small travel-size clothes steamer (they start at 20 dollars) to deodorize, sanitize, and soften your garments and get them looking fresh and pressed for another wearing. Steaming is much faster than ironing. Just be careful steaming delicate materials like acetate that can melt or burn.

HOW TO WASH YOUR SMELLY GYM CLOTHES

Sweaty workout clothes can really stink. It's the combination of the materials we wear to the gym and the way we care for them that is causing this public nuisance. Modern activewear is made with synthetics, and both polyester and nylon trap odors and hold on to them long after a garment is removed.[14] There's evidence that fabric softener and even too much detergent can add to the problem by holding on to the bacteria that causes the odor.[15]

So what to do? Here's one simple way to battle smelly synthetic workout clothes: Don't wait to wash them. It's your sweat that grows bacteria, and it's certain kinds of bacteria that stink.[16] Make it part of your routine to rinse your garments out in cold water and a few drops of detergent in your sink *as soon as you get home from the gym,* or hang your pieces up to air-dry, even if you plan to machine wash them. Resist the urge to throw activewear or any truly dirty clothes in a pile in the laundry room or stuff them into your locker or gym bag.

You should also avoid machine drying gym clothes. High heat amplifies odors in fabrics, whether they're synthetic or natural materials. The heat from the dryer can also break down your technical fabrics. Synthetics dry very fast, so hang them to dry instead, and place them in front of a fan to speed up the process. Last but not least, if you do happen to bake the stink into your yoga pants, try hand washing with clear dish soap or mixing one part vinegar to four parts water and letting the garment soak for half an hour, then wash again. You can of course switch your workout clothes to cotton or merino wool, which resist odors far better.[17] There are improved anti-odor fabrics on the market, but keep in mind that some antimicrobial finishes are made from hazardous chemicals (see Chapter 19).

WASH ON COLD AND USE THE RIGHT SETTINGS

The time will come when it's time to clean your clothes, and I'm as glad as the next person that we have laundry machines that do the work for us. Luckily, there are many ways to use a washing machine that are more sustainable. Ninety percent of the energy consumed in washing clothes is used to heat the water.[18] According to the Department of Energy, switching your temperature setting from hot to warm can cut a load's energy use in half.[19]

But it's even better for the environment and your clothes to wash on cold: Colors will stay vibrant and fibers will last longer. Don't worry about your clothes not getting clean; most modern detergents and machines are designed for lower water temperatures and do a great job when the water is cool.[20] As I'll explain in the care-label section, you can also ignore recommendations on a care label that say wash on warm or hot, as that is the *highest* temperature the fabric can withstand, not a command to wash your clothes in hot water. To green your laundry routine even more, run the machine only when it's full. Waiting for a full load before you run the wash can save thirty-four hundred gallons of water a year, according to the Environmental Protection Agency.[21] And always use the shortest, gentlest, most efficient wash cycle you can.

IS IT TIME TO CHUCK YOUR DRYER?

The real environmental bogeyman lurking in our homes is the dryer. Clothes dryers consume more energy than any other household appliance.[22] In the United States, dryers consume 60 billion kilowatt-hours of energy per year, compared to washing machines' 6 billion kilowatt-hours.[23] If you've traveled abroad, you know that it's not a universal habit to bake clothes in intense half-hour blasts. Only 16 percent of

Polish households own a dryer.[24] Only a third of Brits own one, and the majority of those who do also own a clothes rack or other tool for air-drying.[25]

I know it sounds extreme to ask you to drastically reduce or eliminate your use of a machine many people consider an absolute necessity, but hear me out. There are many unsung benefits to air-drying. It is *much, much* better for your clothes. I can't stress this enough. I've noticed such a dramatic difference in the life span of my air-dried clothes (they look like new for *years and years*) that for the most part I only machine dry my towels and blankets and anything the world won't see, like T-shirts, socks, and underwear—or if I'm in a desperate hurry to wear what I've just washed. American dryers really are the enemy of clothes.

Air-drying is not the tedious household chore it's painted to be, either. In fact, I find it to be convenient. Yes, it takes longer in terms of the length of time it takes to dry clothes, but it takes only five to ten minutes to hang up a large load of clothes to air-dry, and then you're done. No waiting for the dryer to finish. You can go on with your day. If you air-dry your clothes properly, they come out fairly wrinkle-free or can be steamed to touch up right before you walk out the door in the morning.

TAKE THE HANG IT OUT CHALLENGE

I challenge you to try one month of air-drying your laundry, or part of your laundry. Take the Hang It Out Challenge and post it on social media using the #hangitoutchallenge or #hangdry hashtags. To get started, purchase a collapsible drying rack (they start at 15 dollars online) to place inside your home or a clothesline and clothespins for your yard. You can also use the towel racks or shower curtain bar in your bathroom. One of the early hurdles for me was getting used to the presence of clothes drying around the house. But I just reminded myself how charming clotheslines look when I travel! If it's the stiffness of some air-dried clothes you don't like, you can dry your clothes indoors or finish drying them for a few minutes in your machine to soften them. But your clothes will also soften up quickly just by being worn again. Rissanen also recommends adding a half cup of distilled white vinegar to the final rinse for cotton garments to reduce stiffness.[26] Here are additional tips to make the transition to air-drying easier:

AIR-DRYING TIPS AND TRICKS

- Hang items that are damp dry, not sopping wet. Roll garments up in a towel to remove extra moisture if necessary.

- For dense garments that warp when hung, like sweaters or viscose rayon, lay flat to dry. You can buy a flat rack or just lay the item flat on a towel.

- Smooth out wrinkles with your hands and reshape the garment how you want it to dry, and it'll dry that way.

- If you're using clothespins, place them in an inconspicuous spot so they don't leave marks. You can also use hangers on your drying rack or clotheslines to avoid creases.

- If you're drying outside, put whites in direct sunlight to brighten them. Turn dark and bright colors inside out and don't leave them in direct sun, or they'll fade.

- If you need an item to dry faster, place it in front of a fan or near the radiator.

HOW TO MACHINE DRY YOUR CLOTHES SUSTAINABLY

Is there a way to keep using our tumble dryers more sustainably? Yes, but it doesn't look much like how we currently use them.

- **Dry longer and lower.** It's counterintuitive, but *longer* drying cycles on a lower heat setting use *significantly less* energy than short drying cycles on high heat.[27] Many American dryers run very hot (around 125 degrees) on both the permanent-press and high-heat settings.[28] Try the lowest setting first.

- **Use a faster spin setting on your washer.** If your washing machine lets you adjust the speed of the spin cycle, turn it up to wring out more water. The less damp your clothes are, the less energy required to dry them.

- **Dry full loads.** Use your dryer when it's half to two-thirds full so that it works properly and you avoid heating empty space.[29]

- **Don't overdry.** Remove your items when damp dry and lay flat to finish. Every minute the dryer isn't running helps conserve energy, and your clothes.

- **Clean your lint filter often.** This helps keep the machine running efficiently.

- **Buy an energy-efficient dryer.** If you're in the market for a new washer or dryer, look for the most energy-efficient model.

NONTOXIC CLEANING SUPPLIES

Who doesn't like the smell of detergent and the soft, warm feel of freshly washed and dried clothes? We'd be wise to break that association. The smell of laundry detergent is not the smell of clean; it's the smell of synthetic fragrances, and some of them are hazardous to human health. You might already use an eco-friendly laundry detergent. Many consumers started greening household cleaning supplies years ago. All major detergent brands have natural, plant-derived, and fragrance-free options, and there are many popular natural brands to choose from. What counts as an eco-friendly detergent? They are detergents that contain plant-based over petroleum-based ingredients and tend to be free of harsh or hazardous chemicals like chlorine bleach, synthetic fragrance, dyes, and brighteners.

How to choose? Start by picking a detergent that works. There are both conventional and eco-friendly detergents that work no better than water. Mrs. Meyers, Tide PurClean, Method products, and Seventh Generation are all top-performing eco-friendly detergents, according to *Consumer Reports*. The Laundress products are also popular and effective. Do a quick Internet search to find eco-friendly detergents that suit your budget and needs.

How much does choosing a nontoxic detergent matter? I think it's worth making the switch. Green and safe detergents are a simple way to limit exposure to potentially hazardous chemicals in everyday life (see Chapter 19). The fact is that not enough is being done to test and protect consumers from toxic substances in most of the products we buy. What's more, chemicals found in common detergents have been linked to negative impacts on human health and the environment. Among the more alarming studies: Fragrances in many scented laundry detergents, fabric softeners, and dryer sheets emit a cocktail of chemicals, including some that are carcinogenic and toxic to human health.[30] Chemicals used in many common detergents have been linked to endocrine disruption and asthma as well.[31] You might also rethink dryer sheets and fabric softeners. Most are loaded with potentially harmful fragrances and are known to cause asthma, skin irritation, and respiratory problems.[32] You really don't need them anyway.

To reduce static cling, try air-drying your synthetics. It's usually the mix of polyester and cotton in the dryer that causes static.[33]

What about bleach? Bleach is a skin and respiratory irritant and is corrosive to fibers. If you want to switch to something gentler to whiten your clothes, choose chlorine-free oxygenated bleach (the Environmental Working Group website has a list of top nontoxic performers) or use common household items like baking soda and lemon juice to help brighten naturally. You can also try drying your whites in the sunlight. The ultraviolet rays of the sun will lighten your light-colored clothes.

If you want to limit your risk and chemical exposure while doing laundry, here are some additional tips:

- **Go fragrance-free.** Choose unscented and fragrance-free detergents, dryer sheets, and fabric softeners, especially if you have asthma, allergies, or sensitive skin.

- **Check safety risks.** Look up available information about the chemical ingredients and the safety ranking of laundry products online before you shop. The Environmental Working Group's online Guide to Healthy Cleaning, for example, grades products from A to F and makes it easy to find higher-rated, safer alternatives. The U.S. Department of Health and Human Services Household Products Database also carries up-to-date health risk warnings associated with cleaning products.

- **Shop certified.** Shop for laundry products that are verified by a third party as safe for human health and the environment. Some options in the United States include the Made Safe consumer label and the EPA's Safer Choice label.

- **Verify natural claims.** So-called natural ingredients can be as harmful as synthetic ones and fragrances can be just as problematic.

Eco-friendly claims should be verified as safe by a third-party group as well. I use the Environment Working Group and Made Safe websites.

- **Try homemade.** You can also give homemade natural laundry detergent recipes a try, using common ingredients like vinegar, baking soda, and lemons. Google "DIY cleaning recipes" for ideas.

- **Support reform.** Demand regulations protecting us against hazardous chemicals in cleaning products. The Environmental Working Group is one of the leaders of consumer product safety reform in the United States.

GREEN YOUR DRY-CLEANING ROUTINE

A third of consumers avoid purchasing garments labeled dry-clean only.[34] That's a lot of people missing out on some truly beautiful but delicate garments that need a little extra care. As we've discussed, it's okay to skip a few washes before you head to the dry cleaner's. Tailored pieces don't need to be cleaned nearly as often as casual clothes and can be spot cleaned. Natural materials like cashmere and wool, often marked dry-clean-only, resist odors naturally. I'll also show you how to successfully hand wash some of those so-called dry-clean-only items like silk later in this chapter.

But you should also line up a green dry-cleaning routine. Dry cleaners extend the life of quality garments. They save you time on laundry, and sometimes you really need a pro's touch on a tough stain or repair. But don't go to just any dry cleaner. Traditional dry cleaning can be energy intensive and even toxic for humans and the environment. The dry-cleaning process uses chemical solvents to expel dirt from clothes (although dry cleaners also use water to wash basic garments). The most common solvent in use, perchloroethylene, or perc for short, is carcinogenic and toxic to dry-cleaning professionals and anyone living and working near a dry cleaner.[35] The solvent can also remain on clothes taken home from the cleaners.[36]

Luckily, it's getting easier to find nontoxic and greener dry-cleaning options. Many cities and countries are going perc-free. Minneapolis became the first entirely perc-free US city in 2018. Do some research to see what regulations are in place in your area. You should ask your dry cleaner the name of the solvents they use to clean your clothes, and if they're nontoxic (always double-check their claims online). The greenest option is professional "wet cleaning," which uses water and soap in computerized machines instead of chemical solvents, and is more energy efficient than traditional dry cleaning.[37] Bring your own reusable garment bag instead of using the cleaner's disposable plastic, to be extra-sustainable.

THE TAO OF HAND WASHING

I relish hand washing my clothes. It's therapeutic and convenient. I hand wash small batches of clothes throughout the week, so I can skip more laundry days. I also wash silk and cashmere without worry. What can be hand washed at home? Anything that's machine washable is hand washable. And many dry-clean-only items can be hand washed as well. Brands often slap a dry-clean-only label on clothes just to protect themselves; they don't want to get in trouble if you ruin your finest cashmere sweater or silk shirt. But the reality is that *many* delicate garments can be hand washed with ease. Most wool and cashmere sweaters, silk, lingerie, and many viscose rayon fabrics can be hand washed. What *can't* be hand washed? Let common sense guide you. Suede, leather, velvet, fur, and down-filled coats should be taken to the cleaners. Anything that's got lots of layers, linings, and embellishments should be professionally cleaned. Here's how to effectively hand wash your garments at home.

A STEP-BY-STEP GUIDE TO HAND WASHING

1. **Set up.** Use your sink or a bucket. Make sure the basin you choose is spotlessly clean, with no color, dirt, or residue that could transfer to your clothes. Fill your basin with cool water. If you're not sure if the item is colorfast, place a corner in the water without detergent. If it starts to bleed, don't panic: Most items can lose a bit of dye without noticeable fading. If a lot of color comes out, dry clean the garment instead.

2. **Add detergent.** Add a few *drops* of laundry detergent, around a teaspoon or less. If your garment is prone to bleeding, use as little detergent as you can. Too much detergent can pull the dye out of your clothes and leave a residue, and most modern detergents are formulated to work in small amounts.

3. **Lightly stir your garment.** Submerge your garment in the water and swish it around gently by hand until the soapy water covers it. Press on your item, and move it around so the soap and water get on all sides of the garment. If your garment is very dirty, let your garment soak for ten to fifteen minutes. Then agitate again for a few more minutes.

4. **Rinse.** Drain or pour out the soapy water and rinse your garment with clean, cool water until the water runs clear and is free of suds.

5. **Remove excess water.** Gently push down on the garment while it's still in the basin to remove excess water. Do *not* lift up your garment while it's sopping wet or ring it out, as this will warp the fabric.

6. **Hang to dry.** If the garment is still sopping wet, lay it flat on a towel and roll it up. Then hang up or lay flat to air-dry. Do *not* put a delicate garment in a machine to be dried.

DECIPHERING CARE LABELS

Care labels are needlessly confusing nowadays. Who can understand those symbols, with their alien-language mixture of dots, squares, and triangles? The problem with care labels is that they describe the washing conditions a garment *can withstand,* rather than the ideal care methods. A care label's instructions, from advisements on heat settings to the use of bleach, are a garment's *maximum tolerance,* not a recommendation. For example, if a care tag says a garment is bleachable, that doesn't mean it must be bleached, only that it won't fade or disintegrate when bleached. Likewise, a recommendation to "machine wash warm" doesn't indicate that a warm wash is *required,* only that your garment (such as a cotton T-shirt) can withstand warm water without shrinking.

By following the advice in this chapter, you won't need to read between the lines on care labels. Just wash on cold, air-dry, and wash only as needed, and you'll be doing the best thing for your clothes. There are a few exceptions: Anything marked dry-clean only should be handled with extreme care. And outdoor and technical gear that comes with waterproofing and other special finishes often comes with very specific care guidelines that should be followed.

A growing number of conscious brands are redesigning labels so that they're simple and straightforward and the advice sustainable. They are designing labels that mean what they say. Stella McCartney launched a Clevercare laundry campaign in 2014 to simplify laundering instructions and to educate consumers on how to reduce the impact of their laundry routine (you can find more details at clevercare. info). In another example, the care label on my button-down shirt by Grammar, a New York–based sustainable clothing brand, reads "Wash cold and line dry and iron if needed" and has a URL listed on the label for additional care tips.

I think it's a good idea for consumers to *always* read and pay attention to care labels, especially if you continue to regularly use a washer and dryer (as most people do). You do need to know if your garment is machine washable, if it can withstand the heat from a dryer, or if it is dry-clean only. In many cases, our care labels are trying to tell us to be very gentle when washing our clothes; that's one aspect of care labels that I fully agree with.

SUSTAINABLE STAIN REMOVAL

Stains are a part of life. I was inspired to master them both because of my work in the resale industry—there's nothing quite like trying to remove a very old, very yellow mystery spot—and also because of my predilection for eating on the go. Much like our laundry habits, stain removal has moved in the direction of an over-reliance on chemically intensive stain removers and machine washing. A little elbow grease and some basic cleaning supplies work just as well or *better* in most cases. The best way to remove stains is always to remove them fast!

Build a Stain Kit

Make sure you have the tools you need to lift a wide variety of stains, from dirt and grass to oil and food. Every stain is a little different, so here's a list of supplies to gather that'll help you tackle most accidents:

- Cotton swabs or white cotton pads work for blotting stains without transferring color.
- An old toothbrush is perfect for gently scrubbing stains.
- An all-purpose stain remover that can tackle dirt, blood, oil, food, and other protein-based stains. Check the Environmental

Working Group website or the Made Safe website for nontoxic options.

- Clear dish soap is good for removing grease stains, and cornstarch works for absorbing extra oil.

- A gentle bleach alternative like white vinegar, lemon juice, baking soda, or hydrogen peroxide helps lift color from stains. An oxygenated bleach product (like OxiClean) is another option. Just make sure it doesn't lift the color out of your garment, too!

- If you need a higher-powered pretreatment spray for your toughest stains, look for one that's certified as nontoxic by the EPA or the Environmental Working Group. Many of the conventional pretreatment sprays contain hazardous substances and should be avoided.

STAIN-FIGHTING TIPS AND TRICKS

Now that you have your kit together and you know how to find safe cleaning products, here's how to put them into action. The trick with stain removal is to be cautious and gentle but persistent. Otherwise, you risk permanently ruining your garment. Here are some other tricks I've picked up along the way:

- **Start with water.** Plain water is one of the most underrated stain removers. It's a solvent and works on dirt and many common stains that haven't set in.

- **Spit lifts blood.** The proteins in saliva really do work to lift bloodstains.

- **Alcohol works for ink stains.** Rubbing alcohol can help lift pen marks, but use only a small amount to avoid lifting the color from your bag or garment. You can test the alcohol on a discreet part of the piece first, such as the inside seam or underneath a strap.

- **Beware the combo stain.** Some stains like tomato sauce and lipstick are a combination of oil *and* pigment. In these cases, you'll need two different stain removers, one to lift the oil and one to lift the color.[38]

- **Don't dry it until you get it out.** If the stain doesn't lift on your first attempt, never put your garment in the dryer. The stain will set for good. If your first attempt doesn't work, move on to the next method. I've tried as many as four rounds of stain-removal techniques before getting a spot to lift.

- **Consult the Internet.** For tips on stubborn or unusual stains, the American Cleaning Institute, Martha Stewart, and the Laundress websites are all great resources. The proper technique all depends on the color and content of the stain and the type of fabric affected, and you will find detailed information about your specific problem online.

- **Turn damages into design features.** If the stain won't lift or your garment is damaged in the process, see Chapter 24 and turn those damages into a design feature using tricks like visible mending, patching, or natural dyeing.

Call in the Pros to
Fix Your Clothes

I**t's time to** call in the experts! Every person building a conscious closet should have a trusted network of repair professionals to fix and reimagine their shoes and clothes. You'll need both a cobbler *and* a tailor. I have two tailors, one that I trust with basic repairs and another who takes on more complex jobs. The words "tailor" and "seamstress" are used almost interchangeably these days, although historically seamstresses were women who focused on dressmaking and tailors altered tailored clothing, typically menswear, or made suiting from scratch. I'll use the term "tailor," since it's gender neutral.

HOW TO FIND AND BUILD TRUST WITH A TAILOR

Due to our throwaway culture, repair professionals aren't nearly as common as they once were. But we can change that! You're looking for someone who is highly experienced, with broad and deep skill sets for minor and major alterations and repairs. Here are some tips for how to seek them out:

- **Word of mouth.** Since many tailors run a one-person shop or work out of their homes, word of mouth can often be the best way to find a skilled tailor. Ask friends, co-workers, or relatives for recommendations, or turn to Facebook Recommendations.

- **Online reviews.** Look up tailors on Yelp or Google Maps or by simply Googling "clothing repair," "seamstress," or "tailor near me." Online reviews are helpful, as you can get a sense of what types of alterations and repairs are offered and whether or not reviewers are satisfied with the work.

- **Dry cleaners.** Many dry cleaners offer basic repairs and alterations on-site, or they outsource more complicated jobs to a tailor.

WHAT CAN BE FIXED?

A good tailor can address most basic clothing mishaps, from sewing up busted seams and loose stitching to replacing a broken zipper. They can also restore clothing, such as replacing the elastic in a stretched-out waistband or a worn-out lining on a skirt or jacket. If you're looking to have a leather jacket or handbag redyed or repaired, a cobbler is the best professional to use. There are also experts for hire who specialize in denim, leather, and knit repair, and a quick Google search will turn them up.

Once you locate a tailor you want to try out, build a rapport with him or her on something with lower stakes, like hemming your pants, rather than giving them your grandmother's vintage dress to alter from the get-go. Skill levels can vary, but, more importantly, it takes time to learn how to communicate with a tailor, so that you're both on the same page about how your repairs and alterations should go. If you're not quite sure how your garment should be adjusted or repaired, book an appointment with your tailor and try it on. Part of their job is to help you figure out the problem and offer a solution.

HOW TO HAVE YOUR CLOTHES ALTERED AND FITTED TO YOUR FORM

Store-bought clothes are made for an "average" body type that doesn't exist. Luckily, tailors can alter them to fit your form perfectly. Good fit really does make a huge difference in your appearance and the way you feel in your clothes. If there's a garment you love, but the sleeves are too long or the torso is too baggy, it's perfect fodder for alterations. A tailor can take up a hemline, take in a waistband, shorten straps, and slim down a garment to provide a more fitted, flattering appearance. A great tailor can also rebuild or majorly redesign a piece, whether by adding or removing sleeves, changing a neckline, or moving or adding a zipper. When it comes to major alterations, work only with a skilled professional, especially if your garment is expensive or irreplaceable (like a wedding dress or high-end suit).

WHEN IS A REPAIR OR ALTERATION WORTH THE COST?

Prices can start as low as five dollars to have a button replaced or cost many hundreds of dollars to have a suit or gown altered and reworked from top to bottom. One of the reasons I have a whole chapter dedicated to everyday repairs is to save you money spent hiring someone to do basic tasks! Repairs and alterations can be pricey, but they can be well worth the money. It all depends on where you live and the nature of the task at hand. You may ask, "Why not just buy something new?" In my experience, putting in the time to customize a garment results in a perfect-for-you piece that you *want* to wear for years to come. What's more, repairing clothes can help you feel bonded to them. That said, I tend to save alterations for really special garments, ones that I would be hard-pressed to find again in a store or that would be prohibitively expensive to buy new. For example, my grandmother gave me a pair of gorgeous 100 percent silk pants in teal. I had my tailor slim down the entire pant, which suffered from a voluminous 1980s silhouette, for 35 dollars.

How to Care for Cheap Clothes

I'm going to tell you a secret: Cheap clothes aren't disposable. Most of them don't just fall apart at the seams at the slightest provocation. As I mentioned in Chapter 12, we often have a disposable attitude and approach toward low-cost products, but it doesn't have to be this way. We can change our mind-set and treat all clothing, regardless of cost, with respect and care. Here are some tips to make lower-quality pieces last longer:

- **Launder it like it's a delicate.** A bad fabric doesn't have to doom your garment. Wash less, hand wash, or wash on the gentle cycle, regardless of what the care label says. Air-dry to lessen fading, pilling, and misshaping.

- **Treat it like it's expensive.** Carefully hang or fold your pieces when you're not wearing them, remove stains with haste, and care for them like they cost ten times as much as they did.

- **Learn to mend.** Pick up some basic mending skills! Cheap buys can suffer mechanical failures, such as loose buttons and split seams. After you learn the mending skills in Chapter 24, use them to patch up and reinforce your lesser-made buys to keep them going longer.

- **Spend to fix.** Don't let the price you paid factor into your decision of whether to repair. It might cost just a few bucks to have a professional fix a broken buckle, re-glue a sole, or sew up a busted lining.

HOW TO MAKE YOUR SHOES LAST LONGER

The life of a pair of shoes all depends on the shoe, the weather, and the wearer. New Yorkers wear out their shoes in a jiffy because we walk everywhere, but if you live in a car-centric place, your shoes will last longer. As I covered in Chapter 10, high-quality leather dress shoes that come with a good replaceable sole and heel can last for many years, while mass-market and athletic shoes generally have much shorter life spans. Here's how to get the most out of your shoes, no matter what you're wearing or what you paid:

- If you want to use a fabric or leather protector on new shoes, choose one with nontoxic ingredients, using the Environmental Working Group's ratings.

- On dress shoes, consider having rubber half soles or toe taps added to greatly extend the life of the sole.

- Use cheap odor-absorbing insoles to keep your insoles looking and smelling fresh. This is also useful if you plan to resell your shoes.

- Remove salt, stains, dirt, or other marks immediately. I use a toothbrush and clear soap for most marks.

- Never step on the back of your shoes to pull them off; it damages them.

- Give your shoes a break between wearings. The insoles and fabric need time to dry out so that bacteria and wrinkles don't set in.

- Never walk down the heels of your shoes. Get them repaired before they get to this point.

HOW TO WORK WITH A COBBLER AND SHOE REPAIR SHOP

Cobblers are true magicians! There's nothing like picking up a pair of shoes that have been polished and resoled. They genuinely look like new. To find a local cobbler, follow the same advice you'd use to look for a tailor, using word-of-mouth or online review services. It's getting harder to find shoe repair professionals, but it's not impossible, and we can reverse the profession's decline by getting our shoes fixed. There are a few online cobblers who accept mail-ins, like Cobbler Concierge, although they tend to specialize in high-end footwear. It's time to repair your shoes when the sole is wearing thin, the heel is worn down, or your shoes look scuffed and worn-out. Men's and women's leather dress shoes are the easiest to repair, as the cobbler profession was developed around the craft and maintenance of leather shoes. But there are cobblers out there who will fix anything from the broken zipper on your ankle boots to the cork insole of your Birkenstocks and will even repaint the soles of your Louboutins. There's only one way to know if your particular shoe problem can be fixed, and that is to take your shoes to your cobbler and ask (or call ahead). You can also make some shoe repairs on your own. If your sole is splitting from the upper, use shoe glue (I use a brand called Shoe Goo) to reattach it. Shoe glue can also be used to fill in holes on the soles of sneakers. It dries clear and provides an invisible, waterproof seal. Lastly, heel tips and toe taps are cheap to buy online and easy to replace at home.

WHAT CAN BE FIXED?

Cobblers offer a range of services; here are a few of the most common:

- Sole replacement. Protective rubber soles or half soles can be added to provide traction or to preserve leather-soled dress shoes.

- Scuffs and dirt. These can be whisked away with polish and dye, leaving your shoes looking like new.

- Worn, broken, or missing high-heel tips. These can be replaced.

- Fastener repairs. Broken buckles, zippers, or straps can be glued or sewn back together.

- Too-tight leather shoes. These can be stretched a bit, but don't expect miracles. Usually a half size or one width is the most a cobbler can add.

- Color change. If your gold boots don't go with anything in your wardrobe, get them dyed black or brown. Keep in mind that it's much easier to go from light to dark when redyeing footwear.

- In addition to shoe repair, many cobblers can repair and condition leather jackets and handbags.

Mending, Patching, and Everyday Repairs

**With a little mending,
it could be as good as new.**

–DOLLY PARTON

Mending, repairing, and caring for our clothes is the essence of sustainable fashion. Clothes break and burst and wear thin—they just do—and mending is the blissfully simple and economical way to put them back together so that they last. About once a month, I sit down with a needle and thread and mend broken straps, patch jeans, darn holes in sweaters, and connect belt loops back to pants. And I *love* it. Mending is satisfying and fun. It's a way to meditate, appreciate your clothes, and take a break from the world.

In *Overdressed,* I dabbled with the idea of reviving home sewing and making clothes from scratch. There is an incredible movement of people doing just that, and I sew from a pattern from time to time. But the repairs in this chapter are based on very easy hand-sewing techniques that anyone can learn. No advanced skills and no sewing machine are required. There's a powerful reason for this back-to-basics, beginner-level mending chapter: The vast majority of the clothes we get rid of because they're "broken" have very minor flaws, like a missing button, a tiny split in a lining or seam, or loose stitching that just needs to be tightened. These are everyday clothing mishaps that we should *all* know how to repair, both because they keep clothes out of the landfill and because *we can*. It's easy to learn, and I think you just might enjoy it, too.

Build a Mending Kit

To pick up the fundamentals of mending, all you need to know is how to thread a needle, tie off your thread, and push the needle through the fabric. Tutorials for these fundamentals can be found online, including on my YouTube channel. You'll also need to gather some supplies. Basic mending tools are cheap and widely available, and supplies can be found online, in craft or sewing stores, and in some big-box chains. Many stores sell prepackaged mending kits that have thread, scissors, and needles. If you are blessed with an independent knitting and sewing shop in your community, support it! Here's what you need in your mending kit.

- Hand-sewing needles in a few different sizes.
- Thread in a few basic colors, such as black, white, navy, and brown.
- Scissors. Nothing fancy, just a pair that's nice and sharp.
- Straight pins to secure your work while mending. A pincushion is advised (I made mine out of a ball of old socks).
- Seam ripper. A small tool for pulling out old stitches.
- Scrap fabric (from your Conscious Closet Cleanout) to use for patches.
- A thimble to protect your finger.
- A decorative basket or container. Keep your supplies in a festive container to inspire you to do your mending!

FOUR BASIC HAND STITCHES

In this chapter, you'll learn four easy and versatile hand stitches and how to put them into action to fix your clothes. They can be used on anything from a split seam to a hole in your favorite T-shirt. You can practice on a scrap of denim from a pair of worn-out jeans or on an old dish towel before moving on to a real repair, or just jump right in. As you get going, let go of the idea of a perfect mend. It's fine to wing it and just give it a go.

Straight Stitch (aka Running Stitch)

The straight stitch, also called the running stitch, is the most basic hand stitch. You can use it for decorative patching and sewing or as a simple way to close up seams or hems. As you can see in Figures 5 and 6, the straight stitch looks like a dashed line and is created by weaving your needle up and down through the fabric. Keep your stitches and the space between your stitches the same length. I usually keep my stitches between an eighth and a quarter of an inch in length for strength, but feel free to experiment. You'll see the straight stitch in action in both the Easy *Sashiko*-Style Denim Patch and Patchiko tutorials later in this chapter.

Directions: To begin a straight stitch, tie off a knot on the end of your thread and push your needle up through the back of your fabric at point No. 1 (Figure 5). With your needle, come back down through your fabric at point No. 2. Next, weave your needle up and down through the fabric, creating short, evenly spaced stitches. Your results will look like Figure 6. To finish, tie off a knot on the back side of your garment and clip your thread.

Whipstitch

Another easy, versatile, and attractive stitch is the whipstitch. Use it to finish a hem, secure the edges of a patch, or attach decorative patches

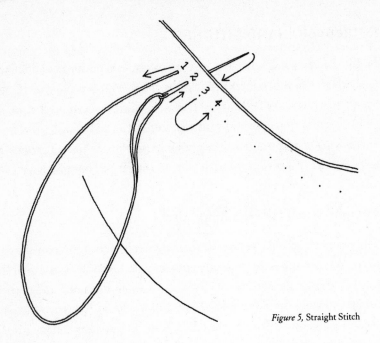

Figure 5, Straight Stitch

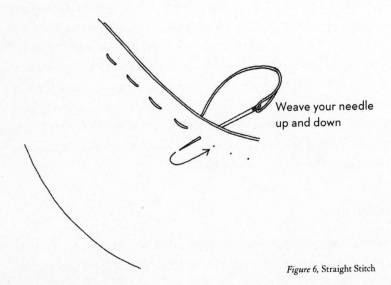

Weave your needle up and down

Figure 6, Straight Stitch

and appliqués. The whipstitch is a vertical stitch that looks like rows of short lines sitting side by side. If you want your whipstitches to stand out, use a colorful or bright-white thread. Otherwise, choose matching thread that blends into your garment. You'll see the whipstitch in action in the Easy *Sashiko*-Style Denim Patch tutorial, where it's used to tidy the frayed edges of a hole on a pair of jeans.

Directions: Figure 7 shows the whipstitch securing a patch to a pair of jeans. To begin the whipstitch, double your thread and tie off a knot at the end. Push your needle up through the back of the fabric at point No. 1, and then bring your needle vertically straight down and push it through the fabric again at point No. 2. You can experiment with your stitch length, but I would suggest keeping them around a quarter of an inch or smaller, so that they're very secure. To take your second stitch, push the needle through the back of the fabric slightly to the right of the previous stitch, at point No. 3, and come back down again vertically at point No. 4. As you'll see in the Easy *Sashiko*-Style Denim Patch tutorial, you can space your whipstitches closer together for added strength or visual effect.

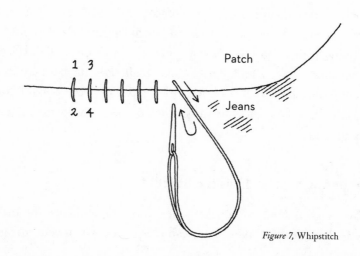

Figure 7, Whipstitch

Backstitch

The backstitch is a strong and versatile hand stitch. It's also a lot of fun. Use it to close up a split seam, finish a hem, secure a patch, and more. It's also a popular stitch in decorative embroidery. I find the easiest direction to learn to backstitch is left to right, as depicted, but you can stitch in either direction.

Directions: To start, tie off a knot at the end of your thread and push your needle up through the back of your fabric. Figure 8 is showing the backstitch in progress, so you can see what it will look like several stitches in. For your first stitch, start out exactly like the running stitch, pushing your needle up through the fabric and back down through the fabric one stitch length to the right. After your very first stitch, your needle will be at the back of the fabric again. From here, bring your needle up through the fabric one stitch length away at point No. 1 as if you're going to make another running stitch. Instead of continuing to the right, bring your needle back one stitch length to the left (closing the space) and to the very edge of your previous stitch. Push the needle down through the fabric at point No. 2, creating your backstitch. Your needle will now be at the back of the fabric at the very edge of your first completed stitch. To take your next stitch, bring your needle back up one stitch length over to the right, bringing it through the fabric at point No. 3 (Figure 9) and back down at point No. 4, and repeat. Make small, tight stitches for added strength or looser stitches on more decorative projects. You'll know you're on the right track if your stitches are perfectly connected in a straight line.

Ladder Stitch (aka Invisible Stitch)

This magical stitch disappears when you're done, hence the nickname. It is ideal for fixing split seams, especially when you can't get

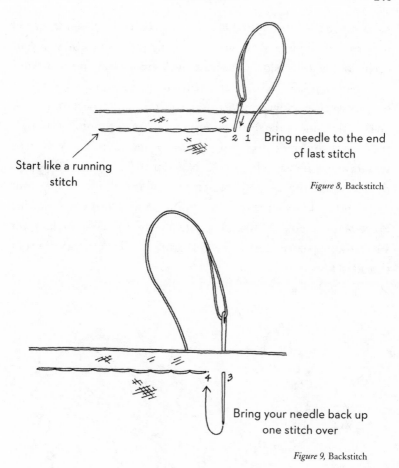

Start like a running stitch

Bring needle to the end of last stitch

Figure 8, Backstitch

Bring your needle back up one stitch over

Figure 9, Backstitch

to the back of the fabric (in the case of a coat, blazer, or skirt with a lining, for example). The illustration (Figures 10–14) shows the ladder stitch sewing up a split seam on the shoulder of a lined jacket. You can also use the ladder stitch to sew up tears, although it will create a bit of a pucker.

Directions: Begin by doubling your thread and tying off a knot. Push your needle up through the fabric along the inside fold of your seam at point No. 1 (Figure 10). Next, cross over the broken seam and pick up a small piece of fabric (about an eighth of an inch) with your needle on the other side, just inside the seam, as seen in point No. 2 and point No. 3. Keep your stitches as close to the inside edge of your seam as you can. Now jump across the opening and repeat the process on the other side of the seam, taking a small stitch running just inside the edge of the fabric (Figure 11). Once you get going, a ladder shape will form, as shown in Figure 12. Now for the fun part: After every three or four stitches, pull your thread tight until it closes up your seam and makes your stitches disappear! When you're done sewing up your seam, pull the thread very taut again to make sure all your stitches disappear into your mend (Figure 13). Tie off and clip your thread to finish.

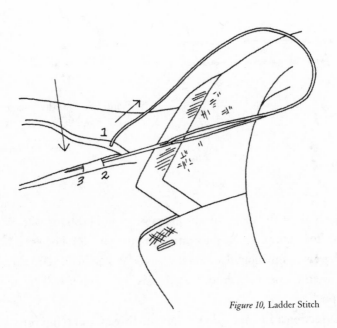

Figure 10, Ladder Stitch

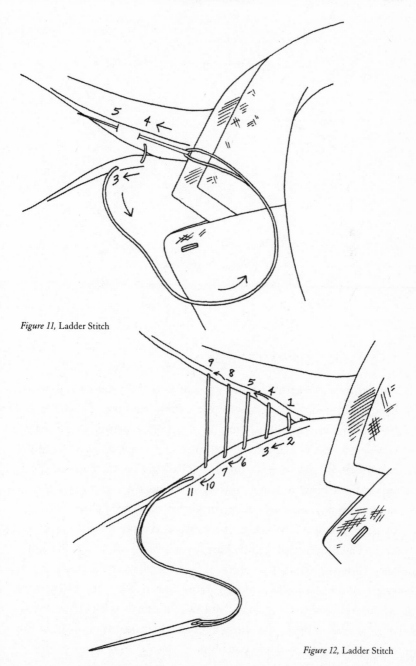

Figure 11, Ladder Stitch

Figure 12, Ladder Stitch

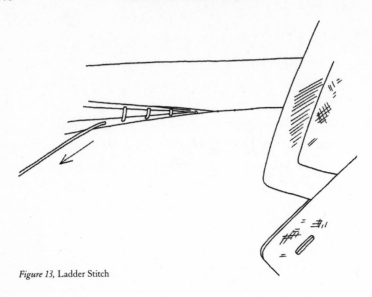

Figure 13, Ladder Stitch

THE BASICS OF PATCHING

Now that you've learned four basic hand stitches, you can put them into action making everyday repairs. First, I'll cover patching, followed by darning, and sewing on a button. Patching is the act of covering a hole or reinforcing a thin place in a garment by sewing a new piece of fabric over or under the damage. While you can speed up your patching by using a sewing machine, I will show you how to do it using the hand stitches you've already learned. I prefer patching by hand because I can sit on the couch and relax while I do my repairs. Patching is what's called for if you need to fix a large hole or a very thin and threadbare area. It is most often used on garments made out of nonstretchy "woven" fabrics, such as blazers, dress pants, button-down shirts, or jackets. But we will start with a hole in a pair of jeans, one of the most common repairs done on one of the most fun and forgiving materials to patch up.

Traditional Denim Patch Tutorial

I adapted this traditional patching technique from the World War II–era Make Do and Mend books. It is a classic patch that all but blends into your garment, disguising the hole or thin spot. You can also use this same technique with a patch in a contrasting color or print for a bold and more customized look. The traditional patch is one of the more advanced repairs in this chapter, but I taught myself how to do it in a matter of hours. It's a lot of fun to learn, and anyone can master it with a little practice.

Directions:

1. With a pair of scissors, cut away the damaged area on your jeans into a tidy square or rectangle. Then measure the dimensions of the hole, and cut your patch to be half an inch larger on all sides than the dimensions of the hole. For material for your patch, use scrap denim from a worn-out pair of jeans, or buy a pair of kids' jeans in a matching color from a thrift store and cut them up. Next, cut quarter-inch diagonal snips at each of the corners of the hole (Figure 14).

2. Fold the snipped fabric back toward the inside of the garment, creating four quarter-inch tabs that are turned to the back of your garment. Turn your garment inside out and press the folded edges down with an iron (Figure 15).

3. Place the patch directly under the hole, with the right side (the side you want to be visible) showing through (Figure 16). Pin the patch to the tabs to hold it in place.

4. With your jeans still turned inside out, fold the fabric of your jeans back along one side of the quarter-inch tabs. Since you've ironed your tabs, you will see a clear crease to sew along. Backstitch along the crease, one tab at a time. Knot and cut your thread,

turn your fabric, knot your thread again, and sew the next tab along the crease. Do this for all four sides.

5. You're done! This patching technique makes your stitches totally invisible from the front or outside of the garment (Figure 17). If you'd like a more finished look for the inside edges of your patch, whipstitch around the patch edges where they are connected to the quarter-inch tabs. Alternatively, sew your patch to your garment using a neat, loose running stitch in a closely matching thread. Finishing the patch edges is not a requirement (as it's not visible from the outside), and your patch will hold just fine using the previous steps.

THE BASICS OF VISIBLE MENDING

Our ancestors were expert menders, able to deftly blend their mends into a garment so they disappeared. But mending is also a perfect opportunity to redesign your garments and get creative, using contrasting denim scraps, a printed fabric, or white or colorful thread. Nowadays, repair is taking on more rebellious and attention-grabbing forms. The visible-mending movement is one group combating throwaway fashion by inspiring people to mend with bright, eye-catching repairs that can be done at any skill level. Instead of mends that disappear, visible menders make repairs that boldly stand out. One of the creators of visible mending, Kate Sekules, offers up her original patching technique, called Patchiko, using a bright printed fabric in just a bit.

There are also menders reviving the Japanese tradition of *sashiko,* a functional embroidery technique that was developed to repair and strengthen clothing and textiles and to make them last as long as possible.[1] Repaired textiles were often passed down *for generations.* Textiles with layers upon layers of repairs are called *boro.* Two recent books, *Make and Mend* by Jessica Marquez and *Mending Matters* by Katrina Rodabaugh, are beautiful resources for *sashiko*-inspired

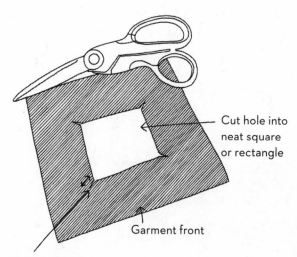

Cut hole into
neat square
or rectangle

Garment front

Make 1/4" snips
at an angle

Figure 14

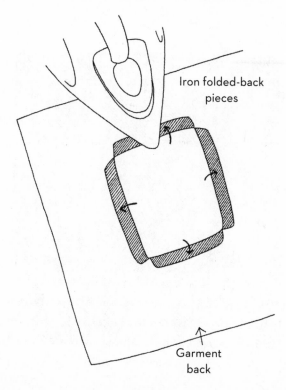

Iron folded-back
pieces

Garment
back

Figure 15

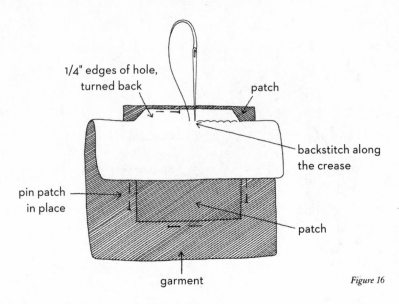

1/4" edges of hole, turned back

patch

backstitch along the crease

pin patch in place

patch

garment

Figure 16

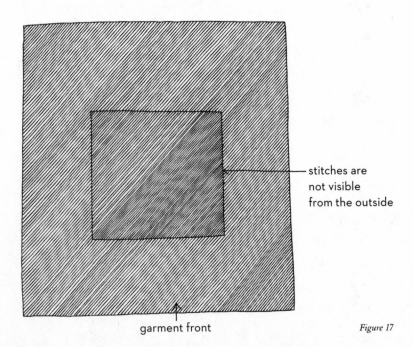

stitches are not visible from the outside

garment front

Figure 17

patching techniques. Modern versions of these techniques deploy the running stitch and fabric swatches of various colors to repair garments again and again, creating a patchwork effect. Just look up the hashtags #sashiko and #borostitch on social media for inspiration.

Easy *Sashiko*-Style Denim Patch Tutorial

This *sashiko*-style denim patch is an ideal way to patch holes or thin spots in your jeans and to decorate and customize them at the same time. To make your repair stand out, use white or contrasting embroidery thread. The thicker strands are bright and strong. For your patch, choose a denim in a contrasting color (either lighter or darker) or choose a bold printed fabric (just make sure the fabric is nice and sturdy). You can also use this technique to patch areas that you don't want to draw attention to, such as the crotch or upper thighs of your jeans. Simply use matching thread and a patch that closely matches your denim in color, so that your repair blends in.

Directions:

1. Clip away loose threads around the hole to keep it from fraying.

2. Cut your patch larger than your hole, both to reinforce the weak parts of the fabric and to give you a bigger canvas on which to make your decorative stitches. In the illustration shown, the patch is about two inches larger than the hole on each side and about an inch and a half wider above and below. The size is really up to you and what you think looks best!

3. Turn your garment inside out and pin your patch in place under your hole to secure it while you sew. Make sure the right side of your patch is showing through the hole. Another way to do this

patch is to sew your patch over your jeans, covering the hole completely. The choice is yours!

4. Using a straight stitch (aka running stitch), create a row of stitches going straight across your patch and skipping over the hole. To create your next row of stitches, jump down one stitch length and stitch in the opposite direction, keeping your stitches and spacing perfectly even. Repeat this step, weaving rows of running stitches, until you've covered your patch.

5. Once your patch is stitched into place, tie off and cut your thread and remove your pins. To finish your mend, whipstitch around the edges of the hole, to prevent it from fraying. It also looks quite nice.

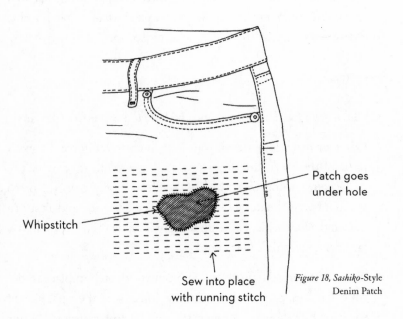

Whipstitch

Patch goes
under hole

Sew into place
with running stitch

*Figure 18, Sashiko-*Style
Denim Patch

Patchiko Patch Tutorial

By Kate Sekules

As a mending addict, evangelist, and historian, I obviously want *everyone* to get into visible mending. Here, I chose a versatile technique any beginner can manage that can also be *zhoozhed up*. I've affectionately titled this the Patchiko: a hybrid of "patch" and "*sashiko*," the Japanese hand-sewing technique from the Edo period that 97 percent of visible menders employ in some way. Though it can get very complex, at its simplest it is just side-by-side rows of running stitch—just up, down, up, down.

This will work on any non-knitwear garment; it's especially good for denims and thicker, less stretchy fabrics. (It is not recommended for wispy things.) For the patch material, select something that's a similar weight and composition to your holey garment. For example, if you're mending jeans, a closely woven cotton or a contrasting piece of denim is great. Do cut up unwanted clothes for patches: never trash your old things!

SUPPLIES

- **Patch.** Use madly contrasting fabric! Cut an even shape about an inch larger all round than your hole. You could use pinking shears, if you have them.

- **Thread.** Select embroidery floss in a color or colors that pop. Do not get cheap stuff in bulk from the Internet—you'll be twisted in knots in no time. The thread will be too. DMC is a good brand available everywhere.

- **Needle.** Select one not too thick or thin, with a large enough eye and a sharp point. An ideal option is an embroidery (or crewel) needle, size 3.

DIRECTIONS

1. Press the garment and the patch with an iron—it saves time and trouble in the end.

2. Carefully position the patch over the hole and pin it. Make sure the hole isn't stretched out beneath. If you're covering a rip, you might tack it closed first. (Tacking or basting is a big running stitch to hold fabric in place, usually removed later.)

3. Tack the patch down nice and smooth. You can skip this step, but it helps.

4. Thread your needle. Embroidery floss has six thin strands. You can use all six or split your length of thread into three or two. I suggest all six to start.

5. Attach the patch. Having knotted the thread, come up through the garment (from the inside) starting in one corner an inch *beyond* the patch. Sew a running stitch in a straight line all the way across, to an inch beyond the patch on the other end. This line will not touch the patch material.

6. Now reverse direction and stitch alongside that line, leaving a quarter-inch gap.

7. Keep going back and forth, back and forth, across the patch, until you've reached an inch beyond the far side. Finish inside the garment, knot, snip: done.

Hints for Success: Don't worry! It'll look great even if your stitches are uneven or crooked. Just keep resmoothing the patch as you go to avoid puckering. If you do go badly wrong, unpick your stitches and start over. Above all, have fun making your enviable, one-of-a-kind couture.

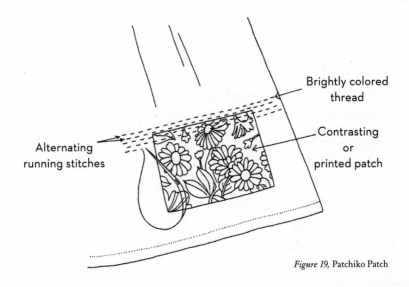

Brightly colored thread

Contrasting or printed patch

Alternating running stitches

Figure 19, Patchiko Patch

DARNING FOR HOLEY SWEATERS AND KNITS TUTORIAL

If your sweaters, socks, and other knits are worn through, it's time to darn them! Darning refers to neatly *reweaving* torn or thin fabric by hand. It is much easier than it sounds and works well even when it's less than perfect. Here are some hints for success: Sit in strong, bright light, keep your tension fairly loose, and don't pull on your thread as you darn, to avoid puckering your mend. I've added visuals on You-Tube and my website as additional resources.

Supplies and Setup

- **Thread or yarn.** Use a thread or yarn that's a similar thickness and color to your garment. Use wool yarn for thick sweaters for example, but regular sewing thread works just fine for thin socks and T-shirts. If you want to do a visible mend, choose a yarn in a contrasting color!

- **Needle.** If it's a chunky knit, you might want to use a longer, thicker embroidery or darning needle that has a bigger eye. Otherwise, a regular sewing needle is fine.

- **Stabilizer.** Keep your fabric taut and secure by stretching it over a darning egg or darning mushroom. But you can also use a cup, plastic bottle, tennis ball, or embroidery hoop. All work well.

Directions

1. Begin your darn by coming up through the back of the fabric a good distance beyond the hole to reinforce the thin parts.

2. Weave your needle and thread up and down in the style of the running stitch, loosely replicating the spacing of the weave of the original garment. Turn the corner and go back in the opposite direction, alternating your stitches. Space your rows evenly and closely together. Staggering or alternating your stitches leaves space to weave perpendicular stitches, which you'll do in step 4.

3. When darning over the hole, you'll pass over it in a straight line (be careful not to pull your thread, or you'll pucker your darn). Stitch past the hole until you've woven a patch of new material with your threads running in one direction (Figure 20).

4. Change directions, weaving over and under your first pass of stitches, and perpendicular (at a right angle) to your original stitches. When you get to the hole, weave under and over your original threads. Keep darning past the hole until you have woven a dense and neat patch of new material and the hole has disappeared (Figure 21).

5. To finish your darn, you can tie off your thread on the back of your fabric. Another method is to simply weave a small tail of your thread through the darn and clip off the end.

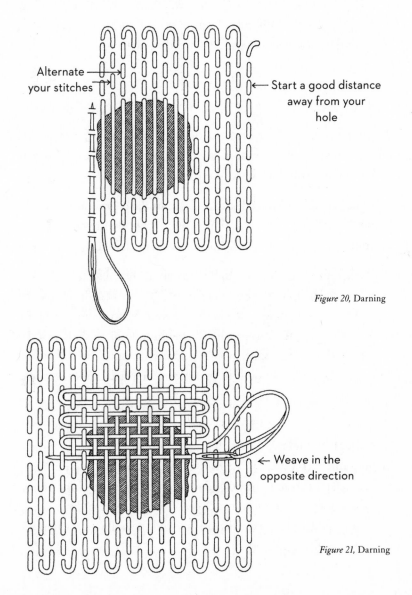

Alternate your stitches

Start a good distance away from your hole

Figure 20, Darning

Weave in the opposite direction

Figure 21, Darning

HOW TO SEW ON A BUTTON TUTORIAL

Sewing on a button isn't particularly exciting, but it's satisfying and everyone should know how to do it. If you don't currently have a loose button, you can carefully cut a single button off one of your shirts and sew it back on to practice. Use a thread that matches.

Directions:

1. Find the spot of the original button. Take the time to get the placement exactly right, so your buttonhole lines up with your button and you don't have to start over.

2. Make a few crisscrossed stitches right in the center of where your button will sit (Figure 22); this is your anchor point and will make your sewing stronger and your button stay on longer.

3. Push your needle up through the back of the fabric and through one of the holes in the button (Figure 22). Use a needle or a toothpick to create some space between your button and the fabric. You'll need it to create a shank, the bundle of threads below a button that creates space between your garment and your button. If your button has a built-in shank, you can skip this step.

4. Bring the needle back down through the hole opposite of the one you came up through and push the needle all the way down through the fabric. Then come back up through the fabric and buttonhole (Figure 23). Repeat this step until you make three to four passes through the holes and fabric on one side of the button. If it's a four-hole button, you'll need to cross over to other side of your button and loop the threads around the holes on the opposite side as well (Figure 24).

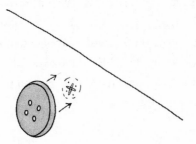

Figure 22

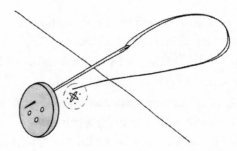

Figure 23

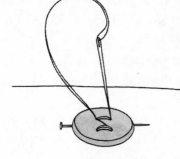

Figure 24

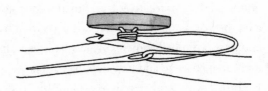

Figure 25

5. Remove the toothpick and pull your needle beneath the button, on the right side of your fabric. Then, tightly wind the thread around the bundle of threads connecting the button to the fabric four to six times, creating your shank (Figure 25). Push the needle back through to the back of the fabric, take a few more stitches, and tie and cut off your thread.

STOP BUYING, START DIYING!

We've covered mending and patching. Now we're onto DIYing. Do-it-yourself, or DIY, is all about giving it a go and reimagining and rebuilding clothes on your own terms and using your own creative inspiration. It's not only *okay* to cut up and transform clothes to make them all your own, it's encouraged! DIY clothing projects vary from simple alterations (cutting a pair of jeans into jean shorts rather than buying them is a basic DIY project) to runway-worthy looks. At the time of this writing, the DIY aesthetic, including patching, mono-gramming, and embroidery, is all the rage, with high-fashion brands like Gucci offering customization for their bags and jackets.[2] You can find professional DIYers who offer customization for jackets, shoes, and tops on a skill level that is mind-blowing on Instagram using hashtags like #diyfashion or #customizer.

But, of course, DIY is by definition something you can do on your own. You certainly don't need a luxury brand to customize your clothes for you. Iron-on patches and lettering are available for cheap on Etsy, an online crafters' marketplace, and in any craft store or sewing section of a big-box chain (it's usually a few dollars for a basic patch). Fabric pens and iron-on embellishments are available in craft stores at very little cost and can be used to add new design elements to otherwise plain clothes. Embroidery is another skill to explore, and it's easier to learn than you might think. In fact, you already have the foundation of it by learning the backstitch. You can use embroidery to customize everything from the back of a jean jacket to a tote bag or T-shirt. You can buy beginner-level embroidery patterns, along with thread and other supplies, on Etsy.

The Internet is full of DIY magic and can provide details and visuals that are beyond the scope of this book. YouTube and Instagram are both great places to look up DIY fashion projects. In this chapter, you'll learn one DIY technique, a tie-dyeing tutorial using natural dyes. Natural dyeing is ideal for reimagining plain garments or covering up dingy or stained pieces. Cara Marie Piazza's tutorial, which is coming up next, shows just how stunning and original naturally dyed clothing can look.

Tips for Success: If you want your DIY projects to come out looking more professional, take the time to plan them carefully. A little preparation can go a long way. Draw up your design on a piece of paper, and make sure to measure and mark your garment before you cut away fabric. If you're altering a garment, use pieces in your wardrobe as a template for the length or shape (you can use a tank top from your own closet as a pattern for your DIY tank tops, for example). But don't be intimidated by trial and error. The process of learning and creating is much of the fun of DIY.

Tie-Dye a T-shirt Using Onion Skins Tutorial

By Cara Marie Piazza

I'm Cara Marie Piazza, a natural dyer and artisan working in New York City. I create one-of-a-kind textiles only using natural dye ingredients such as botanicals, plant matter, minerals, nontoxic metals, and food wastes, working with both designers and artists to realize their natural dyeing needs as well as creating custom pieces for my private clients.

After finding the craft, or the craft finding me, I became instantly addicted to the medium and learning how to cook color from plants. When working with natural dyes properly, they are nontoxic, both to you and to the environment around you. Wearing naturally dyed clothing helps intercept the synthetic dye industry, even through the wash and care of your garments. I also teach workshops on natural dyeing and curate unique experiences merging healing, color, and art.

SUPPLIES

You can commandeer some tools you have from your kitchen, but please remember to keep them separate once you use them for dyeing.

- **Red or yellow onion skins.** This is your "dyestuff" and will produce a burnt-orange color. Collect onion skins after cooking some of your favorite recipes at home or simply by being the funny person at your local grocer collecting them from the bottom of the onion baskets. Stores are typically happy to let you have them! You want to gather enough to fill a large Ziploc bag abundantly.

- **An old garment.** Use a 100 percent silk slip, shirt, or garment (thrift stores are loaded with cheap ones, if you don't have one around).

- **A pot.** Use a large pot that holds twelve quarts, large enough to submerge your entire garment. Choose a nonreactive metal, such as stainless steel or ceramic ware. Iron, copper, and aluminum pots can affect the color of your dye.

- **Tongs**

- **Measuring cups and spoons**

- **Gloves**

- **Vinegar.** Generic distilled vinegar is fine!

- **Binder clips.** Easy to find at big-box stores and office stores, these will create a darker green / black pattern around the folds.

- **Strainer**

DIRECTIONS

1. Fill your pot with your onion skins and cover three-quarters of the way up with warm water.

2. Boil your onion skins for one hour. The longer you boil, the darker your dye will become. Monitor every twenty minutes until the dye is at the level of saturation that you would like! You should note that when the garment is wet, it will be three shades darker than when dried.

3. After the hour is up or your dye is sufficiently dark, strain out your onion skins (it's okay if there are some left in the pot) but leave the water. This will make it easier for you to submerge the garment in your pot.

4. To create the tie-dye effect, fold your garment like an accordion and bind it with your binder clips. There's no right way to do this, so have a little fun! Each garment will turn out differently!

5. Soak your bound-up garment in vinegar in a separate container with your binder clips attached for thirty minutes—this will cause the clips to rust and create a cool pattern around them on your garment!

6. Next, submerge your garment with the clips into the pot of water and dye and leave it for at least two hours on low heat.

7. Remove your garment with tongs. It will be hot! Rinse off with cold water until it's cool enough to handle, and remove the clips.

8. Open up your garment and let it air-dry overnight. Once it's dry, iron on a high heat setting on both sides to set the dye.

9. Wear your new naturally dyed piece with love! Hand washing is recommended to prevent fading, and use a pH neutral soap to help preserve your piece for longer.

HOW TO REVIVE A CULTURE OF REPAIR

I've only scratched the surface of the universe of repair, maintenance, and DIYing that exists out in the world. I encourage you to keep learning and exploring. Let's make it our mission to revive mending and commonsense laundry techniques and to encourage DIYing in our communities, so that fixing clothes and making them our own is the norm. Here are some ideas to make it happen:

- **Share skills.** If you have repair knowledge, skills, or supplies, make it your mission to share with those around you. If you know someone who wants to learn a running stitch or how to darn, take the time to sit down and teach them.

- **Organize a repair café.** Another idea is to organize a pop-up repair café event for your campus or community. Ask skilled volunteers to repair clothes and share know-how and supplies for free.

- **Start sewing circles.** Start a mending or sewing circle or monthly event in your neighborhood, where folks can get together to work on their repair or DIY projects, socialize, and teach others.

- **Start sewing classes, schools, and permanent repair shops.** If you have the resources, start up a permanent sewing school or repair shop in your neighborhood.

- **Offer repairs to your customers.** If you run a boutique or a brand, offer affordable repairs.

- **Start an upcycled or DIY fashion line.** Show the world that broken is beautiful and that customized, DIY clothes can be even more cutting-edge and creative than store-bought fashion.

Reinvent Your Wardrobe with Visible Mending

Q&A with Kate Sekules, Clothing Historian
and Founder of VisibleMending.com

ELIZABETH: You're an expert mender who's also researching the history of mending. How long have humans been mending clothes?

KATE: The history of mending is as old as clothes. What most people don't realize is that, for most of our history, clothes were the most valuable things that any normal person owned. So people had to keep them going because they were terribly costly and they were handmade.

ELIZABETH: When did common knowledge of mending start to die out?

KATE: Even after clothes began to be mass-produced starting in the late 1900s, they were still expensive. So you might have more of them, but you would still need to repair yours, especially if you weren't very rich. By the 1980s [when clothing prices started to drop], most people weren't mending anymore.

ELIZABETH: Why should we mend now when we can just go out and buy something new so inexpensively?

KATE: I feel very strongly about valuing not just our clothes but all of the possessions we share our life with. And there's nothing more intimate than clothes.... One thing I love about mending is that you bond with your clothes; you put this little bit of yourself into it, and then it's really yours and no one else has one like it. It's not just fixed, but it's made into something new.

ELIZABETH: You're one of the creators of what's known as "visible mending." What is visible mending, and how is this different from regular old mending?

KATE: Visible mending is a repair that you can see [typically by using either fabric or thread in a contrasting color to draw attention to the mend]. The point of visible mending is that you're declaring that you are somebody who tends and repairs things. You're saying that without speaking.

ELIZABETH: So there's no pressure for it to look perfect?

KATE: There's no pressure and no rules. My daughter, who doesn't sew, just did a mend and she didn't plan; she just started sewing. And it came out so brilliant.

ELIZABETH: What is the easiest visible-mending technique?

KATE: The most used visible-mending technique is where you just cut out a piece of fabric to make a patch, you put it on top of the hole, and you stitch back and forth, back and forth, back and forth, with a running stitch and with contrasting thread. Anyone can do this repair once they can do a running stitch.

ELIZABETH: What do people think when they see you wearing something with a visible mend? Do they comment?

KATE: Yeah, sometimes they think it's a designer thing! For example, my husband, Scott, had a really holey sweater, and I darned all over it without really thinking—everyone seemed to love it.

ELIZABETH: I find mending to be exciting even when it doesn't come out great.

KATE: Yes, it immediately just makes you feel good. It's a little mysterious why, but it never fails. I just don't remember a single person who hasn't been delighted with their first mend.

ELIZABETH: What would you say to someone who is nervous or thinks they can't learn how to mend?

KATE: Think about that garment. What would happen to it if you didn't mend it? It would go to waste. So you're not going to ruin it. If it's something really valuable to you, then maybe practice a bit, have a plan. But if it's just clothes, then you can always unpick it. It's not permanent. If you don't like what you did, start over or put another patch over the top. There's really nothing you can do to screw it up except not do it.

PART SIX

The Fashion Revolution

**Clothes won't change
the world;
the women who wear
them will.**

—ANNE KLEIN

Welcome to the Fashion Revolution

By this point in the book, you've made incredible changes to the way you buy, wear, and care for clothes. You've harnessed your individual power to reduce your consumption, support better brands, and minimize your footprint on the planet. Now, the bigger fight to fix fashion depends on our coming together to build a movement for change.

You are now part of one of the longest-running and most successful social movements in human history—the fashion revolution. Clothing has been at the very center of the struggle to humanize and democratize society for generations, going back to the abolition of slavery, the rise of labor unions, and campaigns that led to minimum wages and the establishment of the weekend. Clothes—and the people who design them, make them, wear them, and love them—can be a revolutionary tool for social change.

We know from our own history that it's possible to transform bad jobs and dangerous industries into dignified ones. It happened on American soil. The 1911 Triangle Shirtwaist Factory fire killed 146 garment workers, mostly young women, in New York City, and spurred a decades-long movement for workplace rights. Fast-forward to the 1970s, and sweatshops existed only on the margins of the US garment industry.[1] Union garment shops weren't an anomaly. They were the norm! Progress didn't happen organically. Consumers, workers, factory owners, elected leaders, and brands got together and organized to create a more just and fair fashion industry in the United States.

MY FASHION ACTIVISM STORY

I have been a fashion activist since I was fourteen years old, when I first found out that some of my favorite clothing companies, like Gap and Nike, were using sweatshops in Central America and Indonesia. This was in the mid-1990s. I couldn't believe that these brands, which were the epitome of cool to my young mind, were connected to exploitation. Globalization was kicking into high gear and American garment and textile factories, including those in my home state of Georgia, were getting packed up, closed down, and moved to the developing world. But our hard-won labor rights and environmental standards were not extended to these new fashion workers. Time moved backward. Sweatshops returned.

In the late 1990s, the American public rallied around the sweatshop problem. Actress Jennifer Love Hewitt led an anti-sweatshop protest on the popular teen show *Party of Five.* President Bill Clinton established a presidential task force on sweatshops. One of the recommendations (one that's yet to be realized) was the simple and brilliant idea of a government-approved "no sweat" certification label that would verify that clothes sold to consumers were made under safe and fair conditions. The US Department of Labor even launched an educational campaign against sweatshops for youth groups and schools called Getta Clue.[2]

In 1998, I left for college and was swept up in a wave of powerful student-led anti-sweatshop activism. It was one of the biggest social movements of my generation. That year, United Students Against Sweatshops launched and one hundred campuses across the country established chapters, including mine: Syracuse University.[3] Our goal was simple: to demand that clothing bearing college logos be made in sweatshop-free working conditions.

The anti-sweatshop movement was organized and tireless, and we got things done. Across the country, schools held teach-ins to educate fellow students, staged sit-ins in the offices of our campus administrators, wrote op-eds for newspapers, inundated brands with letters and phone calls, and threw rowdy demonstrations when we needed to. Along with some activist pals, I hung a giant hand-painted banner that read I GRADUATED FROM SWEATSHOP UNIVERSITY off the balcony during a basketball game (that's a big deal at a school like Syracuse).

Directly in response to nationwide campaigning, college students won huge victories: It became commonplace for major brands making university apparel to abide by a strict code of conduct regarding labor rights and workplace safety, to publicly list the names and locations of their factories, and to agree to independent monitoring of factories by an outside labor rights group, the Worker Rights Consortium (WRC). To date, the WRC has won 50 million dollars in back wages for garment workers around the world. You'll hear from Scott Nova, the WRC's executive director, later in Part Six. By 2000, *The New York Times* was reporting on noticeable improvements in overseas factories, including safer workplaces and reduced working hours, in response to our highly "vocal anti-sweatshop movement."[4]

What I learned from my time in the anti-sweatshop movement is this: Grassroots, sustained campaigns for change work. Social movements *work*.

RANA PLAZA CHANGED EVERYTHING

Despite the gains of the late twentieth century, it wasn't long before the world changed again. For a decade, the global sweatshop problem mostly flew under the radar. Brands promised they were improving working conditions by monitoring themselves. Western consumers went on with their lives. Many people assumed factories were getting safer, better. *I* assumed things were getting better. The fashion activist movement almost died out.

The façade crumbled on April 24, 2013, when an eight-story building in the capital of Bangladesh fell down, trapping and crushing thousands of seamstresses and workers making clothes for well-known retailers and brands. Rana Plaza was the deadliest and one of the most appalling tragedy in fashion's history, with 1,133 killed and thousands more critically injured. When Rana Plaza came down, people around the world woke up to the fact that sweatshops are alive and well—and that it was long past time to put the great big machine of social progress into motion again. Workers marched and protested in Bangladesh, demanding humane working conditions and reparations for the families of the dead. Globally, millions of citizens signed petitions, wrote letters to brands, and peacefully protested in front of companies that source from Bangladesh, demanding action. A global activist organization called Fashion Revolution launched to organize people to fight for transparency and fairness in fashion.

These renewed efforts paid off: Bangladesh's garment workers saw a near doubling of their wages in 2013 (and are at the time of this writing striking for better pay). And more than two hundred brands and retailers signed a historic workplace safety agreement, called the Accord on Fire and Building Safety in Bangladesh, which has led to dramatic safety improvements in more than 1,660 factories, including workplace-safety training, fire-safety equipment, and even structurally overhauling buildings. The accord has helped to protect the lives of more than 2 million workers to date.[5]

Fashion has the potential to combine different movements, including sustainability, living wages, gender equality, and racial justice, into one globe-spanning force for positive change. And the victories of the labor rights movement of the last two centuries can provide a powerful template for how we can come together to achieve our common goals. With the fashion revolution reignited again, progress won't burn out, as long as we commit to keeping it aflame. In Part Six: "The Fashion Revolution," you'll learn how to start a conversation with brands, hold those in power accountable, put fashion on the agenda of our elected leaders, and join organizations and campaigns making change. You'll also hear from labor rights experts as they talk about their fashion activism journey and how we can work together to end sweatshops, promote social justice, and halt the destruction of our environment for good. With a range of tools and tactics at your disposal, I know you'll discover a way to join the fashion movement that speaks to you.

Where Are You Wearing?

Do you know where this garment comes from—before Old Navy?

—TIM GUNN

Sewing clothes is one of the most common jobs on the planet. The seams on your shirt, the buttons on your jacket, and the hem on your pants, they were all put there by a garment worker. There are an estimated 60 to 75 million garment, textile, and footwear workers around the world today, working in dozens of countries.[1] How can we possibly know what these workers' lives are like, when we're often separated by oceans, language, and culture? It begins by looking at the labels on just a few pieces of clothing in your closet.

Inside your clothes, you'll notice the "made in" label, and you'll start to notice patterns of production. You'll see countries like China, Bangladesh, Vietnam, Indonesia, and India, as Asian countries are where the bulk of our clothes are made. You might also see pieces made in Mexico, Romania, or even Turkey, other garment-producing hotspots. Here's a little more about what it's like to work making your clothes in some of the world's top and most well-known garment-exporting countries; you can also continue your investigation online.

MADE IN CHINA

It is the most ubiquitous "made in" label we buy, found on everything from mattresses and dishes to televisions and toys. Though the garment industry is slowly decamping for lower-cost countries, China is still the largest clothing manufacturer and churns out a third of what the world wears. More than 6 million people work in the Chinese garment and textile industry, which exports 145 billion dollars' worth of apparel and footwear annually.[2] Workers are fighting hard for their rights, and wages have risen in recent years following protests and strikes for better conditions. Chinese garment workers earn the most among Asian countries, at close to 600 dollars a month on the high end in urban areas, but pay varies widely from place to place.[3] And workers do not have meaningful rights to organize unions. Known for decades as a land of sweatshops and cheaply made products, China's manufacturing landscape has evolved dramatically. Some (but far from all) garment and textile workers in China now earn a living wage.[4] Sustainable innovation and ethical production are on the rise, and there's growth in conscious-fashion brands, including American company Everlane, sourcing from here. Redress Hong Kong, Asia's first environmental fashion NGO, is one organization pushing sustainable fashion into the mainstream through its annual Redress Design Award and Frontline Fashion documentary series.

MADE IN BANGLADESH

Bangladesh is the world's second-largest garment manufacturer, employing more than 4 million people in an industry worth 30 billion dollars a year.[5] H&M and the VF Corporation, which owns Vans, the North Face, Timberland, and many other brands, are two of the many well-known clothing companies sourcing from Bangladeshi factories. The 2013 Rana Plaza factory collapse thrust the country into the international spotlight and has led to safety improvements. But the Bangladesh accord hasn't shielded workers from the pressure to keep wages low. Bangladesh's garment workers are among the lowest paid in the world, earning a base minimum wage of 95 dollars a month as of 2019, less than a quarter of a living wage.[6] At the time of this writing, workers are protesting for an almost doubling of wages and are being met with police violence and repression. There are growing ethical and sustainable initiatives coming out of Bangladesh, however. Swallows, a fair-trade worker-owned cooperative in rural northwest Bangladesh, manufactures for conscious brands like People Tree. And a few large companies, like G-Star Raw, are working toward a 100 percent sustainable supply chain and fair wages with the growing number of progressive and sustainable Bangladeshi factories.[7]

MADE IN INDIA

India's deep-rooted garment and textile trades employ a staggering 16 million people (45 million if you count those working in the cotton industry and informal sectors) and export 40 billion dollars' worth of goods.[8] Many Indian workers face forced overtime and pervasive sexual harassment with limited legal protections, and unionization is almost nonexistent.[9] As I mentioned in Chapter 18 (on fibers and textiles) child labor and forced labor are common in India's cotton industry. Pay varies greatly from region to region, but a typical garment worker wage is around 130 dollars a month, less than half a living wage, according to Asia Floor Wage calculations.[10] Progress is being made, however. In 2017, India made a significant advancement by ratifying International Labour Organization conventions banning the worst forms of child labor. India has a long tradition of artisanship, decorative textiles, and small-scale cotton farming and is home to a growing number of fair-trade, artisan, and ethical fashion initiatives. For example, Sudara is a made-in-India brand providing job and skills training to survivors of sex trafficking, MetaWear RESET supports India's tribal cotton farmers using regenerative agriculture techniques, and textile company Pratibha Syntex is setting the bar for sustainable textile manufacturing, by running a solar-powered, low-waste factory and partnering with organic farmers.

MADE IN VIETNAM

Vietnam's garment industry is quickly expanding and is now one of the largest in the world. There are an estimated 3.5 million garment and textile workers in Vietnam, and exports of apparel-related products have reached 36 billion dollars a year.[11] The country is best known for manufacturing outdoor gear, activewear, and shoes, with Nike employing more than 450,000 people there.[12] Vietnam's communist government forbids independent labor unions, and, according to the labor rights nonprofit Fair Wear Foundation, excessive and unpaid overtime plagues the garment industry.[13] The minimum wage recently increased to a high of 171 dollars a month but remains below 60 percent of a living wage.[14] Signs of progress include a 2018 trade deal between the European Union and Vietnam that comes with labor rights and environmental stipulations and could bring a much-needed ethical boost to the supply chain. There are also examples of cutting-edge sustainable production, such as the solar-run, LEED-certified Saitex factory, which manufactures for Madewell, Outerknown, G-Star, Everlane, and Amazon at the time of this writing.[15]

MADE IN CAMBODIA

There are more than seven hundred thousand workers in Cambodia's 7-billion-dollar garment industry.[16] Major brands, from H&M and

Gap to Nike and Puma, source from here. Working conditions are a bit better than in most of Southeast Asia. Minimum wages have almost tripled in the past five years, and the country is home to a vocal and organized labor movement. Despite progress, the current minimum wage of 182 dollars a month amounts to half of a living wage, based on Asia Floor Wage calculations.[17] At the time of this writing, government crackdowns against striking garment workers are increasing again.

MADE IN THE USA

Less than 3 percent of the clothing purchased in the United States is made domestically, down from half in 1990. And a Made in USA garment is no longer a guarantee of ethical working conditions. There are two sides of the garment industry that remain in the United States: New York's storied Garment Center, known for skilled work for higher-end brands, has dwindled to five thousand workers but is still hanging on.[18] The largest part of the business has moved to Los Angeles, where there are roughly forty-five thousand garment workers, many of them undocumented immigrants toiling in sweatshop conditions. A 2016 US Labor Department investigation of LA's factories found that 85 percent of inspected factories violated labor laws. Workers are being paid as little as 4 dollars an hour sewing clothes for well-known fashion brands, including Forever 21, Fashion Nova, Ross Dress for Less, and T.J.Maxx.[19] The Garment Worker Center, an LA-based workers' rights organization, is campaigning for better conditions for LA's garment workers, including 800,000 dollars in back wages owed to them by Ross Dress for Less.

While US garment workers are some of the highest paid in the world by dollar amount, they earn far less than a living wage. There is another picture emerging: Many conscious brands based in the

United States could help revive sweat-free manufacturing. Eileen Fisher produces 25 percent of its clothing in the United States and has living wages as part of its code of conduct.[20] Reformation, which makes about a quarter of its products in its own LA factory, has set a goal to reach a living wage for its factory workers in 2019.[21] Elizabeth Suzann, a popular Nashville-based slow-fashion brand (slow fashion refers to high-quality, timeless clothes made in small batches), pays double the state's minimum wage.[22] Conscious brands are in a strong position to create a hub of ethical manufacturing wherever they operate.

MADE IN ITALY

"Made in Italy" is synonymous with old-world craftsmanship and quality. The country is a fashion and textile-making powerhouse and home to many famous luxury brands, including Armani, Dolce & Gabbana, Prada, Valentino, and Versace. The luxury trade makes up an estimated 5 percent of Italy's GDP and employs nearly half a million people.[23] But the global race to the bottom has taken its toll here, too. A 2018 investigation by *The New York Times* found that thousands of homeworkers in Italy are sewing garments for luxury brands, earning as little as 1 euro per hour (the equivalent of about 1.15 dollars).[24] What's more, poorly paid Chinese immigrants toil in thousands of factories in Italy's Prato region, churning out clothes for mostly mass-market and fast-fashion brands.[25]

No matter where in the world fashion is produced, it can be made under exploitative conditions or it can be made fairly. As you've learned, garment workers have more in common from place to place—in terms of poor pay and paltry conditions—than they have differences: What binds them together are often long hours, lack of workplace power, and wages that fall far below a decent standard of living. These are problems faced by workers in many sectors of the apparel business and in many other industries. In the next few chapters, we'll dig into how we can help ensure that fairness and decent livelihoods prevail.

Living Wages Now

Perhaps you've heard the argument, the one that says sweat-shops are a necessary evil for economic development and that poverty pay is better than the "alternative." You can find it in our history books and in the columns of leading economists today. These same arguments were used for generations to deny workers their rights in Europe and the United States. But by the early 1900s, a full century ago, many Americans had disavowed themselves of the notion that poverty is a necessity for progress. "No man can be a good citizen unless he has a wage more than sufficient to cover the bare cost of living," noted Teddy Roosevelt in 1910. Around the time that factories moved to the developing world, this age-old argument—that sweatshops are good and necessary—got dusted off and put back into action again.

Fashion is a powerful industry, one that can and should lift people out of poverty rather than trap them in it. It is a multi*trillion*-dollar business, with plenty of wealth to go around. And yet, according to Oxfam, the top fashion CEOs earn in four days what the average garment worker will make in a lifetime.[1] And very few retail workers earn a living wage. It's time for the profits of fashion to be shared equally. The time has come for living wages now.

WHAT IS A LIVING WAGE?

While a sweatshop is marked by illegally long working hours and subpoverty pay, a living wage is a wage set high enough to cover housing, food, transportation, health care, schooling for children, and modest savings for a family. A living wage is what a minimum wage intends to be and is calculated based on the local cost of living in a given country or area.

What does the living wage cost? Not much. Labor is often the smallest part of what we pay for clothing, comprising as little as 2 percent of the retail price. To boost garment workers' wages to a living wage in the developing world would require a modest 1 to 4 percent increase in retail prices, according to research by Murray Ross Hall at the University of Queensland and Thomas Wiedmann of the University of New South Wales.[2] Their research shows that it would cost as little as 20 cents more per T-shirt to pay an Indian garment worker a living wage.

Luckily, we don't have to imagine how a living-wage factory works or what it costs, thanks to Alta Gracia, a Dominican garment factory that's paid living wages since 2010. Alta Gracia manufactures hoodies, sweatshirts, and T-shirts for American collegiate and pro sports teams. The Dallas Cowboys are among its many high-profile customers. Alta Gracia workers earn three times more than the local minimum wage, adding up to 442 dollars a month in extra pay. And yet, to pay these higher wages adds only 90 cents to the cost of a sweatshirt. For less than a dollar more per garment, Alta Gracia's workers can live in dignity.

WHO PAYS THE LIVING WAGE?

Who is responsible for paying these living wages and these higher costs? Some might say it's up to factories and local governments to raise their own wages. But there are just a handful of large global fashion brands controlling most of the apparel market. They have *far* more power over setting prices than factories and even the governments in most developing countries they source from. "Brands and retailers control the market and can move to other countries if wages go up, so they set the price," explains John Kline, a business professor at Georgetown University and coauthor of *Sewing Hope: How One Factory Challenges the Apparel Industry's Sweatshops.*[3] Because low-wage countries are effectively in competition with one another to keep prices down, governments often suppress wages to make their countries attractive to brands, working against their own citizens. This leaves brands and retailers responsible for paying the living wage. But how do we really make it happen?

THE FIVE-STEP PLAN TO MAKE LIVING WAGES A REALITY

While writing *Overdressed,* I had the chance to visit the Alta Gracia factory and was invited to garment workers' homes, so I could see for myself how lives are transformed by decent pay. What's so remarkable about Alta Gracia is how unremarkable it is. It's just a good place to work. Workers take turns playing music over a loudspeaker. They have plenty of time off to spend with their friends and kids. They are able to afford enough food for their families. They're able to live in decent housing with things like lights, plumbing, and running water. They have basic health care. "What I love about Alta Gracia is there's nothing complicated about it," says Sarah Adler-Milstein, a labor activist and coauthor of *Sewing Hope.*[4] Adler-Milstein worked for the Worker Rights Consortium and served as Alta Gracia's labor rights monitor for several years.

Alta Gracia has been a huge success, too. Its products are sold in seven hundred school bookstores across the United States. But it's just one factory. While Alta Gracia has room to expand (there's an empty factory right next door), it's important for living wages to be the norm rather than the exception. Here's how we can take the lessons of Alta Gracia and replicate them across the clothing industry:

1. **Establish the living wage in each area.** A living wage is calculated based on the local cost of living essentials like food, rent, transportation, and education. For big brands and retailers that have factories in dozens of countries, it won't be simple, but brands can build on the work done and living-wage calculations made by groups like the Asia Floor Wage Alliance and the Global Living Wage Coalition. From there, brands can increase the price per piece they pay to factories for clothing orders to cover the living wage. They can reduce their profits to pay living wages to retail workers.

2. **Get it in writing.** Alta Gracia is founded on a contractual agreement signed by the Worker Rights Consortium, the factory's union, and the parent company that owns the factory. The contractual, legally binding nature of the agreement ensures that high labor standards are set in stone and everyone shares in the responsibility of keeping the factory going and thriving. The Fair Food Program (which you'll read about in Chapter 29) and the Bangladesh Accord on Fire and Building Safety are other examples of the power of binding agreements.

3. **Establish a union or workers' collective.** Workers are their own best advocates. Each workplace should have a democratically elected workers' group or union that negotiates working conditions, prices, and pay with the factory management and brands.

4. **Appoint third-party inspectors.** A living wage should be verified by an *independent* monitoring organization, such as the Worker Rights Consortium.

5. **Advertise it to consumers.** It's up to brands and retailers whether they pass the living wage cost on to us, the consumers. Retail markup structure can also be changed to make sure that living-wage premiums go directly to workers, instead of increasing profit margins for brands. But many shoppers are happy to pay modest living-wage premiums, as long as they come with a guarantee that the increase is going to workers. Brands should label their product saying it's sweatshop-free and made by workers earning a living wage and make it part of their marketing campaigns!

THE LIVING-WAGE MOVEMENT GOES MAINSTREAM

Living wages have been a rallying cry for decades, and the cause is gaining momentum. Retail and fast food workers in the United States are a few of the groups joining a global movement demanding that workers be paid their fair share of the incredible value and profits they create. H&M made promises to pay a living wage to garment workers by 2017. The date came and went with little progress, but H&M's commitments set off a wave of similar commitments from other brands and opened the door for fashion activists to pressure companies to fulfill living-wage goals. According to Fashion Revolution, thirty-four major brands have made public commitments to paying living wages to workers in the supply chain.[5] Clean Clothes Campaign, International Labor Rights Forum, and Labour Behind the Label are a few of the other activist organizations working to hold brands accountable for their living-wage promises. In the next chapters, you'll meet a few fashion activists and learn more about the organizations and campaigns that you can join to make a difference.

The Small Price to Pay to Ban Sweatshops

Q&A with Scott Nova, Executive Director
of the Worker Rights Consortium

ELIZABETH: What are working conditions like for the people who make our clothes?

SCOTT: Garment workers work all over the world for subpoverty wages. The legal minimum wage in all garment-producing countries is well under what a family needs to live in security and dignity. Workers who try to organize a union are virtually guaranteed to face retaliation. Various kinds of wage theft are common, from underpaying or not paying the minimum wage to not paying workers an overtime premium. And then there's an enormous problem of abusive treatment of workers by supervisors.

ELIZABETH: There are a lot of different countries on the "made in" labels in our clothes. Are there countries where working conditions are better than others?

SCOTT: There are countries where worker protests have pushed up wages some. Cambodia, Indonesia, and China are examples. There are some countries where it's not quite as bad as others in terms of rights to organize. In China and Vietnam, it's illegal to organize an independent union, and those are the two biggest producers of clothing for the US market. But the differences between the countries in terms of respect for labor rights are much less relevant than what they have in common.

ELIZABETH: Give us some good news. What's improved in factories overseas?

SCOTT: There have been modest improvements in certain areas. We see less child labor in the supply chains of major brands and retailers, for example.

ELIZABETH: Why do poverty wages and abusive conditions persist in the garment industry?

SCOTT: It's really quite straightforward. Brands are interested in getting clothing as cheaply and quickly as they can. They have consciously chosen to locate production in countries that do not enforce their labor laws. A factory that scrupulously complied with the labor law, respected the right to organize, paid all required wages, didn't force people to work overtime: That factory will not be able to meet brands' price demands. You can't survive as a supplier unless you operate a sweatshop, because the brands are only willing to pay sweatshop prices.

ELIZABETH: How much more would clothes cost if they were fairly made and workers were paid what they're legally owed?

SCOTT: It would be modestly more expensive. It would vary depending on the country and the product. And to be clear, I'm not saying it would be prohibitively expensive by any stretch of the imagination. You can still make affordable clothing under decent conditions.

ELIZABETH: It's also because all of the promises that brands make to improve conditions are voluntary, right? They don't own the factories; they aren't on the hook for what happens. Can you talk a bit about why voluntary codes of conduct aren't working?

SCOTT: All the brands have codes of conduct, all the factories are monitored over and over again, but by and large that does not lead to improvements. Codes of conduct are unilateral, one-sided promises about what will happen in the supply chain to which the brands cannot be held meaningfully accountable.

ELIZABETH: How exactly is a factory that's monitored by the Worker Rights Consortium different from one that isn't? And how does the WRC improve factory conditions?

SCOTT: The university codes of conduct represented a huge breakthrough. What they meant is that for the first time, the brands' labor rights obligations were a matter of binding contractual obligation. So one difference is that if it's a university factory and workers are seeking to organize a union and management fire the workers, as is typical, they will get reinstated and management will be held accountable for firing them. Another critical difference is if a university factory fails to pay workers money they are legally owed and workers bring a complaint, those workers will get paid.

ELIZABETH: How can we tell if brands are using sweatshops?

SCOTT: Any company needs to be able to answer how much are workers getting paid. Where's the factory? Can workers organize a union? Do they have a union? Are there documents that demonstrate that the building is safe, et cetera?

ELIZABETH: What kind of mechanism could exist to make brands start fulfilling their promises?

SCOTT: The Accord on Fire and Building Safety in Bangladesh has brought about sweeping improvements in safety, in what was the most dangerous country in the world for garment workers. The agreement worked because it is a binding contract between brands and worker representatives, not another batch of unenforceable promises, and because it requires the brands to pay enough to their contract factories so they can afford to operate safely. We need to apply this model across countries and across all labor issues, compelling brands to sign binding contracts that force them to pay a price commensurate with living wages and decent working conditions and that force them to stop doing business with any factory that won't meet these standards. Workers also must be able to organize and bargain.

ELIZABETH: What can we do to help improve working conditions as citizens in our everyday lives?

SCOTT: Brands know that many of their consumers care about human beings and want them to be treated decently and that if a brand is associated with grotesquely abusive conditions, the consumers will turn away from that brand. This gives consumers enormous power, but it is rarely used in an organized fashion. If people want to have an impact, they need to do more than act as individuals; they need to join organizations that are working to hold corporations accountable and support workers, whether it's a union, an anti-sweatshop organization, or a human rights organization.

28

The Campus Activism Playbook

S tudents don't want to hear how bad it is. They always say, 'What can we do?'" says Jason Rhodes, a human geography professor at Kennesaw State University near Atlanta, Georgia, home to a strong student-led fashion activism movement.[1] KSU students take classes on the ethical and environmental impacts of fashion, correspond with Bangladeshi garment workers and academics, and host clothing swaps throughout the semester. They've even launched a campaign to ban sweatshop-made apparel from campus. Students all around the world are participating in the revolution for a more ethical fashion industry. Here are some ideas to get your campus involved:

- **Form a fashion activism group.** Or put fashion on the agenda of an existing campus environmental or labor rights student group. Come up with a name, set up a regular meeting schedule, and develop campaigns and goals for the semester. The agenda is totally up to you! You can look to United Students Against Sweatshops, Fashion Revolution, Clean Clothes Campaign, and the long history of campus activism for campaign ideas. My campus activism group staged sit-ins, wrote op-eds for the campus paper, passed out flyers and petitions, and started a radical cheerleading group that made up our own funny protest cheers, just to give you some ideas.

- **Request classes and independent studies.** For students, ask your favorite professors if they might be interested in teaching about fashion social justice and the environment, and ask them to consider designing a portion of their curriculum or an entire course devoted to the impacts of the fashion industry. Or take your requests to the administration.

- **Banish sweatshop products on campus.** University apparel is big business, and it shouldn't be made under sweatshop conditions. You can establish a local United Students Against Sweatshops chapter on campus. Information is available on the USAS website to get you started. Launch a campaign to have your university affiliated with the Worker Rights Consortium. Or pledge to make your campus fair trade, selling only fair-trade-certified products. You can also ask your campus to source clothes from Alta Gracia, which makes sweatshop-free university apparel.

- **Organize a week of activism and awareness.** Once a year, plan a big week of events to drive your message home. It could be pegged to Fashion Revolution week or Earth Day (both in late April). Pack your week with inspiring and educational activities, such as a documentary film series showing films like *The True Cost,* a hard-hitting investigation into the environmental and social costs of fashion, or *RiverBlue,* an exposé on how fashion is polluting waterways around the world. Invite experts on fashion's impacts to speak, host a campus clothing swap, put on a sustainable-fashion show, or hold a demonstration calling for living wages for garment workers. Ask students to post pictures of their clothing labels to social media, tagging the brand they're wearing and asking #whomademyclothes? Fashion Revolution launched the #whomademyclothes campaign after the Rana Plaza factory collapse. Millions of people have asked brands #whomademyclothes to date, demanding greater transparency and improved worker rights in the fashion supply chain.

29

Road Maps for Making Change

C **ampuses aren't the** only places where change is happening. There are powerful organizations and campaigns already bringing people together to change the fashion industry for the better, from the LA garment workers targeting fast-fashion brands making sweatshop clothes in the United States to Fashion Revolution's viral hashtag campaign, #whomademyclothes. This chapter will provide you with a tool kit for change, including your activist personality type, a list of successful campaigns for social justice in the fashion industry and existing organizations that you can join, and inspiration for how to start your own campaigns.

The Activist Personality Types

You already know whether you're a Minimalist, a Style Seeker, or a Traditionalist, but do you know your activist personality type? Social movements are sustained by all types of people, from creative and practical people and those willing to stand on the front lines, and those who work tirelessly behind the scenes to get things done. Get involved in the fashion movement in a way that fits your strengths and passions. What type of fashion activist are you?

• **The Communicator.** Communicators create and disseminate information about social problems and their solutions. You can organize teach-ins, panels, book clubs, or documentary screenings. You could create your own course, zine, social media posts and stories, YouTube channel, podcast, event series, documentary, book, PhD thesis, research paper, or report.

- **The Advocate.** The advocate creates change through long-term campaigns that pull on the levers of power in government, business, or other dominant institutions. You could join one of the existing human rights, environmental, or labor organizations that I mention in this chapter, or start your own organization. You can design letter-writing, fund-raising, or social media campaigns, or help build a political campaign to elect pro-fashion-movement leaders and put fashion on the legislative agenda.

- **The Artist.** The artist uses creativity and storytelling to make change. This could be through art itself, zine making, culture jamming, slogan tees, videos, creative mending, or whatever else you can imagine. You could become a craftivist, an artist who uses craft-based mediums to get a point across in subtle but thought-provoking ways.

- **The Resister.** The resister pushes progress forward through direct action and by holding brands and institutions accountable in a public way. Resisters don't have to be angry or aggressive; they can join or organize a peaceful march, organize a demonstration in front of a store or company headquarters, pass out flyers or deliver a letter to a store manager or CEO, hang banners and posters in public places, organize a boycott, or look at the generations of history of nonviolent civil disobedience for inspiration.

CAMPAIGNS TO KNOW ABOUT AND JOIN

Luckily, we don't have to imagine what a fashion social movement might look like. There are already a number of successful campaigns in progress that are figuring out how to put pressure where it's needed and achieve the results we're all looking for. Here are just a few campaigns to know about, including some ideas we could borrow for our fashion revolution. I encourage you to come up with your own campaign ideas and organizations.

- **Fashion Revolution and the movement for transparency.** When Rana Plaza collapsed, brands and retailers who sourced from the factory claimed to not know where and how their clothes were made.[1] The transparency movement demands that brands know their entire supply chain and convey that information to the public. Fashion Revolution has been at the forefront of the transparency movement, with its hashtag campaign #whomademyclothes. Fashion Revolution also publishes its groundbreaking *Fashion Transparency Index,* ranking 150 of the biggest global fashion and apparel brands and retailers according to social and environmental disclosure. The good news is that 37 percent of the 150 brands in the *Fashion Transparency Index 2018* are publishing a list of factories and suppliers. Technology firms like Sourcemap are also making it easier for brands to trace their entire supply chain. As a result, transparency is becoming the expectation rather than the exception for fashion.

- **Cities, schools, and sports teams go sweatshop-free.** Large institutions like schools and governments are massive consumers of clothes such as uniforms and logo apparel. The most successful modern anti-sweatshop campaigns have all started by targeting big institutions, starting with the movement on college campuses. There are 45 cities, 7 state governments, and 118 school districts that have adopted sweat-free-sourcing policies through the Sweat-Free Communities movement in the United States. You can get your community or school involved by going to the International Labor Rights Forum's SweatFree Communities website (Sweat Free.org).

- **Crafting new trade deals and electing better leaders.** Our governments have a huge part to play in making fashion a force for good. Government regulates brands, sets standards around climate change, and determines the rules of our trade deals. The United Nations and the European Parliament have both set up working groups to study and set recommendations for the social and environmental impact of fashion. The United States should follow suit. In the United States, the California Transparency in Supply Chains Act, which went into effect in 2012, requires that any company with a turnover of 100 million dollars or more must disclose efforts to prevent human trafficking and slavery in their supply chains. The United Kingdom passed a similar act, the Modern Slavery Act, in 2015. These are all signs of progress.

  I've mentioned ideas for new laws and regulations throughout the book. Here are a few more: Let's get diverse pro-worker, pro-environment people into office. We can lobby for better trade pacts (like a pro-worker, pro-union revision of NAFTA) with strong workers' rights and wage-floor provisions, and punishments for companies that use forced or sweatshop labor. This not only would benefit workers overseas but would help domestic industries compete as well. We can pass laws that ban the importation of sweatshop goods (goods made below a living-wage threshold) and hold brands legally accountable for what happens in their supply chains, including factories and farms. We can also revoke charters for corporations that continuously harm society or the environment.

- **Creating a pool of certified living-wage factories.** We might also resurrect the idea of designated supplier pools of living-wage factories. A decade ago, the Worker Rights Consortium was working toward creating a pool of precertified living wage factories for brands to source from. The idea can be revived to banish sweatshops and finally give consumers the sweatshop-free label they are looking for.

- **Taking inspiration from the tomato workers.** The Coalition of Immokalee Workers fights for the rights of American farmworkers. The CIW's landmark Fair Food Program established a legally binding agreement between Florida's tomato workers and the Florida Tomato Growers Exchange, which supplies huge companies like Whole Foods, Burger King, and Walmart.[2] The initiative requires retailers to pay a mere penny more per pound for Fair Food tomatoes to support the program's code of workplace conduct. The agreement has collected 26 million dollars in fair food premiums since 2011 that go back to workers and the Fair Food Program. Read more about the campaign at FairFoodProgram.org.

- **Internet and online activism.** Social media and the Internet are fast, free, and powerful ways to spread information about the fashion revolution around the world. A photo or video of a small demonstration, an online petition, or a powerful quote or simple fact can be shared online, amplifying its impact many times over and giving people a meaningful way to participate in change. Hashtags can also be leveraged to powerful ends. The hashtag #burnberry, which went viral on Twitter in 2018, helped to encourage the luxury brand Burberry to stop destroying its unsold products. Social media also gives us unprecedented and immediate access to brands. It means that we can hold them accountable in our spare moments by simply tweeting at them or dropping them a comment telling them what we care about, whether it's climate change, gender equality, living wages, diversity, inclusivity—or all of the above! As the #burnberry and #whomademyclothes hashtag campaigns highlight, Internet activism is most effective when it's coordinated. Together we are stronger.

- **Hold celebrities accountable.** With many celebrities launching their own clothing lines (many touting feminist values), it's time to expect that these values extend to the workers sewing, modeling, and retailing celebrity-endorsed products. Let's encourage and pressure celebrities to use their influence to fight for inclusion and workers' rights and to ethically and sustainably source their fashion collections.

FASHION ACTIVISM GROUPS TO KNOW ABOUT AND JOIN

We can build on existing momentum by joining any number of long-standing groups working for labor and environmental justice. Joining an activist organization doesn't have to be a huge, all-encompassing commitment: You can sign online petitions, share campaign updates via social media, help get out the word for actions and demonstrations, make small donations or help fund-raise. If a thousand readers donated 10 dollars each to one of these organizations, we'd raise 10,000 dollars for the fashion revolution. Here are a few fashion activism groups looking to expand their ranks:

- **Clean Clothes Campaign.** This grassroots nongovernmental organization is dedicated to improving working conditions for garment workers around the world. They are currently campaigning for minimum-wage increases in Bangladesh, pressuring H&M to fulfill its living-wage promises, and fighting to protect the Bangladesh Accord on Fire and Building Safety.

- **Fashion Revolution.** This massive open-source activist movement, with headquarters in the United Kingdom and affiliates in more than one hundred countries, mobilizes everyday citizens through educational fanzines, advocacy, and their annual Fashion Revolution Week, held on the anniversary of the Rana Plaza building collapse in April. Fashion Revolution is also the creator of the #haulternative campaign, where YouTubers post haul-shopping videos with swapped, secondhand, mended, and upcycled clothing. Fashion Revolution has graciously supplied its manifesto, a set of ultra-inspirational demands for changing the fashion industry. Read it at the end of this chapter and sign the Fashion Revolution Manifesto online!

- **Garment Worker Center.** This Los Angeles–based nonprofit organizes immigrant labor working in the city's sweatshops and campaigns to raise wages and make LA sweatshop-free. Since 2016, the Garment Worker Center has focused on its Ross Exploits campaign, fighting for back pay and against illegally low wages in factories sewing clothes for Ross Dress for Less.

- **Greenpeace.** This global environmental justice organization advocates for change across a wide breadth of issues impacting the planet. Since 2012, they've tackled chemical usage in the fashion industry with their Detox campaign.

- **International Labor Rights Forum.** This Washington, DC–based nonprofit advocates for better working conditions and labor rights around the world. In addition to SweatFree Communities, they are also fighting child and forced labor in the cotton industry and helping Bangladeshi workers protect the Accord on Fire and Building Safety.

- **Labour Behind the Label.** This UK-based anti-sweatshop campaign works directly with garment workers to improve working conditions around the world. Their campaigns at the time of this writing are living wages for garment workers, a workplace-safety campaign, and a campaign targeting unsafe and toxic conditions for footwear workers.

- **United Students Against Sweatshops.** This student-run organization fights for fair labor in the global garment industry, with more than 150 college campuses involved. USAS leads demonstrations against inhumane working conditions, mainly in factories that produce collegiate and university apparel. If you're a student or faculty member, you can start a USAS chapter on your campus.

KEEPING THE FASHION REVOLUTION AFLAME

In many countries around the world, the apparel industry is *the* top employer. Retail stores in the United States, many of them clothing stores, employ one in ten workers. Clothing provides livelihoods to cashiers, merchandisers, product designers, leather workers, pattern makers, wool and cotton farmers, and countless others. And that doesn't even touch the bloggers, models, magazine editors, designers, and influencers who are firmly linked in our minds with the world of fashion. All of those people are indispensable to fashion and deserve representation, fair wages, and safe, healthy working conditions. In the following pages you'll read an interview with Sarah Adler-Milstein, coauthor of *Sewing Hope*. She will talk more in depth about what it will take to finally banish sweatshops and create a clothing industry that's empowering for everyone involved. I've also included a list of additional organizations, books, videos, and resources at the end of the book so you can continue to seek out the subjects within fashion that interest you. I hope you now feel like you have the tools to join the fashion revolution and help fashion reach it's full and fair potential. Our actions as consumers matter, but coming together and using our voices as citizens is key to lasting and widespread change.

The Conscious Closet

MANIFESTO
FOR A FASHION REVOLUTION

#1 Fashion provides dignified work, from conception to creation to catwalk. It does not enslave, endanger, exploit, overwork, harass, abuse or discriminate against anyone. Fashion liberates worker and wearer and empowers everyone to stand up for their rights.

#2 Fashion provides fair and equal pay. It enriches the livelihood of everyone working across the industry, from farm to shop floor. Fashion lifts people out of poverty, creates thriving societies and fulfils aspiration.

#3 Fashion gives people a voice, making it possible to speak up without fear, join together in unity without repression and negotiate for better conditions at work and across communities.

#4 Fashion respects culture and heritage. It fosters, celebrates and rewards skills and craftsmanship. It recognises creativity as its strongest asset. Fashion never appropriates without giving due credit or steals without permission. Fashion honours the artisan.

#5 Fashion stands for solidarity, inclusiveness and democracy, regardless of race, class, gender, age, shape or ability. It champions diversity as crucial for success.

#6 Fashion conserves and restores the environment. It does not deplete precious resources, degrade our soil, pollute our air and water or harm our health. Fashion protects the welfare of all living things and safeguards our diverse ecosystems.

#7 Fashion never unnecessarily destroys or discards but mindfully redesigns and recuperates in a circular way. Fashion is repaired, reused, recycled and upcycled. Our wardrobes and landfills do not overflow with clothes that are coveted but not cherished, bought but not kept.

#8 Fashion is transparent and accountable. Fashion embraces clarity and does not hide behind complexity nor rely upon trade secrets to derive value. Anyone, anywhere can find out how, where, by whom and under what conditions their clothing is made.

#9 Fashion measures success by more than just sales and profits. Fashion places equal value on financial growth, human wellbeing and environmental sustainability.

#10 Fashion lives to express, delight, reflect, protest, comfort, commiserate and share. Fashion never subjugates, denigrates, degrades, marginalises or compromises. Fashion celebrates life.

SIGN THE MANIFESTO

Join the call for a #FashionRevolution. Let us rise up together and turn this dream into reality!

www.fashionrevolution.org/manifesto

Stronger Together—The Role of Organizations in Fashion Activism

Q&A with Sarah Adler-Milstein, Coauthor of Sewing Hope: How One Factory Challenges the Apparel Industry's Sweatshops

ELIZABETH: I read in *Sewing Hope* that you used to draw fashion design sketches as a kid. What do you love about fashion?

SARAH: It's a really fun form of expression. I really, really enjoy fashion, and that's part of why I wish the industry was different and better.

ELIZABETH: What prompted you to become a fashion activist?

SARAH: My very first introduction to sweatshops was in middle school. The Internet was new; it was hot off the presses, and very exciting. I landed in my Internet searches on information about sweatshops. Particularly in the nineties, there were all of these scandals with Kathie Lee Gifford and Gap saying their clothes were made in the USA and were produced in Saipan under all sorts of abusive conditions. It totally horrified me that these shirts and sweatshirts that I saw every day were linked to these horrible abuses.

ELIZABETH: You worked in Latin America monitoring garment factories from 2008 to 2012. What's the most disturbing thing you saw?

SARAH: The amount of harsh, often violent retaliation that workers would face just for speaking out and trying to organize unions was the hardest to see. That was on top of really harsh working conditions on the factory floor, of workers getting screamed at, yelled at, locked inside factories for long hours. In a lot of cases, once workers organized, they were fired and blacklisted and couldn't get jobs. So getting blacklisted is basically economic violence in that people are not able to find work again.

ELIZABETH: Are the conditions you're describing a rare thing? Or are sweatshops still the norm?

SARAH: Sweatshops are the norm. It's not a couple of bad actors. It's the industry as a whole. And so when people ask me what brands are any worse than any others, it's hard for me to answer because honestly they're all producing from the same factories and all of the factories are paying poverty wages.

ELIZABETH: One thing that I think is important to note is you can go into a sweatshop and it often doesn't look like what we think a sweatshop looks like. There aren't people chained to their sewing machines. But something more insidious is happening in that they're working incredibly long hours almost every day of the week and still can't afford to live. So it's a trap.

SARAH: One visual that really drives this home is you go to many factories on payday and you will see lines of loan sharks, because after working six or even seven days a week and working really long hours, the garment workers have still not made enough money and they have to borrow money in order to pay their rent or put food on the table. Their paycheck ends up going to loan sharks because they get so desperate.

ELIZABETH: What really upsets me is when this type of poverty pay is happening in factories that make clothes from brands that make billions in dollars of profit per year.

SARAH: Yes! And the difference in what it would cost for people to not have to make these kinds of choices between paying rent and putting food on the table is less than a dollar per garment. Why in the world would any company choose every day to prioritize their profits and paying the lowest price possible over ending that kind of human suffering? Especially when it's not complicated or unaffordable to fix it.

ELIZABETH: The fashion industry relies on a type of self-policing called corporate social responsibility, which started up back in the late 1990s. Brands hire these private companies to monitor their factories, and the brands fund these inspections and the organizations that monitor them. It just seems like a massive conflict of interest.

SARAH: Absolutely. Any monitoring organization or industry initiative that's funded primarily through the brands and retailers, I feel very suspect about the credibility of those findings. There is a long history of using corporate social responsibility programs primarily as public relations instead of really trying to address the root causes. So much money goes toward what's called the corporate social responsibility. But if that money went directly into workers' wages or actual safety programs, it would be money far better spent.

ELIZABETH: You worked for the Worker Rights Consortium and were the labor rights monitor for Alta Gracia, a living-wage garment factory, for years. Can brands replicate what Alta Gracia has done?

SARAH: Absolutely. In fact, Alta Gracia had the hardest path imaginable toward setting up a living-wage factory. They had to set up a completely new factory. They had to set up a brand. If you already have a running factory, if you already have an established brand, if you already have a design team and the supply chain, all of that is going to be way easier.

ELIZABETH: Why is it the brand's responsibility to pay the living wage? Shouldn't a factory just pay the workers more?

SARAH: Where the money lies and where the power lies and the ability to change prices is all with the brands and the retailers. It's not a normal supply-and-demand situation where a factory says what they're willing to produce at and the brand pays it. The brands and the retailers set the price and if the factories don't want to produce at the price, then they'll go out of business.

ELIZABETH: Where do we begin to solve the sweatshop problem?

SARAH: A great place to start is in universities, where it would be so easy right now just to say they would designate 20 or 30 percent of their floor space in university bookstores to Alta Gracia, a living-wage, union, and independently verified sweat-free label. It would help Alta Gracia grow and encourage other retailers to step up and do their own versions of what Alta Gracia has done.

ELIZABETH: For people who want to follow in your footsteps and become a fashion activist, where should they start?

SARAH: The first thing to do is to join an organization, like the International Labor Rights Forum, United Students Against Sweatshops, and the Clean Clothes Campaign. They have all been incredibly effective at leveraging collective action to really move some of the biggest brands and retailers in the right direction. You can donate to organizations; you can show up to actions; you can sign letters. There's a million ways, big and small, that you can make a difference, and doing it through an organization is the best way to make sure that your impact is multiplied.

ELIZABETH: How long until we see living wages and the end of sweatshops?

SARAH: Before slavery was abolished, at any point you could have said, How long is it going to take? I think ultimately it just takes enough of a committed core of people who are willing to say that this is no longer acceptable to take action to change it. The collective will has to be strong enough to hold brands and retailers accountable. There was a point where sweatshops were all but abolished here in the United States. I know it's possible because it's been done before.

Conclusion

A fresh generation of women are marching for revolution, and they want to wear clothes that tell a new story.

—NAOMI KLEIN

About eight years ago, I finished writing *Overdressed*. I cleaned out my closet, dropped my clothes off at a charity, and wondered what would happen next. Where would I shop? What would I wear? What would the world think of my little treatise against fast fashion? It turns out that many people are looking for a new and more fulfilling approach to clothing, and I immediately found myself in great company. Soon enough, my life started to change for the better in both small and all-encompassing ways. I think yours will too, and the process has likely already begun.

Almost everyone will tell you that it's exciting and satisfying to build a conscious closet. Being mindful about clothes connects you to new people, ideas, and places around the world and can open up a wellspring of passion and resourcefulness that we don't often get to feel from what we wear. Eight years ago, I couldn't have imagined that I would learn how to darn (and love it) or that I'd relish knowing the differences between fabrics like angora, alpaca, and acrylic. It feels good to know clothes. It feels good to truly know what you're wearing, where it was made, and about the lives of the people who made it.

But it also makes a difference. There is no such thing as a perfectly ethical or sustainable clothing choice or closet. The reality we live in is too complex and multifaceted for that. But it is important and meaningful to make clothing choices that come from a place of greater responsibility to other people and to the environment, even if those choices aren't always perfect. I can't think of a more influential and *necessary* human enterprise than clothing, or one with a bigger potential for positive impact. By buying less, sharing more, choosing sustainably, and acting together, we really can change the world. I've crunched the numbers and done the research, and these are the areas where our actions matter most and can add up to seismic impacts.

Conscious fashion really does look as great as it feels, too. If you've read *Overdressed,* you know that I was once a bit of a fashion victim. I chased trends and shopped on impulse, and it led me further and further away from my personal style. Approaching fashion as a mindful process will over time help you dress better, look better, and feel better in your clothes. I have built a high-quality and one-of-a-kind wardrobe that I deeply cherish. I have a strong sense of personal style that's truly all my own. I've had to work for it, learning to repair pieces, doing my homework on brands and designers, and looking for ways to save money. But that effort, that mindfulness, is what makes it possible to say, "I love my clothes."

I can't wait to hear from all of you about your conscious-closet journey. I hope you've started to discover the incredible benefits of this process, from finding your personal style and building a gorgeous and unique wardrobe that fits your ethics and your values, to being part of a global movement for change. Please share your victories, setbacks, and transformations with one another and with me. There are additional resources in the following pages as well, so you can continue to learn and connect with the many other people and organizations in the conscious-fashion universe.

Our seemingly small everyday actions have so much power. But it's when we use our voices in concert that we can shake the foundations *of* power. It's so important to advocate for widespread change so that ethical and sustainable fashion becomes the way of the world. Climate change and inequality are critical, as are many other social problems. But our collective will to solve these problems is greater than ever. Almost everyone I know is thinking about how they can do better, get more involved, and make a more positive impact on this planet. People are deeply rethinking how they live and what they value. And our clothing is at the center of it all.

RESOURCES

ANTI-SLAVERY INTERNATIONAL
A human rights organization working to free people from all forms of slavery across the world.

ASIA FLOOR WAGE ALLIANCE
An international alliance of trade unions and labor rights activists that set living wage standards for Asian garment workers.

CANOPY
A nonprofit working with the forest industry's biggest customers, including the fashion industry, to protect endangered forests.

CENTRE FOR FASHION DIVERSITY AND SOCIAL CHANGE
Research center focused on fostering diversity, equity, and inclusion in fashion.

CLEAN CLOTHES CAMPAIGN
A grassroots global alliance campaigning for the rights of garment workers.

COMMON OBJECTIVE
A platform that connects professionals looking to create positive impact through business.

COPENHAGEN FASHION SUMMIT
An annual summit and the world's leading business event on sustainability in fashion.

ECO-AGE
A consultancy that works to raise the profile of sustainable fashion; known for their annual Green Carpet Challenge.

ELLEN MACARTHUR FOUNDATION
A charity foundation dedicated to supporting a circular, waste-free economy, with a focus on the fashion industry.

ENVIRONMENTAL JUSTICE FOUNDATION
A charity investigating and campaigning around issues like banning toxic pesticides and protecting human rights in the cotton industry.

ETHICAL FASHION FORUM
A collaborative movement to transform social and environmental standards in the fashion industry.

ETHICAL TRADING INITIATIVE
An alliance of brands, unions, and NGOs advocating for workers' rights around the world.

FAIR WEAR FOUNDATION
An independent, nonprofit organization that works to improve conditions for workers in garment factories.

THE FASHION AND RACE DATABASE PROJECT
Database of research, books, and others resources on fashion and race, curated by fashion studies scholar Kim Jenkins.

FASHION REVOLUTION
A global organization that aims to transform the fashion industry through greater consumer awareness and transparency.

FASHION TAKES ACTION
A Canadian organization promoting sustainability in the fashion industry; host of the annual WEAR Conference.

FREE THE SLAVES
An NGO working to free workers trapped in modern slavery, including those working in the fashion industry.

GARMENT WORKERS CENTER
A workers' rights organization fighting to eradicate sweatshop labor in Los Angeles.

GLOBAL FASHION AGENDA
A leadership forum for industry collaboration on sustainability in fashion.

GLOBAL FASHION EXCHANGE
An international platform promoting fashion sustainability, and host of clothing swaps around the world.

GREENPEACE
A global environmental justice group.

INDUSTRIALL
A global labor union that includes textiles, garment, and leather workers.

INTERNATIONAL LABOR RIGHTS FORUM
A Washington, DC–based nonprofit campaigning for sweatshop-free cities and justice for garment workers, among its many causes.

LABOUR BEHIND THE LABEL
A UK-based campaign that works directly with garment workers and citizens to fight for better working conditions in the garment industry.

THE MODEL ALLIANCE
A nonprofit that promotes fair treatment, equal opportunity, and sustainable practices in the fashion industry, from the runway to the factory floor.

NATURAL RESOURCES DEFENSE COUNCIL
An international nonprofit environmental advocacy group. Its Clean by Design program works with major brands to solve water pollution and climate change.

THE NEW FASHION INITIATIVE
An education nonprofit that raises awareness about the environmental impact of fashion.

PESTICIDE ACTION NETWORK
An international coalition of NGOs and citizens' groups committed to ending toxic pesticide use.

REDRESS
A Hong Kong–based environmental NGO working to reduce waste in the fashion industry.

RESEARCH COLLECTIVE FOR DECOLONIZING FASHION
A global collective of fashion academics challenging Eurocentric fashion discourses.

SLOW FACTORY
Sustainability consultancy that produces global events on the intersection of human rights, sustainability, and culture.

STOP THE TRAFFIK
A campaign coalition that aims to bring an end to human trafficking worldwide.

UNITED STUDENTS AGAINST SWEATSHOPS
The largest student-led campaign for fair labor in the fashion industry.

VERITÉ
A global nonprofit researching supply chains around the world and advocating for fair labor conditions.

WAR ON WANT
A charity organization aiming to address issues of poverty and human rights.

WORKER RIGHTS CONSORTIUM
An independent labor rights monitoring organization.

WRAP UK
A UK environmental charity advocating for sustainable clothing consumption, among other causes.

TO WATCH
Alex James: Slowing Down Fast Fashion
China Blue
"Cultural Appropriation or Cultural Appreciation?: Exploring the Fine Line," UC Santa Cruz (YouTube)
Cotton Road
"Fashion and Diversity Series: Fashion and Race," Parsons School of Design (YouTube)
"Fashion, Culture, and Justice: A NYFW Dialogue," The New School (YouTube)
From Sex Worker to Seamstress (short)
RiverBlue
TED Talk: "Fast Fashion's Effect on People, The Planet, & You" with Patrick Woodyard
TED Talk: "The High Cost of Our Cheap Fashion" with Maxine Bédat

TED Talk: "How to Combat the Lies of the Fashion Industry" with Blake Smith
The True Cost
"Udita" (short, YouTube)
"Unravel" (short, YouTube)

TO READ

Asians Wear Clothes on the Internet—Minh-Ha T. Pham
Behind the Label—Edna Bonacich and Richard Appelbaum
Clothing Poverty—Andrew Brooks
Cradle to Cradle—William McDonough
Craft of Use—Kate Fletcher
The Curated Closet—Anuschka Rees
Deluxe—Dana Thomas
Eco Colour—India Flint
Eco Fashion—Sass Brown
ECORenaissance—Marci Zaroff
Emotionally Durable Design—Jonathan Chapman
Empire of Cotton—Sven Beckert
The End of Fashion—Teri Agins
Factory Girls—Leslie T. Chang
Fake Silk—Paul David Blanc
Fashion and Cultural Studies—Susan B. Kaiser
Green Is the New Black—Tamsin Blanchard
Harvesting Color—Rebecca Burgess
How to Get Dressed—Alison Freer
How to Slay—Constance C. R. White
Liberated Threads—Tanisha C. Ford
Loved Clothes Last zine—Fashion Revolution
Magnifeco—Kate Black
Make and Mend—Jessica Marquez
Mending Matters—Katrina Rodabaugh
The Modern Natural Dyer—Kristine Vejar
Natural Color—Sasha Duerr
No Logo—Naomi Klein
Overdressed—Elizabeth L. Cline
Refashioned—Sass Brown
Representation—Edited by Stuart Hall
Sewing Hope—Sarah Adler-Milstein and John M. Kline
Slave to Fashion—Safia Minney
Slow Fashion—Safia Minney

The Song of the Shirt—Jeremy Seabrook

Stitched Up—Tansy E. Hoskins

Tim Gunn's Fashion Bible—Tim Gunn

To Die For—Lucy Siegle

The Travels of a T-Shirt in the Global Economy—Pietra Rivoli

Wardrobe Crisis—Clare Press

Wear No Evil—Greta Eagan

Worn Stories—Emily Spivack

Why Fashion Matters—Frances Corner

NOTES

INTRODUCTION

1. The $2.5 trillion figure is from "The State of Fashion 2019" report reflecting the industry size in 2018. McKinsey & Company and Business of Fashion, "The State of Fashion 2019," accessed March 19, 2019, https://www.mckinsey.com/~/media/McKinsey/Industries/Retail/Our%20Insights/Caution%20ahead%20Global%20growth%20and%20the%20fashion%20industry/The-State-of-Fashion-2019-final.ashx. Global GDP or Gross World Product passed $80 trillion in 2017, according to the World Economic Forum. Jeff Desjardines "The World's $80 Trillion Economy—in One Chart," The World Economic Forum, October 18, 2018, https://www.weforum.org/agenda/2018/10/the-80-trillion-world-economy-in-one-chart. "Hundreds of millions" is a conservative estimate. Employment in the fashion industry is debated, as fashion can include other industries like cotton farming and chemical companies that service the textile industry.

2. Several reports have come out in recent years measuring the carbon impact of fashion. Due to the complex nature of apparel supply chains, they each show varying results. A low estimate, 3.1 percent, is from the Ellen MacArthur Foundation's *A New Textiles Economy,* which measures only the impact of textile manufacturing; the high estimate, at 8 percent, is from the Quantis report *Measuring Fashion;* it includes measurements for the impact of leather and footwear in addition to apparel and is calculated in terms of CO_2 equivalencies. Ellen MacArthur Foundation, *A New Textiles Economy: Redesigning Fashion's Future* (Isle of Wight, UK: Ellen MacArthur Foundation, 2017), Appendix B.2, https://www.ellenmacarthurfoundation.org/assets/downloads/publications/A-New-Textiles-Economy_Full-Report_Updated_1-12-17.pdf; Quantis, *Measuring Fashion: Environmental Impact of the Global Apparel and Footwear Industries Study* (San Francisco: ClimateWorks Foundation, 2018), https://quantis-intl.com/wp-content/uploads/2018/03/measuringfashion_globalimpactstudy_full-report_quantis_cwf_2018a.pdf.

3. Julien Boucher and Damien Friot, *Primary Microplastics in the Oceans: A Global Evaluation of Sources* (Gland, Switzerland: International Union for Conservation of Nature, 2017), https://portals.iucn.org/library/sites/library/files/documents /2017-002.pdf.

4. Technically, every 1.3 minutes. The assumption is that the average garbage truck holds approximately 13 tons. US Environmental Protection Agency (EPA) figures from 2015 (the latest available) show that 8,240,000 tons of textile clothing and 690,000 tons of leather clothing and shoes, or 8,930,000 billion pounds, are not recovered for reuse and recycling and are going to US landfills. Environmental Protection Agency, *Advancing Sustainable Materials Management: 2015 Tables and Figures* (Washington, DC: Environmental Protection Agency, 2018), https://www.epa .gov/sites/production/files/2018-07/documents/smm_2015_tables_and_figures _07252018_fnl_508_0.pdf. The global statistic of about "one truck per second" is from the Ellen MacArthur Foundation, *A New Textiles Economy*.

CHAPTER 1

1. Nathalie Remy, Eveline Speelman, and Steven Swartz, "Style That's Sustainable," McKinsey, October 2016, https://www.mckinsey.com/business-functions /sustainability/our-insights/style-thats-sustainable-a-new-fast-fashion-formula.

2. Seventy percent (71.45%, to be exact) was arrived at by taking an average of all twenty countries' percentage of wear. Marjorie van Elven, "People do not wear at least 50 percent of their wardrobes, says study," FashionUnited, August 16, 2018, https://fashionunited.uk/news/fashion/people-do-not-wear-at-least-50-percent-of -their-wardrobes-according-to-study/2018081638356.

3. Ibid.

4. Ibid.

5. This calculation is based on the author's use of a thirty-three-piece wardrobe planned out in the wardrobe-organizing app Cladwell. This calculation was arrived at by using a wardrobe of nine tops, three dresses, three skirts, six pairs of bottoms, five pairs of shoes, and five jackets, blazers, and knitwear, which produces 375 unique outfit combinations.

6. Andrea Montali, founder of the Dream Organization, phone interview with the author, June 8, 2018.

CHAPTER 2

1. This is the total amount in the municipal waste stream and doesn't account for recycling and recovery. US Environmental Protection Agency, *Advancing Sustainable Materials Management: 2015 Tables and Figures* (Washington, DC: Environmental Protection Agency, 2018), https://www.epa.gov/sites/production/files/2018-07/documents/smm_2015_tables_and_figures_07252018_fnl_508_0.pdf.

2. Suzy Strutner, "Here's What Goodwill Actually Does with Your Donated Clothes," *HuffPost,* updated April 12, 2019, https://www.huffpost.com/entry/what-does-goodwill-do-with-your-clothes_n_57e06b96e4b0071a6e092352.

3. Savers, *2017 Community Impact Report: A Reuseful Impact,* 2017, accessed January 21, 2019, https://www.savers.com/sites/default/files/community_impact_report_2017-savers.pdf.

4. This statistic is from a phone interview with Jackie King, executive director of Secondary Materials and Recycled Textiles (SMART). The number is also consistent with global averages and SMART's member research, which shows a slightly wider range of 10 to 20 percent. SMART, "The Lifecycle of Rags," accessed March 12, 2019, https://www.smartasn.org/SMARTASN/assets/File/resources/lifecycleofrags.pdf. However, according to King and a phone survey conducted by the author, this statistic varies based on area and location. More remote areas or places where consumers shop less and keep their clothes longer may have higher rates of local reuse.

5. Data is collected from the UN Comtrade Database by searching US reported exports to the world of "Worn Clothing and Other Worn Textile Articles," code 630900, between 2000 and 2017, the last year for which data is available, United Nations, UN Comtrade Data: International Trade Statistics Database, accessed March 12, 2019, https://comtrade.un.org/.

6. Data is collected from the UN Comtrade Database by searching Kenyan imports from the world of "Worn Clothing and Other Worn Textile Articles," code 630900, in 2017. United Nations, UN Comtrade Data: International Trade Statistics Database, accessed March 12, 2019, https://comtrade.un.org.

7. Based on phone interviews and unpublished (at the time of this writing) original research and surveys conducted in Ghana's Kantamanto secondhand market by Liz Ricketts and Branson Skinner of the OR Foundation; for information about their work, visit the project website, Dead White Man's Clothes (https://deadwhitemansclothes.org).

CHAPTER 4

1. Calculations for "fastest-growing" and "almost doubled" are the author's, gathered by looking at the increase of landfilled materials between 2000 and 2015, the last year for which information is available. From US Environmental Protection Agency, *Advancing Sustainable Materials Management: 2015 Tables and Figures,* July 18, 2015, https://www.epa.gov/sites/production/files /2018-07/documents/2015_smm_msw_factsheet_07242018_fnl_508 _002.pdf.

2. Ellen MacArthur Foundation, *A New Textiles Economy: Redesigning Fashion's Future* (Isle of Wight, UK: Ellen MacArthur Foundation, 2017), Appendix B.2, https://www.ellenmacarthurfoundation.org/assets/downloads/publications /A-New-Textiles-Economy_Full-Report_Updated_1-12-17.pdf.

3. Stuart Mitchell, "Vanish Survey Shows That Brits Throw Away £12.5 Billion Worth of Clothing Every Year," *Ethical Marketing News,* March 22, 2018, http:// ethicalmarketingnews.com/vanish-survey-shows-that-brits-throw-away-12-5 -billion-worth-of-clothing-every-year.

4. Alden Wicker, "Fast Fashion Is Creating an Environmental Crisis," *Newsweek,* September 1, 2016, https://www.newsweek.com/2016/09/09/old-clothes-fashion -waste-crisis-494824.html.

5. US Environmental Protection Agency, "Overview of Greenhouse Gases: Methane," accessed January 31, 2019, https://www.epa.gov/ghgemissions /overview-greenhouse-gases.

6. US Environmental Protection Agency, *Municipal Solid Waste Landfills: Economic Impact Analysis for the Proposed New Subpart to the New Source Performance Standards,* June 2014, https://www3.epa.gov/ttnecas1/regdata/EIAs /LandfillsNSPSProposalEIA.pdf.

7. Textile Exchange, "Material Summary: Polyester," Version 1, January 2014, and "Material Summary: Synthetic Rubber," Version 1, January 2014. Resources provided to the author by Textile Exchange.

8. US Environmental Protection Agency, "Municipal Solid Waste Generation, Recycling, and Disposal in the United States: Facts and Figures for 2012," MSW Fact Sheet 2012, https://www.epa.gov/sites/production/files/2015-09/documents /2012_msw_fs.pdf.

9. Ibid.

10. Savers, "Declutter Your Way—Responsibly," accessed January 23, 2019, https://www.savers.com/donate/tips-for-donating.

11. Ellen MacArthur Foundation, *A New Textiles Economy*.

12. Liesbeth Mortier, "France Will Impose Recycling for Unsold Clothing in 2019," Retail Detail, February 5, 2018, https://www.retaildetail.eu/en/news/mode/france-will-impose-recycling-unsold-clothing-2019.

13. Lucas Laursen, "A 'Fast Fashion' Tax? Britain Has a Radical New Plan to Spur Clothing Recycling and Reduce Waste," *Fortune*, February 19, 2019, http://fortune.com/2019/02/19/uk-fashion-tax-recycling.

CHAPTER 5

1. Ellen MacArthur Foundation, *A New Textiles Economy: Redesigning Fashion's Future* (Isle of Wight, UK: Ellen MacArthur Foundation, 2017), 19, https://www.ellenmacarthurfoundation.org/assets/downloads/publications/A-New-Textiles-Economy_Full-Report_Updated_1-12-17.pdf.

CHAPTER 6

1. Patrick Duffy, Global Fashion Exchange, phone interview with the author, January 10, 2019.

2. Ibid.

3. Ibid.

4. Ellen MacArthur Foundation, *A New Textiles Economy: Redesigning Fashion's Future* (Isle of Wight, UK: Ellen MacArthur Foundation, 2017), 73, https://www.ellenmacarthurfoundation.org/assets/downloads/publications/A-New-Textiles-Economy_Full-Report_Updated_1-12-17.pdf.

CHAPTER 7

1. Quantis, *Measuring Fashion: Environmental Impact of the Global Apparel and Footwear Industries Study* (San Francisco: ClimateWorks Foundation, 2018), accessed May 28, 2018, https://quantis-intl.com/wp-content/uploads/2018/03/measuringfashion_globalimpactstudy_full-report_quantis_cwf_2018a.pdf.

2. Wrap UK, *Valuing Our Clothes: The True Cost of How We Design, Use and Dispose of Clothing in the UK,* 2012, http://www.wrap.org.uk/sites/files/wrap/VoC%20FINAL%20online%202012%2007%2011.pdf.

3. The figure for destroyed clothing is calculated by subtracting the $13.76 million in destroyed beauty products from the total of $38 million in destroyed Burberry goods. The Fashion Law, "Burberry Reports that It Has Destroyed Nearly $38 Million in Goods," July 16, 2018, http://www.thefashionlaw.com/home/burberry -reports-that-it-has-destroyed-nearly-38-million-in-goods.

CHAPTER 9

1. Krystina Gustafson, "Retailers Cutting Costs at the Expense of Quality," CNBC .com, April 11, 2016, https://www.cnbc.com/2016/04/11/retailers-cutting-costs -at-the-expense-of-quality.html.

2. Marc Bain, "Pro-tips for Buying Clothes that Will Last Years, Not Weeks," Quartz, December 4, 2016, https://qz.com/823607/pro-tips-for-buying-clothes-that-will -last-years-not-weeks.

3. Sara J. Kadolph and Sara B. Marcketti, *Textiles* (Boston: Pearson, 2012), twelfth edition, 46.

4. Ibid., 182.

5. Karuna Scheinfeld, vice president of design at Canada Goose, e-mail correspondence with the author, January 20, 2019.

6. Textile Exchange, "Preferred Fiber & Materials Market Report 2018," November 2018, https://textileexchange.org/downloads/2018-preferred-fiber-and-materials -market-report.

7. Scheinfeld, e-mail correspondence.

8. Timo Rissanen, associate dean and professor of fashion design and sustainability at Parsons School of Design, e-mail correspondence with the author, January 12, 2019.

9. Scheinfeld, e-mail correspondence.

10. Rissanen, e-mail correspondence.

11. Scheinfeld, e-mail correspondence.

12. Rissanen, e-mail correspondence.

13. Scheinfeld, e-mail correspondence.

14. Ibid.

15. Ibid.

16. Jessica Schiffer, "7 Brands That Will Repair Your Purchase for Free," Who What Wear, July 2, 2018, https://www.whowhatwear.com/brands-that-will-repair-your -purchase-for-free.

17. Bain, "Pro-tips for Buying Clothes That Will Last Years, Not Weeks."

18. Gina Ragusa, "How Do TJ Maxx and Marshalls Sell Designer Clothes So Cheap? 5 Hacks to Save Money on Fancy Duds," *Mic,* November 13, 2017, https://mic.com /articles/185874/5-shopping-hacks-and-secrets-to-save-money-on-designer-clothes-how -tj-maxx-and-marshalls-sell-cheap-discounted-brand-name-clothing#.HTLTbYoh5.

19. Brad Tuttle, "More Retailers Accused of Misleading Customers with Fake Price Schemes," *Money,* January 7, 2016, http://money.com/money/4171081/macys -jc-penney-lawsuit-original-prices.

CHAPTER 10

1. Quantis, *Measuring Fashion: Environmental Impact of the Global Apparel and Footwear Industries Study* (San Francisco: ClimateWorks Foundation, 2018), accessed May 28, 2018, https://quantis-intl.com/wp-content/uploads/2018/03 /measuringfashion_globalimpactstudy_full-report_quantis_cwf_2018a.pdf. The coal equivalency was arrived at by using the EPA "Greenhouse Gas Equivalencies Calculator," United States Protection Agency, accessed March 12, 2019, https:// www.epa.gov/energy/greenhouse-gas-equivalencies-calculator.

2. Alexia Elejalde-Ruiz, "How to Tell It's Time to Throw Out Your Shoes," *The Seattle Times,* March 3, 2011, https://www.seattletimes.com/life/outdoors /how-to-tell-its-time-to-throw-out-your-shoes.

3. National Institutes of Health, U.S. National Library of Medicine, "Polyvinyl Chloride (PVC)," accessed March 12, 2019, https://toxtown.nlm.nih.gov/chemicals -and-contaminants/polyvinyl-chloride-pvc.

4. Joshua Katcher, founder and designer of Brave Gentleman, e-mail correspondence with the author, January 24, 2019.

CHAPTER 12

1. Maybelle Morgan, "Throwaway Fashion: Women Have Adopted a 'Wear It Once Culture,' Binning Clothes after Only a Few Wears," *Daily Mail*, June 9, 2015, https://www.dailymail.co.uk/femail/article-3116962/Throwaway-fashion-Women -adopted-wear-culture-binning-clothes-wears-aren-t-pictured-outfit-twice-social -media.html.

2. Trunk Club, "New Trunk Club Survey Finds Americans Experience 'Wardrobe Panic' 36 Times Annually," Online Press Release, March 12, 2018, https://www.trunkclub.com/press/news/new-trunk-club-survey-finds-americans-experience-wardrobe-panic-36-times-annually.

3. Kit Yarrow, "The Science of Why We Buy Clothes We Never Wear," *Money,* September 20, 2016, http://time.com/money/4499539/why-we-buy-clothes-we-never-wear.

4. Ellen Ruppel Shell's book is a great resource on the psychology of shopping and pricing. This particular phrase is from Ellen Ruppel Shell, *Cheap: The High Cost of Discount Culture* (New York: Penguin Press, 2009), 64.

5. Ibid., 71.

6. There is a lot of research on how choice can block cognition. Here's one excellent study on the subject: Sheena S. Iyengar and Mark R. Lepper, "When Choice Is Demotivating: Can One Desire Too Much of a Good Thing?," *Journal of Personality and Social Psychology* 79, no. 6 (2000): 995–1006, https://www.ncbi.nlm.nih.gov/pubmed/11138768.

7. Rachel Arthur, "This Browser Extension Will Curb Your Impulse Shopping Habit," *Forbes,* August 29, 2017, https://www.forbes.com/sites/rachelarthur/2017/08/29/this-browser-extension-will-curb-your-impulse-shopping-habit.

CHAPTER 13

1. Nathalie Remy, Eveline Speelman, and Steven Swartz, "Style That's Sustainable," McKinsey, October 2016, https://www.mckinsey.com/business-functions/sustainability/our-insights/style-thats-sustainable-a-new-fast-fashion-formula.

2. Ellen MacArthur Foundation, *A New Textiles Economy: Redesigning Fashion's Future* (Isle of Wight, UK: Ellen MacArthur Foundation, 2017), https://www.ellenmacarthurfoundation.org/assets/downloads/publications/A-New-Textiles-Economy_Full-Report_Updated_1-12-17.pdf. The pool estimate is based on the conversion of the report's cited 93 billion cubic meters to about 24 trillion gallons, and the assumption that an Olympic-size pool contains 660,253 gallons of water.

3. Ellen MacArthur Foundation, *A New Textiles Economy,* 21.

4. Idid., 20.

CHAPTER 14

1. thredUP, "thredUP 2019 Resale Report," accessed March 19, 2019, https://www
.thredup.com/resale.

2. Ibid.

3. Poshmark, "What Is Poshmark?," accessed March 20, 2019, https://poshmark
.com/what_is_poshmark.

4. Ellen MacArthur Foundation, *A New Textiles Economy: Redesigning Fashion's
Future* (Isle of Wight, UK: Ellen MacArthur Foundation, 2017), https://www
.ellenmacarthurfoundation.org/assets/downloads/publications/A-New-Textiles
-Economy_Full-Report_Updated_1-12-17.pdf.

5. thredUP, "thredUP 2018 Resale Report," accessed March 1, 2019, http://www
.thredup.com/resale/2018.

CHAPTER 16

1. Rebecca Greenfield, "Inside Rent the Runway's Secret Dry-Cleaning Empire,"
Fast Company, October 28, 2014, https://www.fastcompany.com/3036876
/inside-rent-the-runways-secret-dry-cleaning-empire.

2. Morgan, "Throwaway Fashion: Women Have Adopted a 'Wear It Once Culture.'"

3. Greenfield, "Inside Rent the Runway."

4. Ibid.

5. Mary Pols, "The Truth About Your Online Shopping Carbon Footprint,"
Portland Press Herald, December 17, 2017, https://www.pressherald.com/2017/12
/17/the-truth-about-your-online-shopping-carbon-footprint.

6. Ibid.

CHAPTER 17

1. Sheng Lu, "Latest Trends in the US Apparel Industry (Update: January 2015),"
Sheng Lu Fashion, accessed January 31, 2019, https://shenglufashion.com/2015/01
/15/latest-trends-in-the-us-apparel-industry-update-january-2015.

CHAPTER 18

1. On pages 39 through 51, the *Pulse of the Fashion Industry* report shows the impact of different stages of the apparel life cycle. It is the raw materials and processing phase that show high or very high impacts for water, chemicals, and energy use, as well as in the design and development phase. Global Fashion Agenda and Boston Consulting Group, *Pulse of the Fashion Industry 2017,* https://www.globalfashionagenda.com/wp-content/uploads/2017/05/Pulse-of-the-Fashion-Industry_2017.pdf, 39–51. The Quantis report found that over 90 percent of the fashion industry's water and resource usage, and ecosystem and climate change impact happen in the textile making stages of fiber production, yarn preparation, fabric production, and dyeing and finishing. Quantis, *Measuring Fashion: Environmental Impact of the Global Apparel and Footwear Industries Study* (San Francisco: ClimateWorks Foundation, 2018), https://quantis-intl.com/wp-content/uploads/2018/03/measuringfashion_globalimpactstudy_full-report_quantis_cwf_2018a.pdf.

2. Ellen MacArthur Foundation, *A New Textiles Economy: Redesigning Fashion's Future* (Isle of Wight, UK: Ellen MacArthur Foundation, 2017), Appendix B.2, https://www.ellenmacarthurfoundation.org/assets/downloads/publications/A-New-Textiles-Economy_Full-Report_Updated_1-12-17.pdf. The chemicals figure was arrived at by converting from metric tons to US short tons. The number of barrels of oil is from the same report, 38.

3. Randolph Kirchain et al., "Sustainable Apparel Materials," Materials Systems Laboratory, Massachusetts Institute of Technology, September 22, 2015, https://globalcompostproject.org/wp-content/uploads/2015/10/SustainableApparelMaterials.pdf.

4. Textile Exchange, "Preferred Fiber & Materials Market Report 2018," November 2018, https://textileexchange.org/downloads/2018-preferred-fiber-and-materials-market-report.

5. Ibid.

6. Marc Bain, "If Your Clothes Aren't Already Made Out of Plastic, They Will Be," *Quartz*, June 5, 2015, https://qz.com/414223/if-your-clothes-arent-already-made-out-of-plastic-they-will-be.

7. For a more in-depth look at the links between polyester and the oil industry, see Lucy Siegle's *Turning the Tide on Plastics: How Humanity (and You) Can Make Our Globe Clean Again* (London: Hachette UK, 2018), 24.

8. Ibid.

9. Matthew Taylor, "$180bn Investment in Plastic Factories Feeds Global Packaging Binge," *The Guardian*, December 26, 2017, https://www.theguardian.com /environment/2017/dec/26/180bn-investment-in-plastic-factories-feeds-global -packaging-binge.

10. Textile Exchange, "Material Summary: Polyester," Version 1, January 2014, https:// textileexchange.org/material-snapshots-and-summaries. This chapter draws heavily on in-depth material research conducted by Textile Exchange, a nonprofit organization that develops research and industry standards for sustainable material use in the fashion industry. The research used is contained in Material Summaries and Material Snapshots of twenty-nine materials used in the clothing industry, provided by Textile Exchange at the author's request.

11. N. L. Hartline et al., "Microfiber Masses Recovered from Conventional Machine Washing of New or Aged Garments," *Environmental Science & Technology* 50, no. 21 (2016): 11532–11538, https://brenmicroplastics.weebly.com/project-findings.html.

12. Laura Paddison, "Single Clothes Wash May Release 700,000 Microplastic Fibres, Study Finds," *The Guardian,* September 26, 2016, https://www.theguardian.com /science/2016/sep/27/washing-clothes-releases-water-polluting-fibres-study-finds.

13. Julien Boucher and Damien Friot, *Primary Microplastics in the Oceans: A Global Evaluation of Sources* (Gland, Switzerland: International Union for Conservation of Nature, 2017), https://portals.iucn.org/library/sites/library/files/documents /2017-002.pdf.

14. Brett Mathews, "Study: Cotton Most Prevalent Microfibre in Deep Seas," *Apparel Insider,* November 19, 2018, https://apparelinsider.com/study-cotton-microfibres -most-prevelent-in-deep-seas.

15. Madeleine Smith et al., "Microplastics in Seafood and the Implications for Human Health," *Current Environmental Health Reports* 5, no. 3 (2018): 375–386, https://www.ncbi.nlm.nih.gov/pmc/articles/PMC6132564.

16. Frederic Gallo et al., "Marine Litter Plastics and Microplastics and Their Toxic Chemicals Components: The Need for Urgent Preventive Measures," *Environmental Sciences Europe* 30, no. 1 (2018): 13, doi: 10.1186/s12302-018-0139-z.

17. Deirdre Lockwood, "Ocean Plastics Soak Up Pollutants," *Chemical & Engineering News,* August 22, 2012, https://cen.acs.org/articles/90/web/2012/08/Ocean-Plastics-Soak-Up-Pollutants.html.

18. Statistics refer to mechanically recycled polyester; figures are lower for chemical recycling. Textile Exchange, "Material Summary: Mechanically Recycled Polyester," Version 1, January 2014.

19. Textile Exchange notes that careful management of TDI, a known carcinogen used in spandex production is necessary to avoid this substance being left on final products sold to consumers. Textile Exchange, "Material Summary: Elastane/Spandex," Version 1, January 2014.

20. Textile Exchange, "Material Summary: Polyurethane (PU)," Version 1, January 2014.

21. US Environmental Protection Agency, "Overview of Greenhouse Gases: Nitrous Oxide Emissions," accessed January 31, 2019, https://www.epa.gov/ghgemissions/overview-greenhouse-gases#nitrous-oxide.

22. US Environmental Protection Agency, "Acrylonitrile," April 1992, updated January 2000, accessed February 1, 2019, https://www.epa.gov/sites/production/files/2016-09/documents/acrylonitrile.pdf.

23. Pinar Erkekoglu et al., "Reproductive Toxicity of Di(2-Ethylhexyl) Phthalate in Selenium-Supplemented and Selenium-Deficient Rats," *Drug and Chemical Toxicology* 34, no. 4 (2011): 379–389, doi: 10.3109/01480545.2010.547499.

24. Textile Exchange, "Preferred Fiber & Materials Market Report 2018."

25. "Cotton Growing Industry in China: Industry Market Research Report," *IbisWorld,* February 2019, https://www.ibisworld.com/industry-trends/international/china-market-research-reports/agriculture-hunting-forestry-fishing/cotton-growing.html.

26. Cotton Incorporated, *Life Cycle Assessment of Cotton Fiber & Fabric: Full Report,* 2012, 43, https://cottoncultivated.cottoninc.com/wp-content/uploads/2015/06/2012-LCA-Full-Report.pdf.

27. World Atlas, "Top Cotton Producing Countries in the World," updated April 25, 2017, https://www.worldatlas.com/articles/top-cotton-producing-countries-in-the-world.html.

28. Pesticide Action Network UK, "Pesticide Concerns in Cotton," accessed January 31, 2019, http://www.pan-uk.org/cotton.

29. Ellen MacArthur Foundation, *A New Textiles Economy,* Appendix B.2.

30. United Nations Environment, "Urgent Action Needed to Reduce Growing Health and Environmental Hazards from Chemicals: UN Report," press release,

September 5, 2012, https://www.unenvironment.org/news-and-stories/press
-release/urgent-action-needed-reduce-growing-health-and-environmental
-hazards.

31. Tara Donaldson, "Report: The Truth About Organic Cotton and Its Impacts,"
Sourcing Journal, June 26, 2017, https://sourcingjournal.com/topics/raw-materials
/report-truth-organic-cotton-impacts-68512.

32. Francis Gassert, "One-Quarter of World's Agriculture Grows in Highly
Water-Stressed Areas," World Resources Institute, October 31, 2013, https://www
.wri.org/blog/2013/10/one-quarter-world-s-agriculture-grows-highly-water
-stressed-areas.

33. "Child Labor and Forced Labor Reports: India," United States Department of
Labor Bureau of International Labor Affairs, 2012, https://www.dol.gov/ilab
/reports/child-labor/findings/2012TDA/india.pdf.

34. Textile Exchange, "Quick Guide to Organic Cotton," June 2017, http://
textileexchange.org/wp-content/uploads/2017/06/Textile-Exchange_Quick-Guide
-To-Organic-Cotton_2017.pdf.

35. Sustainable Brands, "World's Largest Rayon Producer Announces
Game-Changing Forest Protection Policy," May 7, 2015, https://sustainablebrands
.com/read/behavior-change/world-s-largest-rayon-producer-announces-game
-changing-forest-protection-policy.

36. "Global and China Viscose Fiber Industry Report, 2012–2015," PRNewswire,
March 19, 2013, https://www.prnewswire.com/news-releases/global-and-china
-viscose-fiber-industry-report-2012-2015-199047751.html.

37. Changing Markets Foundation, "Roadmap Towards Responsible Viscose and
Modal Fibre Manufacturing." Report in collaboration with the Forest Trust,
February 2018, http://changingmarkets.org/wp-content/uploads/2018/03
/Roadmap-towards-responsible-viscose-and-modal-fibre-manufacturing.pdf.

38. Kate Black, *Magnifeco: Your Head-to-Toe Guide to Ethical Fashion and Non-Toxic
Beauty* (British Columbia: New Society Publishers, 2015), 151.

39. "Man-Made Fibers Continue to Grow," *Textile World,* February 3, 2015, http://
www.textileworld.com/textile-world/fiber-world/2015/02/man-made-fibers
-continue-to-grow; Changing Markets Foundation, "Roadmap Towards
Responsible Viscose and Modal Fibre Manufacturing."

40. Sustainable Apparel Coalition, HIGG Materials Sustainability Index, Base Materials, based on a comparison of cotton, polyester, modal, and viscose rayon, accessed February 4, 2019, https://msi.higg.org/compare/209-208-195.

41. For an in-depth look at the toxic history of the rayon industry, see Paul David Blanc, *Fake Silk: The Lethal History of Viscose Rayon* (New Haven, CT: Yale University Press, 2015).

42. Textile Exchange, "Material Summary: Tencel Lyocell," Final Version, November 13, 2015.

43. Canopy, "CanopyStyle," accessed January 2019, http://canopyplanet.org /campaigns/canopystyle.

44. Nicole Rycroft, founder and executive director of Canopy, phone interview with the author, August 8, 2018.

45. Textile Exchange, "Material Summary: Tencel Lyocell."

46. The dollar figure is from Lydia Mulvany and Lindsey Rupp, "Consumers Want to Eat Beef, Not Wear It, Sending Leather Prices Plummeting," *Bloomberg,* June 12, 2018, https://www.bloomberg.com/news/articles/2018-06-12/shoe-shoppers-going -vegan-as-beef-boom-creates-cattle-hide-glut. The amount of leather produced is 4.8 billion square feet, to be exact, as of 2014, per Textile Exchange, "Material Snapshot: Bovine Leather," Final Version, November 13, 2015.

47. "China's Leather Industry Consolidates," APLF, April 9, 2018, http://www.aplf .com/en-US/leather-fashion-news-and-blog/blog/38311/china-s-lather-industry -consolidates.

48. Whether or not cow's leather is a by-product of beef has been extensively debated. In most cases, it is a by-product. In 2018, the European Union Environmental Footprint Steering Committee approved new life cycle analysis rules stating that cow leather is in fact a by-product, and its environmental impact should not include the cattle-raising or live animal phase. Other groups, such as Textile Exchange's Responsible Leather Round Table, do consider the live animal phase in setting standards for leather. Responsible Leather Round Table, https:// responsibleleather.org; "EU Committee Approves Cotance's Leather Carbon Footprint Toolbox," International Leather Maker, April 20, 2018, http:// internationalleathermaker.com/news/fullstory.php/aid/5404/EU_Committee _approves_Cotance_92s_leather_carbon_footprint_toolbox.html.

49. Textile Exchange, "Material Snapshot: Bovine Leather."

50. Converted from kilograms to pounds, so 3 kilograms of chemicals are used to produce 1 kilogram of leather. Ibid.

51. "Commission Regulation (EU) No 301/2014: of 25 March 2014 amending Annex XVII to Regulation (EC) No 1907/2006 of the European Parliament and of the Council on the Registration, Evaluation, Authorisation and Restriction of Chemicals (REACH) as regards chromium VI compounds," *Official Journal of the European Union*, March 25, 2014, https://eur-lex.europa.eu/eli/reg/2014/301/oj.

52. Textile Exchange, "Material Snapshot: Leather," Version 1, January 2014.

53. Quantity in pounds is author's conversion from kilograms shown at International Wool Textile Organization, "Wool Production," accessed January 19, 2019, https://www.iwto.org/wool-production.

54. Ibid.

55. Rob Schmitz, "How Your Cashmere Sweater Is Decimating Mongolia's Grasslands," NPR Morning Edition, December 9, 2016, https://www.npr.org /sections/parallels/2016/12/09/504118819/how-your-cashmere-sweater-is -decimating-mongolias-grasslands.

56. Textile Exchange, "Material Summary: Non-mulesed Wool," Version 1, January 2014.

57. Ibid.

58. Textile Exchange, "Preferred Fiber & Materials Market Report 2018."

59. Textile Exchange, "Material Summary: Linen," Version 1, January 2014.

60. Tom Angell, "U.S. Senate Votes to Legalize Hemp After Decades-Long Ban Under Marijuana Prohibition," *Forbes,* June 28, 2018, https://www.forbes.com /sites/tomangell/2018/06/28/u-s-senate-votes-to-legalize-hemp-after-decades -long-ban-under-marijuana-prohibition/#29b41b77418a.

61. Textiles Exchange, "Material Summary: Linen."

62. Textile Exchange, "Preferred Fiber & Materials Market Report 2018."

63. Textile Exchange, "Material Summary: Silk," Version 1, January 2014.

64. UN Food and Agriculture Organization, *Silk Reeling and Testing Manual* (Rome: Food and Agriculture Organization of the United Nations, 1999), chap. 2, http:// www.fao.org/docrep/x2099e/x2099e03.htm.

65. Textile Exchange, "Material Summary: Silk."

66. Ibid.

CHAPTER 19

1. Converted from 42 million tonnes to short tons. Ellen MacArthur
   Foundation, *A New Textiles Economy: Redesigning Fashion's Future* (Isle of Wight,
   UK: Ellen MacArthur Foundation, 2017), Appendix B.2, https://www
   .ellenmacarthurfoundation.org/assets/downloads/publications/A-New-Textiles
   -Economy_Full-Report_Updated_1-12-17.pdf.

2. Swedish Chemicals Agency, *Chemicals in Textiles—Risks to Human Health and the
   Environment* (Stockholm: Arkitektkopia, 2014), https://www.kemi.se/files
   /8040fb7a4f2547b7bad522c399c0b649/report6-14-chemicals-in-textiles.pdf.

3. National Cancer Institute, "Formaldehyde and Cancer Risk," reviewed June 10,
   2011, accessed January 13, 2019, https://www.cancer.gov/about-cancer/causes
   -prevention/risk/substances/formaldehyde/formaldehyde-fact-sheet.

4. Pinar Erkekoglu et al., "Reproductive Toxicity of Di(2-Ethylhexyl) Phthalate in
   Selenium-Supplemented and Selenium-Deficient Rats," *Drug and Chemical
   Toxicology* 34, no. 4 (2011): 379–389, doi: 10.3109/01480545.2010.547499.

5. Jay Bolus, McDonough Braungart Design Chemistry, phone interview with the
   author, October 27, 2018.

6. Mark Scialla, "It Could Take Centuries for EPA to Test All the Unregulated
   Chemicals Under a New Landmark Bill," *PBS News Hour,* June 22, 2016, https://
   www.pbs.org/newshour/science/it-could-take-centuries-for-epa-to-test-all-the
   -unregulated-chemicals-under-a-new-landmark-bill.

7. Greenpeace, "Greenpeace Exposes Hazardous Chemicals in Clothes Sold by Zara,
   and Other Leading Fashion Brands," press release, November 20, 2012, http://
   www.greenpeace.org/eastasia/press/releases/toxics/2012/toxic-chemicals-detox
   -zara.

8. Bolus, phone interview.

9. Ibid.

10. Greenpeace, "Hazardous Chemicals in Clothing," accessed March 9, 2019, http://
    www.greenpeace.org/eastasia/campaigns/toxics/science/eleven-flagship-hazardous
    -chemicals. ZDHC Roadmap to Zero Programme, "ZDHC Manufacturing
    Restricted Substances List (ZDHC MRSL) & Conformity Guidance," ZDHC

MRSL version 1.1, accessed March 9, 2019, https://www.roadmaptozero.com /programme/manufacturing-restricted-substances-list-mrsl-conformity-guidance.

11. National Cancer Institute, "Formaldehyde and Cancer Risk."

12. Rolf U. Halden et al., "The Florence Statement on Triclosan and Triclocarban," *Environmental Health Perspectives* 125, no. 126 (June 2017), https://doi.org/10.1289 /EHP1788.

13. Erkekoglu et al., "Reproductive Toxicity of Di(2-Ethylhexyl) Phthalate."

14. US Environmental Protection Agency, "Short-Chain Chlorinated Paraffins (SCCPs) and Other Chlorinated Paraffins Action Plan," December 30, 2009, https://www .epa.gov/sites/production/files/2015-09/documents/sccps_ap_2009_1230_final.pdf.

15. United States Environmental Protection Agency, "Brominated Flame Retardants," January 11, 2011, https://cfpub.epa.gov/si/si_public_record_report .cfm?Lab=NHEERL&dirEntryId=226582.

16. National Institute of Environmental Health Sciences, "Perfluorinated Chemicals (PFCs)," accessed January 11, 2019, https://www.niehs.nih.gov/health/materials /perflourinated_chemicals_508.pdf.

17. Ben Mead, representative of the Oeko-Tex Association of the United States, phone call with author, October 8, 2018.

CHAPTER 20

1. Fashion Revolution, "Transparency Is Trending," posted November 2018, accessed January 11, 2019, https://www.fashionrevolution.org/transparency-is -trending.

2. Elizabeth L. Cline, *Overdressed: The Shockingly High Cost of Cheap Fashion* (New York: Portfolio, 2013), 23.

3. Anna Hirtenstein, "Fast Fashion Goes Green with Mushrooms, Lumber Scraps, and Algae," *Bloomberg Businessweek*, April 30, 2018, https://www.bloomberg.com /news/articles/2018-05-01/fast-fashion-goes-green-with-mushrooms-lumber -scraps-and-algae.

CHAPTER 21

1. Rebecca Adam, "Millennials Can't Sew or Do Laundry as Well as Their Parents & Grandparents, Study Says," *HuffPost,* October 17, 2014, https://www .huffingtonpost.com/2014/10/17/millennials-laundry_n_6002244.html.

2. Vanish, "Vanish Survey Shows That Brits Throw Away £12.5 Billion Worth of Clothing Every Year," PR Newswire, March 8, 2018, https://www.prnewswire.com/news-releases/vanish-survey-shows-that-brits-throw-away-125-billion-worth-of-clothing-every-year-676271113.html.

3. Wrap UK, *Sustainable Clothing: A Practical Guide to Enhancing Clothing Durability and Quality,* June 2017, http://www.wrap.org.uk/sites/files/wrap/Sustainable%20Clothing%20Guide%202017.pdf; information on durability also verified in conversations with product developers in the fashion industry.

4. Ellie Pithers, "Are You Guilty of Wearing Things Just Once?," *The Telegraph,* June 14, 2015, https://www.telegraph.co.uk/fashion/style/are-you-guilty-of-wearing-things-once.

CHAPTER 22

1. Life-cycle assessments of clothing rarely include the laundry phase (the so-called consumer use phase of clothing), and those that do exist vary widely in their findings, and further research is needed. As we've established, some clothing is worn only a few times, and in that case, the laundering impact of those garments would be very low but the impact of waste would be high, and demand for new clothing would increase. Some materials also require more laundering, namely polyester, while materials like wool or tailored garments are very rarely washed. Still, most life-cycle analyses that include washing show that laundry has a high impact in terms of both energy and water usage. For further reading: Global Fashion Agenda and Boston Consulting Group, *Pulse of the Fashion Industry 2017,* https://www.globalfashionagenda.com/wp-content/uploads/2017/05/Pulse-of-the-Fashion-Industry_2017.pdf, 11; and Levi Strauss & Co., "The Life Cycle of a Jean," 2015, https://levistrauss.com/wp-content/uploads/2015/03/Full-LCA-Results-Deck-FINAL.pdf.

2. The total impact of washing and drying, based on the latest available data, is 66 billion kilowatt-hours per year. The figure of 60 billion kilowatt-hours on drying is from the Natural Resources Defense Council, and that of 6 billion kilowatt-hours on laundering is from Consumer Reports. I used the EPA's Greenhouse Gas Equivalencies Calculator to convert the total to number of households (5.6 million), which is the population of Minnesota, and to come up with the 46 million carbon dioxide equivalencies; David Denkenberger et al., "Residential Clothes Dryers: A Closer Look at Energy Efficiency Test Procedures and Savings Opportunities," Natural Resources Defense Council, November 9, 2011,

https://www.nrdc.org/sites/default/files/ene_14060901a.pdf; Kimberly Janeway, "10 Ways to Save Energy Doing Laundry," *Consumer Reports,* updated April 24, 2019, https://www.consumerreports.org/laundry/energy-saving-laundry-tips.

3. Timur Senguen and Ethan Wolff-Mann, "How Dryers Destroy Clothes: We Delve into the Research," Reviewed, Science Blog, August 8, 2013, https://www.reviewed.com/science/how-dryers-destroy-your-clothes.

4. Ibid.

5. Timo Rissanen, Parsons School of Design, e-mail correspondence with the author, January 12, 2019.

6. Corinne Purtill, "One Household Staple Sums Up Why Americans and Brits Will Never See the World the Same Way," *Quartz*, July 20, 2017, https://qz.com/1034914/it-doesnt-matter-where-brits-keep-their-dryers-the-point-is-they-dont-work.

7. Energy Star, "ENERGY STAR Facts & Figures for Your Co-Branded Material," updated September 2014, accessed January 2019, https://www.energystar.gov/index.cfm?c=ppg_cobrand.ppg_cobrand_3c.

8. Based on the assumption that the average American does three hundred loads a year and laundry machines use nineteen gallons of water per load (the average for an agitator top-loader machine, according to *Consumer Reports*). Kimberly Janeway, "Yes, Your Washing Machine Is Using Enough Water," *Consumer Reports,* March 9, 2017, https://www.consumerreports.org/washing-machines/yes-your-washing-machine-is-using-enough-water.

9. Ashley Lutz, "Levi's CEO Explains Why Jeans Should Never Go in the Washing Machine," *Business Insider,* July 15, 2014, https://www.businessinsider.com/levis-ceo-dont-wash-your-jeans-2014-7.

10. Chris Callewaert et al., "Microbial Odor Profile of Polyester and Cotton Clothes After a Fitness Session," *Applied and Environmental Microbiology* 80, no. 21 (November 2014), https://doi.org/10.1128/AEM.01422-14.

11. Elise Stolte, "Not Washing Jeans for 15 Months OK, Health-wise at Least: Study," *National Post,* January 19, 2011, https://nationalpost.com/news/canada/not-washing-jeans-for-15-months-ok-healthwise-at-least-study.

12. S. N. Patel, J. Murray-Leonard, and A. P. Wilson, "Laundering of Hospital Staff Uniforms at Home," *Journal of Hospital Infection* 62, no. 1 (January 2006): 89–93, https://www.ncbi.nlm.nih.gov/pubmed/16214262.

13. Kim Corollo, ABC News Medical Unit, "Dirty Laundry? How Nasty Germs Survive in Your Washer," ABC News, May 27, 2010, https://abcnews.go.com /Health/Wellness/washing-machines-loaded-bacteria-dirty-clothes/story?id =10751420.

14. Ingun Grimstad Klepp et al., "What's the Problem? Odor-Control and the Smell of Sweat in Sportswear," *Fashion Practice* 8, no. 2 (2016): 296–317, doi: 10.1080/ 17569370.2016.1215117; Mohammed M. Abdul-Bari et al., "Synthetic Clothing and the Problem with Odor: Comparison of Nylon and Polyester Fabrics," *Clothing and Textiles Research Journal* 36, no. 4 (2018): 251–266, https://doi.org/10.1177 /0887302X18772099.

15. Jolie Kerr, "How to Clean Your Gross Workout Gear," *The New York Times,* May 30, 2018, https://www.nytimes.com/2018/05/30/smarter-living/how-to-clean-your -gross-workout-gear.html.

16. Amanda L. Chan, "Why You Should Wash Those Dirty Gym Clothes Immediately," *HuffPost,* September 8, 2014, https://www.huffpost.com/entry /polyester-sweat-smell-odor-stink-cotton_n_5774984.

17. Mark Witten, "Scientist Offers 6 Tips for Keeping Your Workout Clothes from Smelling Permanently Bad," Phys.org, June 26, 2018, https://phys.org/news /2018-06-scientist-workout-permanently-bad.html.

18. US Environmental Protection Agency, "Earth Month Tip: Wash Your Clothes in Cold Water," EPA Blog, April 30, 2014, https://blog.epa.gov/2014/04/30/earth -month-tip-wash-your-clothes-in-cold-water.

19. Energy.gov, "Laundry," US Department of Energy, accessed February 1, 2019, https://www.energy.gov/energysaver/appliances-and-electronics/laundry.

20. Kimberly Janeway, "Don't Bother Using Hot Water to Wash Your Laundry," *Consumer Reports,* August 25, 2016, https://www.consumerreports.org/washing -machines/dont-bother-using-hot-water-to-wash-your-laundry.

21. EPA, "Earth Month Tip: Wash Your Clothes in Cold Water."

22. Natural Resources Defense Council, "A Call to Action for More Efficient Clothes Dryers: U.S. Consumers Missing Out on $4 Billion in Annual Savings," NRDC Issue Brief, June 2014, https://www.nrdc.org/sites/default/files/efficient-clothes -dryers-IB.pdf.

23. Denkenberger et al., "Residential Clothes Dryers."

24. Kirsi Laitala, Ingun Grimstad Klepp, and Beverley Henry, "Does Use Matter? Comparison of Environmental Impacts of Clothing Based on Fiber Type," *Sustainability* 10, no. 7 (2018): 2524, https://www.mdpi.com/2071-1050/10/7/2524.

25. Levi Strauss and Co., "The Life Cycle of a Jean"; Luke Yates and David Evans, "Dirtying Linen: Re-evaluating the Sustainability of Domestic Laundry," *Environmental Policy and Governance* 26, no. 2 (March–April 2016): 101–15, https://doi.org/10.1002/eet.1704.

26. Timo Rissanen, Parsons School of Design, e-mail correspondence with the author, February 10, 2019.

27. Energy Star, "Laundry Best Practices," accessed January 11, 2019, https://www.energystar.gov/products/laundry_best_practices.

28. "Explanation of Dryer Temperatures," GE Appliances, accessed January 11, 2019, https://products.geappliances.com/appliance/gea-support-search-content?contentId=20985.

29. NRDC, "More Efficient Clothes Dryers."

30. Carol Potera, "Indoor Air Quality: Scented Products Emit a Bouquet of VOCs," *Environmental Health Perspectives* 119, no. 1 (January 2011): A16, https://www.ncbi.nlm.nih.gov/pmc/articles/PMC3018511.

31. Robin E. Dodson et al., "Endocrine Disruptors and Asthma-Associated Chemicals in Consumer Products," *Environmental Health Perspectives* 120, no. 7 (July 2012): 935–943, https://www.ncbi.nlm.nih.gov/pmc/articles/PMC3404651.

32. Ibid.

33. "'Greener' Laundry by the Load: Fabric Softener versus Dryer Sheets," *Scientific American*, March 12, 2019, https://www.scientificamerican.com/article/greener-laundry.

34. Care Label Project, "The Care Label Project: Designers Join the Fight Against Fast Fashion," AEG, March 21, 2017, https://www.notjustalabel.com/editorial/care-label-project-designers-join-fight-against-fast-fashion.

35. Nina Shen Rastogi, "Dirty Laundry: Should I Give Up Dry Cleaning?," *Slate,* March 9, 2010, http://www.slate.com/articles/health_and_science/the_green_lantern/2010/03/dirty_laundry.html.

36. Katy S. Sherlach et al. "Quantification of Perchloroethylene Residues in Dry Cleaned Fabrics," *Environmental Toxicology and Chemistry* 30, no. 11 (November 2011): 2481–2487, https://doi.org/10.1002/etc.665.

37. Laitala et al., "Does Use Matter?"

38. "Removing Stains: The Basics," MarthaStewart.com, accessed January 9, 2019, https://www.marthastewart.com/265555/removing-stains-the-basics.

CHAPTER 24

1. Jessica Marquez, *Make and Mend: Sashiko-Inspired Embroidery Projects to Customize and Repair Textiles and Decorate Your Home* (New York: Watson-Guptill, 2018), 1.

2. Matt Sebra, Noah Johnson, and Samuel Hine, "Now You Can Collaborate with Gucci, Hermès, and Dolce & Gabbana Through Their Insane Custom Ateliers," *GQ Style,* December 4, 2017, https://www.gq.com/story/gucci-diy-hermes-sur-mesure-dolce-and-gabbana-alta-sartoria-labels-on-fire.

CHAPTER 25

1. Edna Bonacich and Richard P. Appelbaum, *Behind the Label: Inequality in the Los Angeles Apparel Industry* (Berkeley: University of California Press, 2000), 242.

2. Ibid.

3. Stephanie Gutmann, "Half a Century of Student Protest," *The New York Times,* November 11, 2001, https://www.nytimes.com/2001/11/11/education/half-a-century-of-student-protest.html.

4. Steven Greenhouse, "Anti-Sweatshop Movement Is Achieving Gains Overseas," *The New York Times,* January 26, 2000, https://www.nytimes.com/2000/01/26/us/anti-sweatshop-movement-is-achieving-gains-overseas.html.

5. "Achievements 2013 Accord," Accord on Fire and Building Safety Bangladesh, accessed January 11, 2019, https://bangladeshaccord.org/resources/press-and-media/2018/07/20/achievements-2013-accord.

CHAPTER 26

1. The Circle, "Fashion Focus: The Fundamental Right to a Living Wage," May 2017, https://www.thecircle.ngo/wp-content/uploads/2015/11/Fashion-Focus-The-Fundamental-Right-to-a-Living-Wage-1.pdf.

2. International Labour Organization, "Developing Asia's Garment and Footwear Industry: Recent Employment and Wage Trends," *Asia-Pacific Garment and Footwear Sector Research Note,* no. 8 (October 2017), https://www.business -humanrights.org/sites/default/files/documents/wcms_581466.pdf; Ian Colotla et al., "China's Next Leap in Manufacturing," Boston Consulting Group, Publications, December 13, 2008, https://www.bcg.com/en-us/publications/2018 /china-next-leap-in-manufacturing.aspx.

3. International Labour Organization, "Developing Asia's Garment and Footwear Industry."

4. Oxfam Australia, *What She Makes: Power and Poverty in the Fashion Industry* (Carlton, Victoria: Oxfam Australia, October 2017), https://whatshemakes.oxfam .org.au/wp-content/uploads/2017/10/Living-Wage-Media-Report_WEB.pdf.

5. International Labour Organization, "Developing Asia's Garment and Footwear Industry"; "Baton-Wielding Bangladesh Police Fire Tear Gas to Break Up Garment Pay Clashes," Reuters, January 10, 2019, https://www.reuters.com/article /us-bangladesh-garments-protests/baton-wielding-bangladesh-police-fire-tear-gas -to-break-up-garment-pay-clashes-idUSKCN1P41D7.

6. Based on the 2017 Asia Floor Wage Alliance calculation for Bangladesh, which is 37,661 taka (450 US dollars). Asia Floor Wage Alliance, "Asia Floor Wage: What Is It and Why Do We Need One?" accessed January 1, 2019, https://asia.floorwage.org /what.

7. "G-Star Raw to Boost Further Sustainable Denim Sourcing from Bangladesh," *Textile Today,* October 14, 2018, https://www.textiletoday.com.bd/bridge-needed -textile-industry-education.

8. Anuradha Nagaraj, "India's New Deal for Textile Workers Could Add to Risks, Campaigners Say," Reuters, June 24, 2016, https://in.reuters.com/article/india -textiles-labour/indias-new-deal-for-textile-workers-could-add-to-risks -campaigners-say-idINKCN0ZA2X2.

9. Anuradha Nagaraj, "Take Teen Girls Off Night Shift, Indian Factories Told," Reuters, January 7, 2019, https://www.reuters.com/article/us-india-manufacturers -workers/take-teen-girls-off-night-shift-indian-factories-told-idUSKCN1P11BE.

10. International Labour Organization, "Developing Asia's Garment and Footwear Industry."

11. Nguyen Thi Lan Huong, "Vietnamese Textile and Apparel Industry in the Context of FTA: The Labour and Social Impacts," March 16, 2017, accessed via

the United Nations Economic and Social Commission for Asia and the Pacific website, https://www.unescap.org/sites/default/files/DA9%20Viet%20Nam %20Session%207%20-%20textile%20and%20apparel%20industry.pdf; "Vietnam's Garment-Textile Export Turnover $36 Billion," Fibre2Fashion, December 29, 2018, https://www.fibre2fashion.com/news/apparel-news/vietnam-s-garment -textile-export-turnover-36-billion-246483-newsdetails.htm.

12. Nike Manufacturing Map: Vietnam, Nike Inc., accessed November 20, 2018, http://manufacturingmap.nikeinc.com.

13. Fair Wear Foundation, "Vietnam," accessed January 9, 2019, https://www .fairwear.org/country/vietnam.

14. Tara Donaldson, "Vietnam Will See 6.5% Minimum Wage Increase Despite Concerns About Competitiveness," *Sourcing Journal,* December 19, 2017, https:// sourcingjournal.com/topics/labor/vietnam-minimum-wage-increase-76233; Research Center for Employment Relations, "Living Wage Report," March 2016, https://www.isealalliance.org/sites/default/files/resource/2017-12/Urban _Vietnam_Living_Wage_Benchmark_Report.pdf. Calculations in the report put the living wage for Ho Chi Minh City at $290 a month.

15. Angela Velasquez, "Madewell Joins the Growing List of Brands Tapping Saitex and Candiani for Eco Denim," *Sourcing Journal,* August 31, 2017, https://sourcingjournal .com/denim/denim-brands/madewell-saitex-candiani-eco-denim-117099.

16. Prak Chan Thul, "Cambodia's Garment Workers Fear EU Trade Threat but Producers Optimistic," Reuters, October 17, 2018, https://www.reuters.com/article /us-cambodia-eu-garments/cambodias-garment-workers-fear-eu-trade-threat-but -producers-optimistic-idUSKCN1MR0HN.

17. The current minimum wage of 182 dollars is 37 percent of the living wage, at the time of this writing, based on the 2017 Asia Floor Wage for Cambodia, set at 1,939,606 riel (483 US dollars).

18. Deborah Belgum, "2018 Retrospective: Rising Minimum Wage Contributes to Decline in California's Apparel-Factory Employment," *Apparel News,* December 13, 2018, https://www.apparelnews.net/news/2018/dec/13/2018-retrospective -rising-minimum-wage-contributes.

19. Natalie Kitroeff, "Factories That Made Clothes for Forever 21, Ross Paid Workers $4 an Hour, Labor Department Says," *Los Angeles Times,* November 16, 2016, http://www.latimes.com/business/la-fi-wage-theft-forever-ross-20161116 -story.html.

20. Eileen Fisher, "Behind the Label: Labor Rights," accessed February 6, 2019, https://www.eileenfisher.com/labor-standards.

21. Reformation, "The Sustainability Report: 3rd Quarter, 2018," July–October 2018, https://www.thereformation.com/pages/q3-sustainability-report.

22. Elizabeth Suzann, "Money Talk," January 2, 2017, https://elizabethsuzann.com /blogs/stories/money-talk.

23. Elizabeth Paton and Milena Lazazzera, "Inside Italy's Shadow Economy," *The New York Times,* September 20, 2018, https://www.nytimes.com/2018/09/20 /fashion/italy-luxury-shadow-economy.html.

24. Ibid.

25. D. T. Max, "The Chinese Workers Who Assemble Designer Bags in Tuscany," *The New Yorker,* April 16, 2018, https://www.newyorker.com/magazine/2018/04/16 /the-chinese-workers-who-assemble-designer-bags-in-tuscany.

CHAPTER 27

1. Oxfam International, "Reward Work, Not Wealth," January 2018, https://www .oxfam.org/en/research/reward-work-not-wealth.

2. Murray Ross Hall and Thomas Wiedmann, "It Would Cost You 20 Cents More Per T-Shirt to Pay an Indian Worker a Living Wage," Fashion Law, June 18, 2018, http://www.thefashionlaw.com/home/it-would-cost-you-20-cents-more-per-t-shirt -to-pay-an-indian-worker-a-living-wage.

3. John Kline, coauthor of *Sewing Hope: How One Factory Challenges the Apparel Industry's Sweatshops,* phone interview with the author, November 19, 2018.

4. Sarah Adler-Milstein, coauthor of *Sewing Hope: How One Factory Challenges the Apparel Industry's Sweatshops,* phone interview with the author, November 19, 2018.

5. Fashion Revolution, Wages Archive, accessed January 11, 2019, https://www .fashionrevolution.org/category/wages.

CHAPTER 28

1. Jason Rhodes, professor of human geography at Kennesaw State University, phone interview with the author, October 10, 2018.

CHAPTER 29

1. Matthew Mosk, "Wal-Mart Fires Supplier After Bangladesh Revelation," ABC News, May 15, 2013, https://abcnews.go.com/Blotter/wal-mart-fires-supplier-bangladesh-revelation/story?id=19188673.

2. Sara Adler-Milstein and John M. Kline, *Sewing Hope: How One Factory Challenges the Apparel Industry's Sweatshops* (Oakland: University of California Press, 2017), 138–39.

ACKNOWLEDGMENTS

There are so many people who helped to bring *The Conscious Closet* to life, beginning with my early fans and readers of *Overdressed* and the New York conscious-fashion community, which embraced me early on, especially Sass, Tara, Anthony, Amy, Timo, Bob, Gretchen, Kate, Celeste, Carmen, Tabi, and Deb.

Thank you so much to my agent, Larry Weissman, and his wife and editor, Sascha Alper, for seeing potential in *Overdressed* (before most people understood that conscious fashion was going to be *a thing*) and for shepherding this new project through its lengthy germination phase. To Stephanie Kelly, my editor, thank you for being my champion and for understanding the vision for this book from the beginning. Working hand in hand with someone with a love of style, an appreciation of the power of books *and* fashion, and a decisive yet patient approach to editing has been a joy. You've given this idea the support it needed.

To Keri Wiginton, thank you for being my trusted reader and for making time in general, no matter what was going on. I really couldn't have gotten this done without your help. To Melanie Koch, thank you for your magic, for your industry wisdom, and for the wine and sewing parties. To Felicia, thank you for your styling talents, for your friendship, and for helping me look the part. One day I'll get the Armani suit tailored. To my illustrator, Alexis Seabrook, thank you for working with grace under pressure and elevating a last-minute assignment into work that I can't imagine *The Conscious Closet* without.

I relied on a range of experts for background information on everything from fibers and leather, chemicals and quality, to how to organize a closet. I'm indebted to all of you. They include Karuna Scheinfeld, who advised extensively on quality; Kate Black from Magnifeco on chemicals in textiles; Jesse Daystar from Cotton Incorporated on cotton; Alex Bass from District Leathers on leathers; Nicole Rycroft from Canopy on the viscose rayon industry; Blake Smith from Cladwell on consumer habits and wardrobe building; Eric Henry from TS Designs on cotton and organic fibers; Anthony Lilore on pricing and retail structure; Jay Bolus from Cradle to Cradle and Ben Mead from Oeko-Tex on hazardous substances; Andrea Montali from Dream Organization New York on closet organizing; La Rhea Pepper from Textile Exchange on the sustainability impacts of fibers; Timo Rissanen from Parsons on quality and laundry habits; and Gabriella Arenas on fashion finances and thrifting.

A special thanks to Céleste Lilore, La Rhea Pepper, and Textile Exchange for generously providing access to in-depth research materials on fabrics, which helped make the book as accurate and current as possible. To Kim Jenkins, thank you for access to the Fashion and Race Database.

Thank you so much to the companies and their brilliant representatives who participated in this book: thredUP, Reformation, Eileen Fisher, Sorel, Canada Goose, and Cladwell. Thank you for spreading a message of change and for showing readers that sustainable and ethical fashion can be beautiful and accessible.

To my mom, Rebecca Cline, thanks for the peptic piddling genes and a superbly peaceful place to write: a porch in south Georgia overlooking our pond and its creatures. To my dad, thank you for always telling me to think big. To Routh, who isn't with us anymore, thank you for giving me permission to write. To Adam Baruchowitz, your open-mindedness, enthusiasm for change, and willingness to share New York's clothing garbage with me were the foundation of this book. To *all* my friends and family, Mary Shell, Katie Van Syckle, Mosi Secret, Jonathan Clasberry, Peter Brandvold, Erinmichelle Perri, Katrina Schaffer, Margaret Baker, John and Carol Ann Rowland, and Grams—thank you for vetting my ideas, reading drafts, and brainstorming ideas. To Jill Schwartzman, thank you for remembering the gray gingham dress and for giving me another shot at this inimitable and worthy process. To everyone at Dutton and Plume, thank you for taking risks and bringing new writers to market. They matter now more than ever.

Amy DuFault, you've been my friend and champion since *Overdressed*. Thank you for your PR and social media savvy and for your expertise vetting my content on fabrics and materials. Let's go on alpaca-farming and thrifting journeys together. To my research assistants, you've been invaluable: Mareesa Nicosia, Faye Lessler, and Alya Albert, your work and diligence kept this project on track. Thank you to Kate Sekules for your mending genius and friendship. Thank you to Cara Marie Piazza for her contribution and expertise on natural dyeing. To Megan Snow, I so enjoyed perfecting our darning skills together. Thank you for your insights on art direction. To Barbara Bourland, thanks for the IG pep talks and support.

To the activists and labor rights organizations and their representatives who appear in these pages, thank you: Sarah Adler-Milstein and John Klein of *Sewing Hope* and Scott Nova of the Worker Rights Consortium. To Fashion Revolution, including Orsola de Castro, Carry Somers, Sarah Ditty, Emily Sear, and Tamsin Blanchard, thank you for inspiring a new generation of fashion activists and for your contributions to and support for this book. To Lauren Fay of the New Fashion Initiative, much love for sparking so much organizing and change in New York City.

To my partner, Joseph Rowland, you are a supremely talented, supportive, supernaturally sweet, patient, and grounding force in my life. You're the world's best partner. You inspire me to focus on what

I truly love and show me how to be confident in my creativity. Thank you for enduring the many months I spent blindly focused on this, including the phase where I mostly talked to myself. Thank you for making me cocktails, bringing them to me in bed after a long day of writing, and gently suggesting that I put on something other than sweatpants while writing a book about fashion. Let's go on vacation now.

ABOUT THE AUTHOR

Elizabeth L. Cline is a journalist, public speaker, and the author of *Overdressed: The Shockingly High Cost of Cheap Fashion*. Her writing has appeared in the *Los Angeles Times, The Atlantic, The Nation*, and *The New Yorker,* among others. She is an expert on fashion industry waste, runs a clothing resale business, and is the director of research and reuse at Wearable Collections, one of New York City's largest used-clothing collectors. She lives in Brooklyn with her partner, Joseph D. Rowland of the band Pallbearer, and their cat, Lily.